THE PLAYS OF EURIPIDES

TROJAN WOMEN

General editor

Professor Christopher Collard

EURIPIDES
Trojan Women

with translation and commentary by

Shirley A. Barlow

ARIS & PHILLIPS LTD

Greek Text © Oxford University Press 1981. Reprinted from the Oxford Classical Texts edition by permission of Oxford University Press.

 British Library Cataloguing in Publication Data

Euripides
    Trojan Women. – (Classical texts)
    I. Title   II. Barlow, Shirley   III. Series
    882'.01   PA3975.T7

ISBN 0 85668 228 4 *cloth*
ISBN 0 85668 229 2 *limp*

Cover illustration taken from Vase E643, the Louvre is reproduced with the kind permission of the Département des Antiquités Grecques et Romaines (photographer M. Chuzeville).

Printed and published in England by ARIS & PHILLIPS Ltd, Teddington House, Warminster, Wiltshire. BA12 8PQ, England.

CONTENTS

GENERAL EDITOR'S FOREWORD

Euripides' remarkable variety of subject, ideas and methods challenges each generation of readers – and audiences – to fresh appraisal and closer definition. This Series of his plays is in the general style of Aris and Phillips' Classical Texts: it offers university students and, we hope, sixth-formers, as well as teachers of Classics and Classical Civilisation at all levels, new editions which emphasise analytical and literary appreciation. In each volume there is an editor's Introduction which sets the play in its original context, discusses its dramatic and poetic resources, and assesses its meaning. The Greek text is faced on the opposite page by a new English prose translation which attempts to be both accurate and idiomatic. The Commentary, which is keyed wherever possible to the translation rather than to the Greek, pursues the aims of the Introduction in analysing structure and development, in annotating and appreciating poetic style, and in explaining the ideas; since the translation itself reveals the editor's detailed understanding of the Greek, philological comment is confined to special phenomena or problems which affect interpretation. Those are the guidelines within which individual contributors to the Series have been asked to work, but they are free to handle or emphasise whatever they judge important in their particular play, and to choose their own manner of doing so. It is natural that commentaries and commentators on Euripides should reflect his variety as a poet.

This volume includes a General Introduction to the Series, on Greek Tragedy and Euripides; a General Bibliography; a Bibliography special to the play; and a short Index. I must explain why the General Introduction has been written not by myself but by Dr Shirley Barlow (who is by happy arrangement the editor of the first volume published, *Trojan Women*). I asked her to undertake it for two reasons: first, because I was sure that Euripides – and all Tragedy – in this Series would be illuminated by her distinctively open approach; second, because I had myself recently published a brief *Greece and Rome* 'New Survey' on Euripides (1981), and I hoped that her general essay would usefully complement my mainly factual chapters. I am most grateful to her for accepting the invitation. The General Bibliography, however, is my responsibility, and will be updated for each volume; the special Bibliography and the Index are compiled by individual editors.

For most plays in the Series the Greek text is reproduced from the new Oxford Classical Text of Euripides, edited by Dr James Diggle, with his own and the publisher's generous permission; an explanatory note will be found at the end of the Introduction.

University College of Swansea   Christopher Collard

PREFACE

Greek Tragedy was a genre which made great use of formal structural divisions, variety of mode and calculated metrical controls. It was sensitive to the many resources for changing pace and to building climaxes. This is certainly not obvious to the Greekless reader, and often not to classical students either. For this reason I have tried, generally in the Introduction, and more specifically in the Commentary, to give both for the Greekless and for those with Greek, what are often quite extended literary and dramatic assessments of key structural or stylistic points in the play rather than to run on without pause with detailed line comments from beginning to end. It has seemed to me that sometimes in the past commentaries in their excessive focus on small detail have allowed this to overbalance larger perspectives of a whole scene, speech or ode. Of course one wants both, but since space is rationed, there has had here to be necessarily less comment of a strictly philological, historical, or textual nature than is often customary. I have however commented on the text in places where the recently published O.C.T. Vol.II introduces a new reading, and it has been a very rewarding experience to work with such a clear and imaginative new text.

My debt to the general editor, Professor C. Collard, is very great. In fact, if there are model editors then he is surely one. He has managed to pounce on things with his unerring critical eye and to make encouraging noises at the same time. This commentary would have been the poorer without the benefit of his comments.

Thanks are also owing to Dr D.C. Innes who read parts of the manuscript at different stages and made many helpful suggestions.

I am grateful also to Miss J. Woodyatt for some checking of the typescript at an earlier stage, to Mrs Pat Gibb for typing the Commentary and to Miss Linda Harty for coping with the rest.

Eliot College,   Shirley Barlow
University of Kent at Canterbury

ix

FOR

Paolo, Lucasta, Christopher, Jean-Luc,
Judith, Charles, Vanessa, Mary Emma,
Sarah and Samantha

(Cheltenham Greek Summer School 1984)

GENERAL INTRODUCTION TO THE SERIES

I. The Ancient Theatre

The contemporary theatre consists of many different types of performance, and these are on offer most of the time at numerous small theatres up and down the country, particularly in centres like London where the cultural choice is vast. Audiences go to only one play at a time – unless, that is, they are attending something special like Wagner's *Ring Cycle* – and they go primarily for entertainment, not to be overtly instructed or to discharge a religious obligation. The choice includes musicals, ballets, operas, variety shows, classical plays, contemporary plays, thrillers, serious prose plays, verse dramas, domestic comedies and fringe theatre. Audiences range from the highly intellectual, who might be devotees of serious opera, or of Becket or Eliot or Stoppard, to the self-acknowledged low-brow, who go to the theatre to escape from real life and have a night out away from the harassments of home and work. In spite, however, of this range in type of audience, the English theatre-going public has long been, and probably still is, predominantly middle class. It is not representative of all strata of the population.

I mention all these obvious things merely to draw a contrast with the ancient theatre. For the classical Greek theatre did not have this fragmentation of genre, location or audience. The genres were few, all in verse, consisting of only four types – tragedy, satyric drama, comedy and dithyramb. There were neither scattered small theatres, nor performances on offer all the time. Theatres were outdoor, few and far between, and performances were concentrated into one or two dramatic festivals held at select times of the year. One could not go to the theatre all the time in ancient Greece. Audiences were vast mass ones (probably 14,000, for instance, at the theatre of Dionysus in Athens) and were drawn from a wide section of the population. Moreover their reasons for going were as much religious, or to glean instruction, as for pure entertainment. They would not have expected their tragedies to allow them to escape into a fantasy world which

1

bore little relation to reality – or to escape into another *private* domestic world which had no public relevance.

Greek Tragedy was in no way portrayed on a small canvas, nor was it personal in character. It was grand and large, and it dealt with elevated social, political, religious, and moral issues in elevated poetic language. It conveyed these themes through traditional myth, and was thus communal in another sense than just having a mass audience – it had a mass audience with a shared heritage about to be presented on stage. This heritage had both religious and secular associations.

First, religious. Tragedy, like the other dramatic genres, was an offering to the God Dionysus whose statue stood in the theatre throughout dramatic performances. The main festival at Athens, the Great Dionysia, happened once a year for a few days in the Spring when tragedies, comedies, satyr plays and dithyrambs were performed in open competition in Dionysus' honour. The occasion was for the whole community and a kind of carnival air reigned. The law courts were closed. Distraints for debt were forbidden. Even prisoners were released, according to Demosthenes, and any outrage committed during the performance was treated as a sacrilegious act.

Although such *religious* ceremonial was essential to the presentation of drama at Athens, it was the state which managed the production side. A selected official, an archon, in charge of the festival, initially chose the poets and plays, and was responsible for the hiring and distribution of actors. Thus the theatre was also a state function.

Peisistratus had been the one to institute tragic contests recognised by the state, and the first competition was held in 534 B.C. when Thespis won first prize. At each festival from then on, three poets were appointed as competitors, and each exhibited four plays (three tragedies and a satyr play). The general name for the group of plays was *didaskalia* or teaching, because the author taught (*edidaxe*) the plays to the actors.

A herald proclaimed the victorious poet and his choregus (trainer of the Chorus), and these were crowned with ivy garlands. The poet and choregus who won a prize were listed on public monuments, and in later times actors' names were also recorded on official lists. The monuments of stone erected near the Theatre of Dionysus at Athens, as well as private monuments set up by the choregus, or the dedication of masks, marble tablets or sculptural reliefs and the *didaskaliai*, show how high a place the tragic poet held in society. The place of the poet in ancient fifth century society is thus different from the way poets or dramatists are regarded by most people today. His place was in a context of the whole community and so was the subject matter of his plays.

Note

The most scholarly and detailed discussions and evidence for the festivals, staging and performances of the ancient Greek theatre may be found in A.W. Pickard-Cambridge, *The Dramatic Festivals of Athens* and *The Theatre of Dionysus in Athens*. Shorter and more easily digestible treatments, also suitable for the Greekless reader, may be found in P.D. Arnott, *Introduction to the Greek Theatre*, H.C. Baldry, *The Greek Tragic Theatre*, E. Simon, *The Ancient Theatre*, and T.B.L. Webster, *Greek Theatre Production*. (See General Bibliography, Section VIII). A.E. Haigh's *The Attic Theatre* (Oxford, 1907[3]), though very old now, and in many ways superceded, has some very useful details on ancient sources.

II. Greek Tragedy

Greek Tragedy treats passions and emotions of an extreme kind (fear, anger, hate, madness, jealousy, love, affection) in extreme circumstances (murder, suicide, incest, rape, mutilation). Its potency is felt all the more because such circumstances and such emotions occur within the close confines of a family.[1] Were the protagonists unrelated, such intensity would be lacking. Yet offsetting all this violence is the concentrated and controlled form of the plays which serves as a frame for the action. Of all art forms Greek Tragedy is one of the most formalised and austere. The combination of such formality with the explosive material it expresses, is what gives this drama its impact.

In life, extremes of emotion do not often have shape and ordered neatness. They are incoherent and chaotic. The newspapers show everyday the havoc wrought by acts like murder, incest, rape and suicide – the very stuff of Greek Tragedy. Amid such havoc the perpetrators or victims of violent deeds seldom have either the temperament or the opportunity to express in a shaped form how they feel or felt

3

at the time. Lawyers may later impose an order for them, but it cannot be *their own* response as it was at the actual moment of disaster. What Greek Tragedy does is to create an imagined action, through myth, where the characters *are* able to articulate the thoughts and emotions which drive them, and where the audience is given also the thoughts and emotions of those involved with the main actors, i.e., relatives, friends, outsiders. It does this moreover in such a way that the lasting effect is not one of repugnance, but of acceptance and understanding.

The material of Greek Tragedy is shaped and transformed into art in two main ways. One is through the creative harnessing of ancient myth and more modern insights. The other is through the formal conventions of language and structure.

First the combination of myth with more contemporary elements. By this I mean the blending of traditional stories, the shared heritage, with the perspectives which come from the city state, particularly fifth century Athens. This means an explosive mixture of past and present. Consider first the mythical element:-

1) Myth means *the past* to a Greek tragedian, a past which he has inherited over centuries, ever since the earliest stories were recited to his ancestors.
2) This past myth is usually concerned with the *heroic* – the great heroes as they are presented in epic and lyric poetry.
3) In this telling of the heroic, the *individual* is important. It is the single figure and his greatness which stands out, whether Achilles or Agamemnon or Odysseus or Ajax or Philoctetes or Heracles.
4) This single figure is so glorified that he may often have become, in epic and particularly in lyric poetry, a *model*, an archetype of heroic qualities.

Against this let us set the other side – the contemporary world of the poet which must confront this mythical material.

1) It is the present with present values and attitudes.
2) It is not a heroic world – it is the *city state* with its keen interest in contemporary politics and social issues.
3) It is interested in *collective values* much more than in the lone outstanding individual. The community matters.

4

4) It is interested in asking *questions*, not in eulogising the great heroes – at least not exclusively. As Vernant says, when past heroes become incorporated into contemporary tragedy, they turn into problems and cease to be models.

In the creation of tragedy, therefore, we have the meeting of the mythical past, with its stress on the greatness of the hero, with the contemporary present, with its stress on collective values and the asking of fundamental questions. Vernant puts it very elegantly. "Tragedy is a debate with a past that is still alive" and "Tragedy confronts heroic values and ancient religious representations with new modes of thought that characterise the advent of law within the city state".[2]

So too Nestlé, "Tragedy is born when myth starts to be considered from the point of view of an (ordinary) citizen".[3]

The heritage of myth is well represented by epic poetry in the shape of Homer, and lyric poetry in the shape of Pindar.

Tragedy borrows heavily from the stories told by Homer. In fact Aeschylus was said to have called his plays "rich slices from the banquet of Homer".[4] From the *Iliad* we meet again in tragedy the heroes Agamemnon, Ajax, Menelaus, and Odysseus, as well as Hecuba, Andromache, Helen and Clytemnestra. Other figures from the other epic cycles such as Philoctetes, Heracles, Theseus and Oedipus form the main subject of tragedies.

Agamemnon for instance plays a leading role in Homer's *Iliad* and Aeschylus' *Oresteia*, yet in the transformation from one author to another, setting, concept and climate have changed. Agamemnon is no longer seen as prestigious leader against the backdrop of a glorious war. The new domestic situation in which he is depicted strips him both of prestige and of a glorious cause. The righteousness of the Trojan war is questioned, Agamemnon's motives are questioned, his weaknesses dwelt upon rather than merely lightly indicated. In this new setting our concept of the hero is found to undergo a change, but it is not only that the setting alone brings about that change, it is that the tragic poet explores a complexity of motive, both human and divine, which would have been inconceivable in Homer's day. It is not simply the *greatness* of the heroic figure which interests Aeschylus, but the weakness and complex negative traits which underlie the *reputation* of

5

that heroic greatness. He uses the familiar epic frame in which to paint a new picture in a dramatic form.

In Homer, whatever the heroes' faults, they are unquestionably great and glorious. Eulogy is implicit in the very epithets used to describe them. Pindar also eulogises several of the great hero figures which become later the subject of tragedies. Among them are Ajax, Heracles, Jason and Philoctetes.

Homer and Pindar both celebrate Ajax's greatness, particularly his physical strength. Homer calls him "great", "huge", "strong", "tower of defence", "rampart of the Achaeans", "like a blazing lion".[5] He defended the ships against the onslaughts of Hector. He was pre-eminent in the battle for the body of Patroclus. He held a special place of honour at one end of the Greek encampment.[6] Even in the *Odyssey*, in the Underworld, where he turns his back on Odysseus, his silence is majestic and impressive.[7] Pindar glorifies Ajax in the fourth *Isthmian* and pays tribute also to Homer's celebration of the hero's greatness. Neither Homer nor Pindar, however, ask fundamental questions about the nature of the man – they are content merely to celebrate him as a hero. But Sophocles begins from where Homer and Pindar left off. He too acknowledges this hero's greatness, but he asks stringent questions at the same time. His play *Ajax* is the vehicle for such questions: How can the world comfortably contain such an individual? How can society function properly with one such as him in its midst? How can Ajax himself survive when he confuses so tragically the rôles of comrade-in-arms and arch enemy? What does it mean to him mentally to take the decision to kill himself?

In this play we see Ajax not only as a glorious single heroic figure, but also as a tragic character who is so because he is isolated from others, and is unable to communicate with them successfully. He is seen in the perspective of those around him – Odysseus, Tecmessa, Teucer, Agamemnon and Menelaus. Undoubtedly he has that epic *star quality* which the others do not possess and the continuity with the heroic past is important and a fundamental part of the whole conception – but that is not the whole of it. He is a problem both for himself and for others, and because he is a problem we see the tragedy unfold. The heroic individual is balanced against the collective values of a more modern society, represented particularly by Odysseus, and to some extent by

Agamemnon and Menelaus – odious though they are.[8] What makes the drama of the play is precisely this tension between the old heroic individual concerns (the core of the myth), and the newer collective values of society which had more relevance to Sophocles' own time. Of course this is an over-simplification – there are problems *implicit* in epic too, as in Achilles' case, but they are not articulated as problems, they are just told and the audience must draw its own conclusions.

One of the most eulogised heroes in Pindar is Heracles. He is celebrated as the glorious hero *par excellence* – monster-slayer and civiliser of the known world. In the first *Nemean* Pindar introduces him, and then goes on to describe his miraculous exploits as a baby when Hera sent snakes to destroy him in his cradle.[9] In the ninth *Pythian* are the words:

> Stupid is the man, whoever he be, whose lips defend not Herakles,
> who remembers not the waters of Dirke that gave him life, and Iphicles.
> I, who have had some grace of them, shall accomplish my vow to bring them glory; let only the shining light of the singing Graces fail me not.[10]

In the fourth *Isthmian* he speaks of Heracles' ascension to Olympus after civilising the known world, and in the second *Olympian* he greets Heracles as the founder of the Olympic games.[11]

Euripides takes the spirit of the Pindaric celebration and incorporates it early in his play, *The Mad Heracles*, in an ode somewhat reminiscent of Pindar.[12] In it the chorus eulogises the great labours of Heracles, stressing his superhuman strength and effortless valour. But this dramatist too is concerned ultimately not with mere celebration but with problems. The end of the play shows a transformation: not the glorious invincible hero, but a vulnerable human being struck down by madness. This is a disgraced and humiliated Heracles who is broken and dependent. It is society who rescues him in the shape of Theseus his friend and Amphitryon his father. As the hero is brought down to the level of others, the superhuman isolation goes and human social values are seen to count. Once again the tension between the lone heroic figure and socially co-operative values are worked through in the course of the drama.

7

Perhaps nowhere is this blend of archaic myth and more recent thought, of the clash between the heroic individual and collective co-operation, seen more clearly than in Aeschylus' *Oresteia*. There, an archaic story of the heroic Mycenaean age ends up in Athens - not famous in Mycenaean times at all, and an Athens, at that, with contemporary resonances. The old story of a family's blood feud is played out in the *Agamemnon* and *Libation Bearers* where the tribal law of vendetta rules, and blood is shed for blood in seemingly endless succession. In the last play of the trilogy - the *Eumenides* - a modern legal solution is imposed, and by means of a new jury system at the court of the Areopagus at Athens, a public not a private judgement is made on the crime of murder. The setting up of this court in the play reflects a historical event, the confirmed attribution to the Areopagus of homicide cases in 462 B.C. by Ephialtes, and the patronage which Athene, the patron goddess of Athens, extended to this institution and to Athens as a whole. Thus the present community of the whole city is inextricably blended with what is ostensibly an archaic drama recounting an ancient myth.

Thirty two tragedies survive, and of these, nineteen have as their setting a city or *polis*, a *polis* with a ruler, a community and political implication which have a bearing on contemporary issues. Of these nineteen, the *Eumenides* is set in Athens itself, Sophocles' *Oedipus at Colonus* is set at Colonus, very near Athens, Euripides' *Suppliants* is set at Eleusis very near Athens, and his *Heracleidae* is set in Athens itself. The rest are in Greek cities like Corinth, Thebes, Mycenae, or Troizen. All these cities have a *turannos* or sole ruler.

The setting and the form of rule are ostensibly archaic to fit the traditional myth, but again and again the dramatist imports contemporary resonances which will be of particular interest to his audience.

Two of Sophocles' plays - the *Antigone* and *Oedipus the King* - are set in a *polis*, though that of Thebes not Athens, and both, particularly the *Antigone*, are to some extent concerned with the question of rule in relation to the ruler and his citizens.

Sophocles was not on the whole aiming to make *specific* references to the contemporary political scene[13] although the plague at Thebes in *Oedipus the King* will have awoken familiar echoes in the audiences' minds of their own privations from plague at Athens in the opening years of the Peloponnesian War.[14] But this aside, Sophocles was concerned in these plays much more with general questions of what makes a good ruler in a city, what stresses affect him and what should be his relations with the citizens. Such questions would be of perennial interest to the inhabitants of a city like Athens, even though the mechanisms of rule were no longer the same as they had been under the tyrants, and even though the dramatic location was Thebes not Athens.

Such examples show that in Greek tragedy the archaic myths are transmitted not only to preserve their traditional features – though this transmission of the past is a vital ingredient of the dramatic conceptions and indeed forms an assumption from which to view the whole dramatic development[15] – but they are also permeated by a sense of what the present and the city state mean. The old hero is put in a new context where new judgements are made on him. There is a sense of the community, sometimes represented by the comments of the chorus as ordinary citizens, e.g. in the *Antigone*, *Oedipus the King*, *Medea* and *Hippolytus* and sometimes by the comments of other characters who represent the common good like Odysseus in the *Ajax*, Theseus in the *Heracles*, the messengers in the *Bacchae*. The hero may have greatness, as he often has in Sophocles, but the greatness does not go unchallenged. It is not flawless. In Euripides the greatness may disappear altogether, as in the case of Jason, once the great hero of the Argonauts, and now a paltry mean-minded person caught in a shabby domestic situation, or Menelaus as he appears in the *Helen* or Agamemnon in the *Iphigenia in Aulis*.

This questioning spirit so characteristic of Greek Tragedy is also important when one considers it as a religious event. It has often been said that tragedy's origins lie in ritual.[16] This may be true. But that implies repetition, dogma and unquestioning belief, and classical tragedy was never like this, although its performance was sacred to a god, and its content still reflected to some extent the relations between gods and men. For gods as well as heroes were inherited from earlier myth and the innovations the dramatists bring to religious consciousness are just as important as the developing complexity in their grasp of human behaviour. In fact the two are inextricably linked. It is not too much to say that the gods dominate the world of tragedy and those gods are no

9

longer the sunny Olympians of Homer. In the interval between the eighth century and the fifth, moral consciousness has been born and the gods become associated with the implacable punishment of men's wrongdoing. Whether Aeschylus' all-seeing Zeus who is associated with Justice, or Sophocles' relentless oracles which always come true in the fulness of time, or Euripides' pitiless Aphrodite or Dionysus, the gods hover above the heroes' actions watching men trip themselves up. And whether it is the passionate belief of Aeschylus, or the inscrutable acceptance of Sophocles, or the protesting criticism of Euripides, the gods are always there at the heart of tragedy and the new problematic lives of the heroes must be seen against this divine background. But tragedies are not sacred texts. By classical times the art form was emancipated, and the authors free to change traditional treatments, criticise even the divine figures and sometimes, as Euripides did, show radical scepticism about the gods, their morals and even their very existence. This is all the result of a creative meeting between two worlds – the archaic, traditional, aristocratic, heroic world of myth, and the newer contemporary values of the democratic, highly social city state where the ordinary citizen's views counted in the general reckoning of human conduct and achievement, and where contemporary thinkers were questioning moral and theological issues.

The tragedians had available to them all the resources of inherited myth which they incorporated into their own experience as beings within the *polis*. They also had to work through the contrived shapes of language and structure which conventionally belonged to the dramatic genre of tragedy. As we see them, these contrived shapes are overt and analysable, and their variety of style and development is largely responsible for the rich and complex experience which comes from watching this drama. Through them the dramatic action is assimilable: through them the reactions of those watching and listening are orchestrated. In other words they filter through their disciplined structures the inherent turbulence of the basic material, thus controlling by form and pace the responses of the audience.

First the verse form. Greek Tragedy was written in verse in an elevated and traditional poetic language. Most translations, even the verse ones, are misleading in that they do not record the variety of verse forms employed in the different sections of the plays. Spoken dialogue was in iambic

10

trimeter. The sung portions, choral odes and solo arias, and some exchanges between actor and chorus, were in lyric metres of which there was a wide range and variety to express different moods. Rhyme was not used. Music would accompany the lyric portions, often on the pipe but the music accompanying the drama has unfortunately not survived except for tiny almost unintelligible fragments.

The long spoken episodes, rather like acts, stand between shorter sung choral odes, or *stasima* as they are sometimes called, of which there are usually three or four in the course of the play. A processional song called the *parodos* marks the first entrance of the chorus into the orchestra and the name is clearly associated with that of the *parodoi* or side-entrances.

The choral odes were danced as well as sung, and had elaborate choreography which again has not survived. Modern productions have to use imagination in providing steps and music in which to express the lyric parts of tragedy, but they can on the whole successfully reproduce the basic metrical rhythms and recurring patterns of the words themselves. The language in which iambic speech and choral lyric are written, differs. The former is in the Attic dialect, the latter includes elements from a Doric form of Greek, perhaps reflecting the Peloponnesian origins of choral songs. There is the utmost contrast in Greek Tragedy between the spoken portion and the lyric. The former, though in verse, resembles more nearly ordinary conversation and, with occasional colloquialisms, particularly in Euripides, its language also owes much to rhetoric, particularly in the set debate and the longer speeches. Euripides' language here is outstanding for its fluency and clarity of diction whether employed in argument, appeal, statement of feeling or philosophical reflection.[17]

The lyrics on the contrary are in more elaborate metres and highly poetic language containing more ornament, more images, more condensed syntactical structures and more compressed thought patterns.[18] They are composed in the tradition of the great lyric poets, particularly Pindar whose somewhat obscure but highly colourful and elaborate style was famous in antiquity and would have been familiar to the dramatists' audience.

It is hard to communicate in a few words just what the lyric metres achieve in Greek Drama. And indeed we do not always know. But one can say that they characterise and control pace, mood, and tone. They act as a kind of register

11

of emotion. Certain metres, like the dochmiac, for instance, are associated with high points of excitement, others like the ionic rhythms have cult associations, others, like the dactylic, convey a strong sense of insistent and forward movement, or may recall the hexameter beat of epic. Frequently it is the subtle blend and changing of rhythms which create special effects as for instance when the opening ionics of the *Bacchae parodos*, evoking religious and cult associations, turn eventually through choriambs and glyconics to excited dactyls as the pace gathers momentum and the women sing of rushing off to the mountains,[19] or when the primarily iambic first *stasimon* of the *Trojan Women* is given an epic flavour at the beginning by its opening dactyls.

The lyric metres, more emotional than iambic trimeters, are often used in contrast with the trimeter in mixed dialogues where one actor sings in lyrics and another replies in spoken utterance or where an actor will speak his lines and the chorus reply in sung lyrics. In this way the different emotional levels are offset as for instance at *Alc*, 244, where Alcestis, in a semi-delirious trance, as she has a vision of approaching death, is given lyrics, and the uncomprehending Admetus speaks in iambics.

The chorus are always at the heart of the play. Singing and dancing to music, they have a function which is both a part of, and yet slightly separated from, the main action. Placed in the orchestra, the circular dancing space, the chorus are physically distanced from the actors and like the messenger they are usually, though not always, outsiders who look at the happenings from a slightly different point of view from the protagonists. They are ordinary citizens,[20] the protagonists are not. The chorus' task is to change the gear of the action, interrupting its forward flow and examining it in new perspectives. Their look at events allows time for reflection and judgement, leisure to consider motivation and causal explanations. They may as so often in Aeschylus - e.g. in the *parodos* of the *Agamemnon* (40 ff.) - bring to light a whole realm of background material which sets into relief the immediate events, or they may as in the ode on Man in the *Antigone* (332 ff.), cast specific actions in a more universal context. Their rôle is that of an interested commentator who is able not only to reflect, but to look *around* as well as directly *at* an action, providing a sort of philosophical pause in highly poetic form. But sometimes, as in the *Bacchae*, for instance, they are strongly involved in the action as participants, and

12

here their songs actually enact the religious rituals which are at the heart of the play's experience. Here there is no detachment, only devotion to the god. The choral function is complex and multiple, and varies from context to context, particularly in Euripides. The varied lyric metres show a fine register of different emotions and indicate tone and mood. Frequently they change as an ode proceeds.

Lyric is however not restricted to the chorus, and the solo aria is often a *tour de force* in the play and associated with high emotion expressed through the lyric metres in which it is cast. This actor's song in lyric is called a monody. Not all plays have one but some, as for instance the *Ion*, *Trojan Women* and *Phoenician Women* of Euripides, have two or more. The monodies of Greek tragedy formed high points of sympathetic identification with hero or heroine – more usually the latter since only a very few male characters are given one to sing in all of extant Greek tragedy. Here the author sought to move his audience with stirring music and words that excited pity. The monody is often designed to present a subjective and partial point of view which reflects the strong preoccupations of the singer, but which may be at variance with other views presented in the play. Euripides, the most renowned composer of monodies, gives his singers just such passionate commitment and bias.[21] Examples are Ion's adoration of Apollo, Creousa's blasphemy against the same god, Hecuba's aching despair, Cassandra's delirious wedding song, or Electra's passionate grief.[22] The monody has a lyric non-logical structure with images, personal apostrophes, laments and prayers predominating.[23]

Among the spoken parts of the play are certain set pieces, easily recognisable in formal terms, such as the messenger speech, *agon* (debate), *rhesis* (single set speech) and *stichomythia* (one line dialogue). In Euripides these are much more obviously marked off than in Sophocles and Aeschylus so that they sometimes seem almost crystallised and isolable in themselves rather than merging into one another or growing naturally. Euripides no doubt had his own reasons for this and indeed often the sharp contrast between modes creates a dramatic excitement of a peculiarly impelling kind.[24]

The messenger speech, much beloved by Euripides, is one such spoken device.[25] It is a set narrative speech in iambics, reporting offstage action to the actors on the stage and to the audience. Perhaps here the rôle of the imagination for the audience is at its height. A whole scene is set for the

13

spectator with exact detail sketched in so that visual and auditory images etch themselves sharply on the mind. Gone are the personal apostrophes, images, laments and prayers of the lyric style. Here, instead, is ordered narrative in strict chronological sequence, full of verbs of action and graphic physical detail. Unlike the monodist, the messenger is an outsider, a third person objective witness who records events in an unbiassed way and in such a manner that the audience can make their own judgements.

It would be a mistake to think of the messenger's report as a poor substitute which fails to make up for what cannot be shown on the stage. On the contrary it is superior to spectacle. The Greeks delighted in narrative ever since the performances of the epic rhapsodes were formally instituted by Peisistratus, and long before that no doubt, and such extended reports will have given special pleasures in themselves. As Aristotle saw, there were disadvantages to mere horror spectacles even had it been feasible to stage them.[26] For they produce confusion and shock – so that their impact would preclude proper assimilation of the events. What the messenger does is to control and stage the experience so that it is assimilable to the spectator bit by bit in an ordered way.

Euripides' messenger speeches with their quiet pictorial beginnings, their slow build-ups, their fragments of recorded conversation, and their graphic descriptions of the climactic acts of horror in visual terms, are masterpieces of the art of narrative. The two in the *Bacchae* for instance not only tell the audience *what* has happened, but make imaginable through pictures the whole Bacchic experience. Here the narrative is indispensable, for it is inconceivable that the audience would ever be able to view directly the mass attack of the women upon the cattle or upon Pentheus. It would be utterly beyond stage resources. But if by any chance they were allowed to view it, it is unlikely that they would emerge with as clear and as objective a picture as the messenger is able to give. Narrative enables greater total understanding than mere spectacle, and can condense more into a short space of time. In that it is one degree removed from direct sight, and is delivered by an impartial witness, it practises a kind of *distancing* which reduces the crude horror of the tragic action and requires balanced judgement as well as an emotional response.

Many tragedies contain a set debate or '*agon*' where one

14

character presents a case in formal terms, and another, as adversary, responds point for point in a counter speech. Euripides, particularly, formalised such debates, so that they often resembled law-court speeches, and they are indeed sometimes cast in formal rhetorical terms.[27] Examples are Medea's great debate with Jason, or Hecuba's with Helen in the *Trojan Women*. In these, logical and orderly exposition is more important than naturalism. It is never possible entirely to separate feelings from reasoned thought – nor should it be. But the modes of tragedy assault both, in differing degrees, by different routes. The solo aria is a direct appeal to the feelings through emotive sound and image, through words of personal address and reaction. The messenger speech appeals to the audience's consciousness through an ordered evocation of the senses so that one perceives and hears a chronological sequence of events in the mind's eye and ear. The *agon*, on the other hand, captures the audience's hearts and minds by persuasion through reasoned argument. Although the result may involve the emotions, the method is more intellectual than in either the aria or the messenger speech. Thus the *agon* in the *Trojan Women* with its sharp development of points of debate gives an academic edge to an action which is otherwise predominantly lyric in mood.

The *rhesis* is a set speech of an actor which works by persuasive and ordered logic and which may none the less often make strong appeal to the emotions. It is the commonest of all dramatic forms and one of the most varied, and overlaps with other parts. It may, for example, form part of a debate scene, it may convey extended dialogue or it may stand on its own in monologue. Its tenor may be argumentative, reflective, pathetic, informative or questioning. Many set speeches take the form of a monologue where the speaker examines his or her motives and actions in an intense process of self-examination.[28] Such are Medea's speech to the women of Corinth at *Med.* 214 ff. or her monologue at 1021 ff., Phaedra's speech at *Hipp.* 373 ff. or 616 ff., Hecuba's speech at *Hec.* 585 ff.

Often it is hard to separate the emotional element from the thought element when the poet gets the balance right. For instance Medea's speech at *Med.* 1021 ff., where she debates whether she can bring herself to kill her own children, has a tight logical structure, but through this makes strong appeal also to the emotions.[29] There is a delicate balance between direct apostrophe, a simple expression of raw feeling, and reasoned alternatives which are worked out logically. But the

15

dramatist brilliantly gives the impression that the logic is forced out desperately by a person fighting for control in a situation where the emotions threaten to take over. The result is a powerful speech which assaults both our emotional and our thinking faculties, made no less effective by the violent swings of stance which Medea takes as she is torn between the immediate sight of her children before her, and the more long-term thought of her future life as it must follow from present circumstances.

Stichomythia is a special kind of formal dialogue where the characters speak in single line exchanges. It is not the only kind of dialogue or even the commonest in tragedy but I single it out here bcause of its regular and easily identifiable form. Such a tight and formal framework permits speed, concentrated and pointed utterance within its compass.[30] It is particularly suited to scenes of interrogation such as we see in the *Bacchae* where it communicates with its economy and rapid pace, the extreme tension and changing shifts between the god Dionysus and Pentheus the King.[31]

All these items, monody, choral ode, messenger speech, set debate, *rhesis* and *stichomythia* make up the 'formal' elements of Greek Tragedy. Now 'formal' sometimes conjures up an image of fossilisation and aridity, but this is far from the case. On the contrary, the variety of metre, language, dialect and mode within the compass of one tragedy, and the alternation of song and speech, and of lyric and dialogue, made Greek Tragedy a rich experience offering a range seldom even dreamt of today. Each mode approaches the same dramatic action in a new way, with its own perspective and its own style, so that the audience is constantly exposed to shifts of perception, and the contrasts such shifts imply. Moreover each mode would have had its own associations – lyric arousing echoes of the great lyric tradition in Greece, narrative, reminiscent of epic, catering for the pleasure in story-telling the Greeks always had. And each mode carried with it its own responses which contrasted with others. Thus the great debates provided intellectual stimulus and were set off against the more emotional colouring of choral odes and arias. All were combined within the one dramatic action.

With great range of form went an economy and concentration lacking in much modern drama. The action was usually confined to twenty-four hours in one place, and was so arranged that all the parts could be taken by three actors. Scenery was sparse, subtle gestures and expressions were precluded by masks, heavy costumes and the sheer size of the theatre. But these things in themselves explain why the burden must be on the language (speech and song) and why the words were so important. In them were all the things which today are done by elaborate costume, make-up, close-up photography, lighting, scenery, stage directions, and all the rest. To the Greeks the expressed utterance was all – or almost all.[32]

So it was that the very great range of form in Greek Tragedy evinced in the different modes of speech and sung lyric, was matched by an equal range of expressions of complex human emotion, action, and thought made to fit those forms and channelled into patterns of plot, setting and action of extreme economy. It was this rich content within a controlling structure which involved too a creative harmonising of past and present attitudes through use of myth, as I outlined at the beginning, which gave, and still does give, Greek tragedy its forceful, concentrated impact.

III. Euripides

Euripides was the youngest of the three great Athenian tragedians (c.484-406 B.C.) although Sophocles, his slightly older contemporary, outlived him by a few months. In his lifetime he was not as popular with the Athenian public as the others, winning fewer prizes (four first prizes out of twenty two occasions) and ending his life in voluntary exile away from Athens at the court of Archelaus of Macedon.[33] More of his work has survived than the meagre seven plays each we have of Aeschylus and Sophocles. Nineteen plays entire have come down to us under his name, including the satyr play *Cyclops*, the *Alcestis*, a substitute for a satyr play, and the probably spurious *Rhesus*. Perhaps because of the wider sample known to us, part of which has been preserved by accident and not by deliberate selection, his work seems uneven and diverse in range.[34] There are the great tragedies of a very high order such as the *Medea, Hippolytus, Trojan Women* and *Bacchae*. But there are also plays where tragic themes mix with lighter elements and the ending is happy, such as the *Alcestis, Ion, Iphigenia in Tauris, Helen*. Attempts to categorise Euripides' style and plot by chronological criteria, thematic groupings, or structural elements, have largely failed, since there always seem to be exceptions which prevent such categories being

17

watertight.[35] Euripides is the most elusive of dramatists and the most resistant to fixed labels.

Not that his contemporaries hesitated to fix labels upon him. The comic poet Aristophanes was one such, a sharp critic who parodied him for his choice of subject matter, characters, plots, opinions and style.[36] Aristophanes saw him as ultra-trendy, undermining traditional religious and moral beliefs in a dangerous way and introducing outrageous musical innovations. He saw Euripides' characters, particularly his women characters, as unprincipled and shameless, too clever for their own or anybody else's good. He thought that Euripides elevated the ordinary to an absurd degree, making the trivial seem important, and low characters appear too significant. He therefore saw him as destroying the old heroic values and introducing instead ambiguous moral standards.[37] A rebel in fact of a most subversive kind.

This is quite a catalogue of blemishes. How misleading is it? Aristophanes is concerned of course mainly with raising a laugh – and for this, gross exaggeration is necessary. None the less much of his criticism is apt, if in a superficial way.

Euripides does introduce women characters who are criminal in their actions, like Medea who kills her children and two others, or like Phaedra who falsely incriminates her stepson thus indirectly causing his death. But Aeschylus had portrayed Clytemnestra – surely a woman of towering criminality. Why the fuss now? Perhaps because Euripides led the audience to see the action from these characters' points of view, whereas Aeschylus hardly encourages us to sympathise with Clytemnestra. Euripides was able to show what it *felt* like to have to kill your children or your mother; to be consumed by devouring jealousy or a desire for revenge; to fight an overmastering love and struggle with the consequences of madness.[38] And in so doing, unlike Sophocles, who on the whole portrayed characters who retained their wholeness and integrity throughout their tragedies, he explored weakness not strength, and exposed those elements in character which revealed disintegration and the split *persona*. Electra, Orestes, Pentheus, Phaedra, Admetus and even Medea or the great Heracles all reveal in some degree traits which characterise such disintegration and a nature divided against itself.[39]

To say that in so presenting his characters Euripides was debunking the heroic is only part of the truth. Undeniably in a play like the *Electra* all the old heroic assumptions and

18

settings are undermined or changed. Electra and Orestes are no longer the single-minded champions of justice. Clytemnestra and Aegisthus are no longer the uncompromising villains they were in Aeschylus. The murders are no longer performed in such a way that they can be seen as heroic actions. Even the setting has changed from grand palace to impoverished hovel.

And in other plays too such as *Iphigenia in Aulis*, great leaders of the heroic tradition like Agamemnon and Menelaus appear in particularly despicable lights, shifting their ground, arguing for expediency and promoting personal ambition at the expense of principles.

Yet it would be a mistake to say that Euripides had no concept of what it meant to be heroic if we think of this word not in its narrow archaic sense of military and physical valour, but in more general terms. It is that often he redefines traditional heroic qualities or else transfers them to *women*, placed in different situations from male heroes. Medea for instance, although a woman, shows many of the great heroic qualities of say an Ajax or an Achilles: bravery, desire to preserve her own honour, refusal to be laughed at by her enemies, the decisive nature to act in revenge.[40] What makes her interesting is the combination of these traditional qualities with her rôle as a woman and mother.

In the *Trojan Women*, Hecuba the old queen of Troy is heroic in her endurance of the sufferings inflicted on her by the Greeks, and in her fight to preserve her family. And when Euripides in the first stasimon makes the chorus "Sing, Muse, of Ilium, a lament consisting of *new* songs"[41] he is redefining the old epic notions of glorious war and transferring them to a setting where it is the victims who are seen as the true heroes – a point Cassandra also makes in her speech at *Tro*. 365 ff.

Several women characters voluntarily surrender their lives for a noble cause – such as Iphigeneia in *Iphigenia in Aulis*, the *parthenos* in the *Heracleidae*, or Evadne in the *Suppliants*, not to mention Alcestis who dies to save her husband. These are all examples of heroism, though not in the traditional masculine mould.

In the *Heracles* where the protagonist is male, Euripides contrasts the old traditional and active heroism of Heracles in performing the labours, with the more passive qualities of endurance he must display in facing up to the terrible consequences of his subsequent madness. He rejects the

19

traditional hero's solution to disgrace, namely suicide – the way Ajax had taken – and decides to live on in the company of his humiliation and misery. A new heroism perhaps for a newer age.[42]

Aristophanes, through the mouthpieces of Aeschylus and Dionysus in the *Frogs*, regretted the passing of the old standards and saw nothing but demeaning and undignified negativism in their place. *"Oikeia pragmata"*, "ordinary things", to him were not worthy of tragedy. But Euripides' celebration of the ordinary, if so it may be called, is often a positive and important part of the way he saw events and actions.

It is not only in settings and small actions we see it at work,[43] but also in characters. Again and again relatively humble characters play a significant rôle in a play's events. The former husband of Electra is arguably the only sane person in the *Electra*. The old servant in the *Hippolytus* has the wisdom Hippolytus lacks. The two messengers in the *Bacchae* grasp the truth of the Dionysiac phenomenon with an instinctive sense denied to all the other characters in the play.[44] They in fact carry the message of the play – that it is dangerous to deny such instinctive wisdom and to mock at belief. Aristophanes was therefore right when he said that Euripides introduced the ordinary into tragedy. He did. The ordinary person is listened to and often proved right. And if this is regarded as an overturning of values, it is a positive and significant one, and should not be dismissed as mere rabble rousing.

What Aristophanes saw as frivolity and irresponsibility in Euripides in fact sprang from a deep care for the world and a wish to protest at its wrongs. This is what his characters show. It was not to abandon a portrayal of the heroic but to redefine it. And all the charges of agnosticism or heresy which the comic poet loved to heap upon Euripides' shoulders are likewise superficially true, but in a deeper sense misleading.

Aristophanes was wrong to see Euripides' own views in every character who railed against the gods. Indeed his own views are difficult to recognise since he is usually much too good a dramatist to intrude his own *persona*. His characters display many different beliefs as their rôle and the occasion demands. It is true however that attack on the gods is a persistent and recurring theme from major characters. Repeatedly his leading characters – Hecuba, Iphigeneia, Amphitryon, Heracles, Ion, Creousa, Electra, Orestes –

20

express their despair at a Universe negligently managed by divine beings.[45] But this despair springs not from a reluctance to believe at all on their part, but from an outrage that gods, as they are commonly understood, can be so amoral and utterly uncaring of human well-being. It is the disillusion of the perfectionist that Euripides so often portrays. As Heracles is made to say,[46]

> but I do not believe the gods commit
> adultery, or bind each other in chains.
> I never did believe it; I never shall;
> nor that one god is tyrant of the rest.
> If god is truly god, he is perfect,
> lacking nothing. These are poets' wretched lies.

Such sentiments come not from the frivolity of his characters, but from their taking the Universe too seriously. If there is a fault it is the latter not the former, that should be laid against Euripides' door. And no one who has heard or read the *Bacchae* could possibly accuse its creator of either agnosticism or superficiality. There are depths in it still being explored today.

The very characteristics in Euripides' work which disturbed Aristophanes and his contemporaries – his moral ambiguity, his scepticism, his anti-heroic stance and his common touch – are what appeal to the modern reader for they seem more in keeping with our own age. In the twentieth century we have been preoccupied with doubt and disintegration, demythologising and rationalising, and this is what Euripides epitomises. We can admire the sheer brilliance with which he manipulates the myths in a way which both uses and exposes their assumptions. While keeping the traditional stories as a frame, he yet undercuts them by rationalising many of the attitudes which have previously underpinned them. Notions of the very gods he uses come under attack: old conceptions about pollution and guilt are questioned; traditional criteria for judging character are scrutinised and found wanting. And in this problematic climate his characters like Electra, Orestes, Medea, Phaedra or Pentheus, pick their way, on the verge of collapse under the strain, as their rational grip loses the battle with the forces of disintegration.

But the drama he created did not always offer purely negative perspectives. Again and again positive human values are seen to triumph over divine neglect or apathy – the friendship of Amphitryon and Theseus, the supporting love of

21

Hecuba for her family and her courage, the integrity of Ion, the compassion of Cadmus and Agave, the selfless sacrifice of Iphigeneia, Alcestis, the *parthenos* in the *Heracleidae*, and the cheerful sanity of ordinary people like messengers, or servants.

In the importance he attached to supporting rôles and to the close interaction between his characters, Euripides prefers not to focus upon one dominating protagonist. The *whole* social context is what matters, and environment and social factors play a much larger part in determining the main character's rôle and the course of the action than they do in Sophocles (with the exception perhaps of the *Philoctetes*).[47]

In short Euripides was adventurous – adventurous above all in his treatment of myth. And adventurousness here meant an entirely new perspective on plot, character, moral and religious values, and social factors. But he was adventurous too in treatment of form and structure. He experimented with music and lyrics, with metrical forms and with the breaking up of dialogue. He increased the rôle of the solo aria and messenger speech and he sometimes changed the traditional function of the chorus. He introduced more colloquialism into the dialogue and more elaboration than Sophocles into the late lyrics, thus increasing contrasts between the modes.

What is clear is that he reshaped tragedy in a radical way so that it could never be quite the same again. He went as far as he could in giving it a new image without abandoning its basic conventions. And there is common agreement that his work is, at its best, of the first rank.

Of course there are faults and unevennesses in the plays: echoes from the soap-box occasionally, irrelevant rhetorical excrescences sometimes, self-indulgence in over-elaborate ornamentation of some of the later lyrics, too blatant melodrama perhaps in certain plays, loose plot construction in others.[48] But informing all is an understanding of a very powerful sort, a mind which for all its critical sharpness, also knew the human heart and dissected it not only with uncanny perception but also with compassion. It was Aristotle who called Euripides *tragikōtatos tōn poētōn*, "the most emotionally moving of the poets",[49] a paradox one might think for one who was also the most intellectual of dramatists, but a paradox that for him somehow makes sense.

Shirley A. Barlow

Notes to General Introduction

1. Aristotle, *Poetics*, ch. XIV, 1453 b, 19-22.
2. Vernant & Vidal-Naquet, 10; 4.
3. Cited *ib.*, 9.
4. Athenaeus, 347e.
5. Homer, *Il.* 23. 708, 842; 3. 229; 7. 211; 17. 174, 360; *Od.* 11. 556; *Il.* 3. 229; 6. 5; 7. 211.
6. *Il.* 11. 5-9.
7. *Od.* 11. 543 ff.
8. See especially Soph. *Aj.* 121 ff. where Odysseus rejects the traditional Greek view of the rightness of hating one's enemies and 1067 ff. where Menelaus complains of the problems an individual such as Ajax poses for the army as a whole and its discipline.
9. Pindar, *Nem.* 1. 33 ff.
10. *Pyth.* 9. 87 ff., transl. by R. Lattimore.
11. *Isth.* 4. 56 ff. *Ol.* 2. 3 ff.
12. *H.F.* 348 ff.
13. Unless the use of *ton stratēgon* 'the commander' *Ant.* 8, and *andrōn prōton* 'first of men' *O.T.* 33 are veiled references to Pericles who was *stratēgos* 'general', and whose influence was very much that of first citizen. See Thuc. II.65.10; V. Ehrenberg, *Sophocles and Pericles* (Oxford 1954) 105 ff.
14. *O.T.* 168 ff.
15. In fact Aristophanes set great store by what he saw as the rôle of tragedy to preserve traditional heroic features and criticised Euripides strongly for debasing such features. See next section.
16. For a recent analysis of ritual elements in Greek Drama see F.R. Adrados, *Festival, Comedy and Tragedy* (Leiden, 1975), chs. II, VII, VIII, XI.
17. Collard (1981) 20-23, 25-27.
18. *ib.* 26-27.
19. *Ba.* 64 ff. and Dodds' analysis, *Bacchae* (1960) 72-74.
20. Not in the technical sense of course since women were not full citizens but in the sense of people concerned at issues in the community.
21. On the function of the monody see Barlow, ch. III, 43 ff.
22. *Ion* 82 ff., 859 ff.; *Tro.* 308 ff., 98 ff.; *El.* 112 ff.
23. e.g. *Hipp.* 817 ff.; *Ion* 82 ff., 859 ff.; *Tro.* 98 ff. See also Barlow, 45 ff.

24. See for instance the contrasts in *Trojan Women* between the prologue and Hecuba's monody, between Cassandra's monody and her iambic *rhesis*, between the great debate and the subsequent choral ode, between the iambic dialogue at 1260 ff. and the lyric *kommos* which ends the play.
25. On the messenger speech see Barlow 61 ff.
26. Aristotle, *Poetics*, ch. XIII, 1453 b, 8–10.
27. On the *agon* see C. Collard, *G & R*, 22 (1975), 58–71; J. Duchemin, *L'Agōn dans la tragédie grecque* (Paris, 1945).
28. Collard (1981) 21–22.
29. I am assuming here that 1056–80 are genuine as it seems to me they must be (*pace* Diggle, Tomus I (1984) of his Oxford Classical Text).
30. Collard (1981) 22.
31. *Ba.* 463–508, 647–655, 802–841. N.B. the change to *two*-line dialogue, i.e. *distychomythia*, at 923–962.
32. But for the rôle of the non-verbal in theatrical performance see Taplin (1978) *passim*.
33. See the chart of chronology and award of prizes in Collard (1981) 2.
34. Collard (1981) 3; Barrett, *Hippolytos* (1964) 50 ff.
35. Collard (1981) 5.
36. Criticisms of Euripides occur extensively in *Frogs, Thesmophoriazusae*, substantially in *Acharnians* and in scattered references throughout Aristophanes' other works. See G.M.A. Grube, *The Greek and Roman Critics* (London, 1965) 22–32; P. Rau, *Paratragodia* (München, 1967); K.J. Dover, *Aristophanic Comedy* (London, 1972) 183–189.
37. Religious beliefs: *Frogs* 888 ff. Immorality: *Frogs* 771 ff., 1079 ff., *Thesm.* 389 ff. Musical innovations: *Frogs* 1298 ff., 1331 ff. Women characters: *Frogs* 1049 ff., *Thesm.* 389 ff. Cleverness: *Frogs* 775 ff., 956 ff., 1069 ff. Stress on the ordinary or sordid, the antiheroic: *Frogs* 959 ff., 1013 ff., 1064, *Ach.* 410 ff.
38. A point made by Vickers 563–4 and 566 (apropos of the *Electra*). See Medea's agonised speech at 1021 ff., Electra's remorse at 1183 ff., Hermione's vindictive jealousy expressed in the scene at *And.* 147 ff., Hecuba's gloating revenge over Polymestor *Hec.* 1049 ff. and her justification before Agamemnon 1233 ff., Phaedra's

struggle with her love at *Hipp.* 373 ff. particularly 380-381 and 393 ff., Heracles' struggle to face the consequences of his madness from *H.F.* 1089 to the end.

39. Electra and Orestes in the *Electra* both suffer remorse for their murder of their mother. Orestes in the *Orestes* is reduced to madness through guilt and tormented by conscience (*sunesis*). Pentheus is destroyed by the very thing he professes to despise, ending his life as voluntary spectator at a Bacchic revel from which he had previously dissociated himself. Phaedra knows how she should be but cannot achieve it. Her love overrides her better judgement as does Medea's hate (*Hipp.* 380-381, *Med.* 1078-9). Admetus suffers acute remorse for letting Alcestis give her life for him (*Alc.* 861 ff. and 935 ff.). Heracles is on the brink of total disintegration (*H.F.* 1146 ff.).

40. B.M.W. Knox, 'The *Medea* of Euripides',*YCS* 25 (1977), 193-225, esp. 198-9.

41. *Tro.* 511 ff. See my note on this passage.

42. See esp. H.H.O. Chalk, 'Arete and Bia in Euripides' *Herakles'*, 82 (1962), 7 ff.

43. Settings such as the farmer's cottage in the *Electra* or the drab tents of the Greek encampment in the *Trojan Women*. Often ordinary actions are described such as when the chorus and companions are doing the washing (*Hipp.* 121 ff., *Hel.* 179 ff.) or Ion is sweeping out the temple with a broom (*Ion* 112 ff.) or Hypsipyle sweeping the step (*Hyps.* fr. 1. ii Bond), or the chorus describe themselves getting ready for bed (*Hec.* 914 ff.).

44. *Ba.* 769 ff., 1150 ff.

45. *Trojan Women* 469 ff., 1240 ff., 1280 ff. *I.T.* 384 ff. *H.F.* 339 ff., 1340 ff. *Ion* 435 ff., 1546 ff., 911 ff. *El.* 979, 981, 1190, 1246.

46. 1341-1346 transl. by W. Arrowsmith, cf. *I.T.* 384 ff.

47. See n. 43.

48. These points are covered by Collard (1981) e.g. rhetorical excrescences 25-26, over-ornamentation of lyrics 26-27, melodrama to be seen in last minute rescues or recognitions 6. Many plays have been criticised for their plot construction in the past; see my article on *H.F.* in *G & R* 29(1982), 115-25, although, as I have pointed out, opinions on this subject are now changing.

49. Aristotle, *Poetics*, ch. XIII, 1453 a, 28-30.

INTRODUCTION TO *TROJAN WOMEN*

Almost all Greek Tragedy is concerned not with miniature experiences and feelings, but with large scale basic and essential ones, less with shades than with strong colours. This is particularly true of the *Trojan Women* where one finds in the women who dominate its cast, no room for "sensibility" in the 18th and 19th century senses of that word, but a more raw and unexpendable sort of emotion which is unequivocally stark and is a response to an extremity of physical existence. In the play we see women who had once been happy, secure and prosperous, facing now the problem of self-survival and the preservation of what remains of their families. We see them on the outer edge of despair as they face deprivation, slavery, rape or death. Their will and capacity for emotion under these extreme circumstances is what interests the dramatist. Responses of grief, madness, love, hate, anger, despair, compassion, as well as the powers to rationalise and to reflect, are articulated by the tragedian through the separate characters and the established dramatic modes with a range and balance which is enormously impressive. It is true that more hideous events than these have been represented on the stage since, but suffering does not have to be sensationalised and multiplied a thousandfold to make an impact. Aristotle, and the Greeks, knew that mere spectacles of violence, although capable of shocking, could also distract and interfere with true artistic interpretation.[1]

The play was produced in 415 B.C. when the poet was 69 years old, and won a second prize at the Great Dionysia. It was the third play in a trilogy consisting of the *Alexandros - Palamedes - Trojan Women*. The accompanying satyr play was *Sisyphus*.[2] Several things make this production distinctive. The first is that there appears to be some thematic connection between the three plays – something very unusual at this date. Was Euripides trying in some sense to revive the connected trilogy which Aeschylus favoured? The second is that the political context of the time at which it was written seems to be significant, and to have some bearing on why it was written as it was. The Athenians' destruction of Melos had

26

occurred in the previous year, and the enslavement of its women and children and the slaughter of its male population might have influenced Euripides in his presentation of the Trojans' predicament at the hands of the Greeks. Also in the same year as the production, the expedition to Sicily was voted and there is a reference to Sicily by the chorus which seems to be somewhat clumsily brought into the Trojan context.[3] Was Euripides alluding to his countrymen's planned enterprise here?

The third unusual feature is that Euripides in the earlier *Hecuba* and in this play is breaking new ground in treating the destruction of Troy dramatically – neither Aeschylus nor Sophocles wrote a *Trojan Women* – and also in treating it exclusively from the point of view of a group of women. Deserting the usual stance of playwrights to represent male warriors like Agamemnon, Odysseus, Eteocles, Polyneices, Ajax or Philoctetes, Euripides instead allows his audience to look at the effects of war through women's eyes. In this he is also striking a blow at old epic values which saw war as men's business and as glorious. Epic was not without its women – and they are important – but their views would hardly have been elevated to carry the major impact of the work as they do here where a political statement about war in general, and more specifically the conduct of the Greeks, is made by their victims.

The Trilogy

The scene of the *Alexandros* is Troy at an earlier stage. Hecuba and Priam had exposed their son Paris at his birth because of the prophecy that he would destroy Troy when he grew up. Hecuba had dreamt that she was giving birth to a firebrand when she was pregnant with him. The child was exposed, but like many babies in legends, he was not killed, but brought up in secret by a shepherd. When of age, he comes to Troy to compete in the games as an unknown competitor. To everyone's astonishment he wins and eventually – after much discussion and intrigue – his true identity is discovered. The play deals with these latter events – the Trojan games and the recognition.

As it happens, extensive fragments of the *Alexandros* have come down to us – some from quotations from ancient sources, some from Ennius' translation of the play quoted by

27

Cicero, and some from a papyrus.[4] The hypothesis to the play has also been found on an Oxyrhynchus papyrus discovered by Grenfell and Hunt in 1905-6 and published by R. Coles in 1974.[5] From these separate pieces some notion of what the play contained can be gleaned.

Hecuba and Cassandra play major rôles in the *Alexandros* as they do in the *Trojan Women*, and Cassandra prophesies the future in this play as she does in the third.[6] The things she describes in the prophecy – the burning firebrand – the Greek fleet – the Judgement of Paris – Helen as one of the Furies, the death of Hector and the Wooden Horse – are all either alluded to or described in detail in the *Trojan Women*.

The plays however are very different both in perspective and structure. The *Alexandros* is a play of intrigue and action, not of suffering like the *Trojan Women*. There are sudden reversals – Paris winning the games incognito – Hecuba's and Deiphobus' plot to kill him – last minute recognition and rescue. The hypothesis shows that Hecuba takes the initiative in attempting to kill the victorious stranger, so that her rôle is not that of victim as it is in the third play.

In fact in the *Alexandros* the Trojans were tragically in error. First Hecuba and Priam disobeyed the oracle of Apollo which ordered them to forbear from raising Paris, for he would be "the destruction of Troy and the ruin of Pergamum". This Cassandra relates in a prologue speech.[7] Secondly, when Paris does appear, Hecuba fails to recognise him as her own son and tries to murder him – only to draw back when his true identity is revealed.

Such muddles on the part of the Trojans in this play surely make more intelligible the criticisms of Helen in the debate of the third play. To the audience who had a little while earlier sat through the *Alexandros*, the sufferings of the Trojan Women in that name-play had a context which they could not entirely forget. The perspective had merely shifted – but some of the characters were shared and their fate had already been prophesied earlier in the trilogy. Cassandra's vision in the *Alexandros* must surely relate to her appearance in the *Trojan Women* and to the subject matter of that play as a whole.

But what of the *Palamedes*, the second play? This took as its subject the Greeks before Troy and their false condemnation at the instigation of Odysseus of one of their number, the wise Palamedes. Unfortunately almost nothing survives of this play and attempts to reconstruct it have necessarily had to be even more speculative than in the case of the *Alexandros*.[8] They have rested on versions from the mythographers, from Servius and from the scholia on Euripides' *Orestes* 432. But one or two things are of interest for the trilogy. First the characterisation of Odysseus. He was the arch villain of the *Palamedes* and responsible for planning the false evidence which condemned the innocent man. His capacity there for treachery and machination accords with the strong outburst against him by Hecuba in the *Trojan Women* which is less explicable without the context of the *Palamedes*.

> Must I?
> To be given as slave to serve that vile, that slippery man,
> right's enemy, brute, murderous beast,
> that mouth of lies and treachery, that makes void
> faith in things promised
> and that which was beloved turns to hate. Oh, mourn,
> daughters of Ilium, weep as one for me.
> I am gone, doomed, undone,
> O wretched, given
> the worst lot of all.[9]

There is no particular reason for Hecuba to be so vehement about him at this point, since it is only later that he emerges as the instigator of Astyanax' death. He has not even been mentioned as the architect of the plot to take the Wooden Horse into Troy. But if the audience had just witnessed a play in which his villainy was manifestly demonstrated, this outburst would make more sense. Secondly, in the *Palamedes*, according to the scholium on Aristophanes' *Thesmophoriazusae* 771, Palamedes' brother engraved the story of his death on oar-blades and threw them into the sea that they might be carried to reach Nauplios their father. The tradition says that Nauplios revenged himself on the Greek army by setting false beacons to wreck the fleet during the storm which attacked the ships as they sailed from Troy.

This storm, raised by Poseidon, who, interestingly, was Palamedes' ancestor, is referred to in the prologue of the *Trojan Women* and two places are named which are specifically associated with Nauplios – Euboea (see 432) and the Capherean cliffs.[10] Again the references become more intelligible in the context of the *Palamedes* although it is fair to say that other places are also mentioned and that Poseidon's motive for

29

raising the storm in the *Trojan Women* is not linked directly to Palamedes.

There can be no question here of a trilogy in the Aeschylean sense with very tightly linking plot, themes, language, and characters. But there seems to be some thematic connection between the three plays and some sharing of character.[11] The third play encompasses the fate of both Trojans and Greeks and fulfils prophecies made about both in *Alexandros* and *Palamedes* respectively. The structure of the third play is in strong contrast to the plots of action and intrigue of the first two. Perhaps in all three there is some sense that public judgements are illusory – Paris was falsely judged several times and not recognised for the destructive agent he was going to be. Palamedes was falsely judged and not recognised for the innocent man he was. The Greeks were falsely thought to be victorious when defeat was awaiting them. Nothing is what it seems. Such ironies are not unusual for tragedy but they are developed here in different ways in all three plays.

The *Trojan Women*

The *Trojan Women* may be only partly intelligible in the context of the *Alexandros* – Ruth Scodel puts enormous weight on their inter-connection, too much in my opinion, but it stands as a play in its own right also and has stood the test of many performances in modern times. In my view it is one of the greatest tragedies. Can one say why? It is certainly different in structure, form, and content, from most other extant works by the three tragedians. It has a less intricate plot than many, is more static and it differs markedly from other Euripidean episodic representations too in its representation of character. It is not only that most of its characters are women but also that those rôles are on the whole interpreted as those of *normal* people caught up in abnormal circumstances. There is an ordinariness about Hecuba and Andromache which cannot be said about Electra, or Orestes, or Medea, or Phaedra, or Pentheus. These women's feelings for their children and grandchildren, husbands and parents, are the feelings of millions of people for their families – not feelings out of balance, as are so often depicted elsewhere in Euripides – but feelings *naturally* felt. The

30

tragedy occurs not from some neurosis in them, but from cruelty imposed from outside which draws out their natural responses of love, protectiveness, and grief. The germ of naturalness must be there in all tragedies, but often in Euripides it is distorted, so that it becomes something else – an obsession, a pathological condition. Here there is none of that in the case of Hecuba, Andromache or indeed Talthybius. Only Cassandra's reaction is one peculiar to her special function as priestess. This normality in the midst of cruelly imposed circumstances somehow gives hope in the midst of an otherwise bleak play. For as the women work through their natural emotions, so they become for the audience more than just passive victims. They *do* respond – they *do* articulate, they *do* rationalise and they *do* grieve. And even if they face only despair, the play had brought them to vibrant life for the audience even in that expression of despair. And in that vibrant life is a tribute to the human spirit in the face of cruelties imposed upon it.

As for the process itself of working through the grief – it seems to me to be wholly successful on the dramatist's part. For he has achieved a miraculous balance of purely emotional and reasoned utterance, using the different dramatic modes to effect this. The result is a blending so skilful that the impact on feeling and thought at once is complete. Some earlier scholars saw the play as a mere series of laments. Recently Ruth Scodel has pointed to the large component of "dry and analytic rhetoric" in the drama. "Although a love of arguments which are not entirely suited to their contexts is a notorious characteristic of the Euripidean stage, this play may carry it further than any extant work of its author". She finds that the *rheseis* of the four main characters are "not at all pathetic in either tone or content, but logical and disputatious. These speeches, moreover, seem inappropriate to both characters and situations".[12] I have tried to show at relevant points in the commentary that this is far from the case – that the speeches of Cassandra and Andromache for instance are entirely germane to the situation. Scodel is right in drawing attention to the analytical quality of many of the speeches, but wrong in assuming that they are irrelevant, dry, or lacking in emotional impact. The impact of a powerful argument may be an emotional one, and the pure sound of lamentation may provoke thought. The boundaries are not so clear. And in this play both modes work to produce a composite effect.

The *Trojan Women* is neither a soggy emotional mess nor an art form weighed down by too much "dry and analytic rhetoric". It is a delicate balance of composite modes, composite moods, and varied responses.

It has both unity and extraordinary diversity. The unity is tonal, and also consists in the cohesive rôle the central character Hecuba plays throughout. She is the only figure to be on stage throughout from beginning to end, and to some extent all the other characters are a foil for her. But all characters except Talthybius, Menelaus and Helen are caught up in the same situation which binds them and gives a common focus to the action. The chorus play a significant rôle here for they too are Trojan captives and all their odes except one, have Troy as their subject. Troy itself is almost like one of the Trojan Women, frequently addressed by the women as if it were a person.[13] Its fall determines their fate. Lyric laments are thus shared by the chorus and main characters in a harmony which is no less a harmony because it is concerned with grief.

Poetic unity is also achieved by a network of connecting images running through the play. Ships – walls – fire are recurring themes used both symbolically and literally to generate action. All are part of the imagined set – the Greek ships offstage to take the women away – the walls in the background, the scene of Astyanax' death and the last symbol of Troy's greatness – the fire the one which engulfs the city at the end of the play. But as well as their literal rôle here, and connected with it, these items are also used allegorically – ships form part of the images the women use to express their fear, walls are employed in images of "building tower high" men's hopes and ambitions, fire is described as a sinister destructive agent which attacked Troy on an earlier occasion, appeared too in the shape of a burning brand which presaged Paris' birth to Hecuba in the *Alexandros*, and reappeared as an emblem for Cassandra in the mad scene. I have pointed out the way these recurring images are developed in the commentary.[14]

But in spite of this unity and harmony of mood there is diversity too. The women are sharply differentiated from one another, and each great scene containing first Cassandra, then Andromache, then Helen, in conjunction with the ever present Hecuba and chorus, provides a contrast with the one which precedes and follows.

Each of these three episodes presents a spectacle which erupts into the general scene of mourning with a startling impact: Cassandra enters, hair streaming like a bacchant, brandishing torches, dancing and singing wildly: Andromache and her son enter on a cart piled high with Trojan loot: Helen enters beautifully dressed in contrast to the Trojan women who are in rags. Cassandra, Andromache and Helen are different in their responses to their situation, and Hecuba's response to her daughter and daughters-in-law also differs as each confronts her. I have tried to show in the commentary how this is so. I do not agree with Lee that Hecuba "is more of an abstraction than a person" nor that she is "a pathetic and moving figure but little more".[15] He contends that her "reactions are too predictable and her emotions too unbalanced for her to be an absorbing personality". I do not understand this at all. The reactions of any mother or grandmother to events such as are depicted here *would* be predictable, and Euripides has perfectly captured this. As for her emotions "being unbalanced" – what does he suppose extreme grief to consist of? If one's daughter and grandson are killed – would one's emotion be moderate? Hecuba seems to me to be a strong character, naturally and powerfully drawn.

Nor do I agree with Lloyd's general conclusion that Hecuba is the idealist throughout – that in her scene with Andromache she "takes an idealist attitude to the future", and that in her scene with Helen her "view of the gods is idealistic".[16] On the contrary she seems to me to have a firm grip on reality throughout. She has no illusions about her own state, both present and future (see esp. 99 ff., 487 ff.). While Cassandra is obsessed with the future, and Andromache fixed in the past, Hecuba retains a strong grasp on the possible and the present. Her concern for Cassandra is to prevent her doing herself and others some harm (348 ff.): her advice to Andromache is to adapt to present circumstances in the interests of survival (698 ff.). It is she who takes leave of the child when Andromache almost flings him at the guards in her despair (774 ff., 790 ff.) and she who sees to his burial and gives the lament over his body. She sees through Helen's rhetoric and she remains wary and sceptical of the gods – an attitude borne out of bitter experience as time and again they have failed her and Troy. (See 612 n. and esp. 1240 ff., 1280 ff.) In spite of a momentary impulse to despair, thwarted by Talthybius at 1285 ff., the last lines of the play show her still in control of herself and the women, still resolved to survive, though aware that the future will mean slavery and degradation. The old perhaps have fewer illusions, and so it is appropriate, one might think, that Euripides gives to Hecuba's daughter and daughter-in-law and not to herself, the refuge of madness and the hope of glory in Cassandra's case, and the clinging to the past and the abandonment to total despair in Andromache's case. But even that is an oversimplification, for Hecuba too, to some extent, idealises the past, and Cassandra and Andromache in their own different ways are capable of confronting the situation in which they find themselves. Human attitudes are complex and it is thus the poet represents them.

Diversity, but also to some extent harmony of mood, is also provided by the interesting character of Talthybius who comes from the outside with an alien's reactions yet is finally drawn into the tragedy of the women. What does Lee mean, "without a will of his own"?[17] The whole point is that he develops initiative when he prepares the child's body for burial.

Those who have adapted and produced the play have often seen it as primarily political propaganda. Jacqueline Moatti, Sartre and later Frank Dunlop through Ronald Duncan's version of Sartre, have set it in specific political contexts – that of the Algerian colonial crisis or that of Vietnam – and used it to make modern political points.[18] More recently to be seen, Tadashi Suzuki's adaptation has set the play at the end of the last war in the context of the Hiroshima bomb.

It is a tribute to the original that such adaptations have been very successful. But when all is said and done, Euripides' play is so much more than mere political propaganda. It is a humane play where there are not mere villains and heroes, and where the time scale encompasses very much more than the present. The choral odes introduce dimensions of myth and religion which can be of no interest to the political propagandist. Attitudes to the past for instance are often complex and ambivalent – Troy's past, Hecuba's past, Greece's past. And certain images of that past – Troy's links with Olympus, the former prosperity of the Trojan royal household, Telamon's and Heracles' expedition to Troy – are counterbalanced against the present with an irony which points the starkness of Troy's ruin in the play's time but leave unanswered some difficult questions about root causes. It is the second *stasimon* which particularly stresses this,[19] but all three main choral odes move through different time dimensions while focussing all the time on Troy itself. They somehow manage to create, through a series of brilliant images, the extraordinary physicality and intimacy of that place – its houses, its acropolis, its gates, its temples, its beaches, its altars, its graven images. The Greek invasion of it, which involves both symbolic and literal rape, is likewise purveyed through tangible and visual pictures – of the Wooden Horse being dragged into a shrine, of the red blast of enemy fire against the walls, of terrified children clutching their mothers' skirts.

These odes not only give the play unity and harmony of mood by their imaginative description of Troy as a presence. They also, by their own peculiar visual and textural quality, contribute to the overall richness of experience which the different modes produce and which ensure that this play communicates more than a simple and crude message. To reduce it to that, is to miss the poetry and the total context and humanity which goes beyond mere victims and enemies.

Notes to Introduction to *Trojan Women*

1. Aristotle, *Poetics*, Ch. VI, 1450 b, 17-19; Ch. XIV, 1453 b, 3-14.
2. Aelian, *Var. Hist.* 2.8. The *Alexandros, Palamedes* and *Sisyphus* exist only in fragmentary state.
3. 220 ff.
4. Snell, Scodel Ch. I, p. 20 ff.
5. R. Coles, *A New Oxyrhynchus Papyrus*, B.I.C.S. Supp. 32 (1974).
6. Snell frag. 10.
7. Snell frag. 1.
8. For a reconstruction see Scodel Ch. II, p. 43 ff.
9. *Tro.* 281 ff., transl. R. Lattimore.
10. *Tro.* 89 ff. cf. *Hel.* 1126 ff.
11. G. Murray, (1946) 128-48 and (1932) 645-56. Thematic unity for the Trojan plays of 415 is however denied by G.L. Koniaris.
12. Scodel. p. 11.
13. e.g. 780, 1278, 1324.
14. e.g. pp. 158, 162, 163, 164, 185, 189, 203, 218, 226, 227. See also Barlow 117 ff.
15. Lee xxiv.
16. Lloyd 313.
17. Lee xxv.
18. *Les Troyennes*: adaptation de J.P. Sartre, 1966. *The Trojan Women* by J.P. Sartre, English version by Ronald Duncan, 1967.
19. A. Burnett has an interesting article on the second *stasimon* in which she argues that the dramatist there - largely through the mention of Laomedon - stresses the Trojan city of the past as "a place of bad faith and effeminacy, impiety and arrogance" (308). She makes a great deal of what she calls "the negative traits of Troy", i.e. materialism and lack of faith, and argues that these extend to Hecuba (310-311). I think she overdoes these features. The focus in this play is not Trojan misdemeanours but largely undeserved suffering. That Ganymede and Tithonus betray Troy does not implicate all other Trojans. Divine indifference to a city that should be cherished is the point. None the less, things are never that simple, and their mention here together with the context of the trilogy as a whole, at least points to a past that has at times been filled with division and treachery.

TRANSLATOR'S NOTE

The *Trojan Women* is a play about acute suffering – about pain, damage, loss and violence, and in attempting to translate it the translator has particular difficulties in addition to the usual ones associated with rendering Greek Tragedy. For so much of this play is prolonged lament for that suffering and the expression of concentrated grief. The Greek consists of a rich range of words expressing the emotions of grief. Yet when we examine our own vocabulary we are hampered at every turn in trying to find modern equivalents. Consider for instance the many verbs describing the utterance and feeling of lament. *Thrēneō, thrēnōdeō, aiazō, throeō, stenazō, katastenō, iacheō, thōussō, kōkuō, olophuromai, apolophuromai, oimōzō, katoimōzō, exoimōzō, goaomai, dakruō, klaiō.*

If one looks these up in the dictionary one finds that the same English words are given again and again to translate them.

Thrēneō : wail, bewail
aiazō, exaiazō : bewail, bemoan
olophuromai : bewail, lament, mourn.
iacheō : cry, shriek in pain.
stenazō : bewail, bemoan, groan,
and so on.

It is partly that we lack the range in English to cope with these words and partly because where we *do* find equivalents they sound outdated and lacking in weight. "Lament", "bewail", "bemoan" do not have a contemporary ring. And many words which in Victorian times did justice to the emotion of grief, particularly abstract nouns, now sound old-fashioned. Notice that I chose factual words just now to describe the play's action; "pain", "damage", "loss" and "violence" still have some impact. But consider others more emotional, now outworn. What a hollow ring they have: "affliction, anguish, woe, sorrow" and even "care, distress, grief" and "agony". Our vocabulary has grown tired and only a few words in this area still carry their full weight. "Pain" is one. "Hurt" is another. But those words have factual as well as emotional connotations. It is the words for *feelings* which have shrunk. Take also the Greek apostrophes *aiai, pheu, e e, oimoi, iō, ototoi* which in that language express so adequately raw feelings. "Alas", "alack", "woe is me" sound ludicrous. And how is one to differentiate between them? I admit defeat here. Sometimes one can give a

37

periphrasis like "How wretched I feel", but at other times I have kept the Greek sounds transliterated. There simply are no modern substitutes.

Take another area – that of religious feeling. Part of the point of this play is that the characters feel that even the Gods have deserted them. "The gods loved Troy once. Now they have forgotten". (857-8). The power of that sense of loss resides in the assumption that the Trojans *believed* in their gods, performed their sacrifices, were devout, but in spite of this were let down by them. This is the point of the rich description of Troy's altars burning with incense and sacrifices, and the images in the third *stasimon*. Zeus betrayed all this devotion *houtō dē ... proudōkas ... ō Zeu* (1060-3) the ode begins. It is very difficult for a modern audience to capture the impact of this betrayal when deep religious feeling today is on the whole rare. Once again words for religious experience in English sound tired and outmoded; "reverence, veneration, devotion, devoutness, sanctity, sacredness, piety, holiness, godly, blessed, pious, holy". It was because the Greeks had such a strong sense of the gods and the supernatural at work that they used words like *dusdaimōn, barudaimōn, dusmoros, dustuchēs*. Yet English equivalents like "hapless", "ill-starred", "ill fated" sound quaint today and purely secular words like "miserable" and "wretched" do not get that sense of the supernatural.

This poverty of words available to express religious feeling and the poverty of the concepts behind the words is particularly evident in a context like Cassandra's aria where there is a great concentration of Greek words for religious observance, and for the ceremony of marriage within a religious context, e.g. *hieron* (309), *sebō* (308), *hosios* (378), *thuēpolō* (330), the five times repeated refrains to the Marriage God, *O Humenai' anax*, the address to Hecate and Apollo and the Bacchic cry *Euhan Euhoi* as well as words with religious connotations like *makarios*, four times repeated, and stressed through being at the beginning of lines (3 times) and once a superlative at the end. The ode is saturated with the vocabulary of worship and the effect of this aria depends upon the frenzied religious fervour of this priestess which has become distorted through madness. To make this song live for a modern audience with the same obsessive power that it presumably once had is extremely difficult.

I asked my students which areas they thought in our own

language *did* still carry a richness of emotional association where words still carried some force, and they said those of fear and horror. "Fear: fright: terror: panic, alarm, shock, scare: consternation: dismay, qualms, misgivings, apprehension: unease: worry, nerves. Being petrified, terrified, panic-struck, flabbergasted, stunned, appalled, numbed, paralysed", and so on. These words they said had not lost their impact. I suspect too that very physical words for violence of various kinds are still strong. Messenger speeches are, therefore, interestingly, less of a problem for us than lyric laments.

It is with such shifting values of words that the translator has to contend, in addition to all the other difficulties which the conventional and stylised language of Greek Tragedy presents. (On some of the difficulties in translating a choral ode for instance see my introductory note on the second *stasimon*).

It was a highly artificial poetic vocabulary and style removed from everyday naturalism, and yet at the same time it was a language which lived, and whose resonances were full of familiarity with earlier poetical forms. A prose translation has to contend not only with loss of metre, verse form, and poetic style, but also with these resonances in a medium where the language is many-layered and uneven in style. There is the utmost distinction between the lyric and the iambic portions. This can be rendered in verse by different metres, but in prose it is more difficult to mark. However I hope that the condensed poetic artifices of the lyric sections make themselves felt even through the medium of prose, and that some of their beauty becomes apparent.

For this is the miracle – that with all these limitations of language and changed conventions the power of the Greek still comes across to modern audiences. The *Trojan Women* continues to be re-translated, and adapted, so that this century alone has seen many versions which although they may differ one from another, all retain something of that tremendous power which resides in the original.

(N.B. : the contents of this Note appeared as part of a paper delivered to a Hellenic Society Colloquium for Professor R.P. Winnington-Ingram in February 1985.. The paper will appear in *JHS Supplementary Papers* no. 15.)

NOTE ON THE GREEK TEXT

The text in this volume is reproduced, with permission of editor and publisher, from J. Diggle, *Euripidis Fabulae*, Tomus II, Oxford Classical Texts, 1981. The brief *apparatus* too is drawn from that edition, but in a heavily reduced form, on the responsibility of the editor of this volume; its purpose is to provide the basic information for a critical reading of the edited text, and to serve the occasional text-critical discussion in the Commentary.

The text of *Trojan Women* depends primarily upon three medieval manuscripts:

V = Vatican Library, Codex Graecus 909 (late 13th Century)

P = Vatican Library, Codex Palatinus Graecus 287 (early 14th Century)

Q = London, British Library, Harley 5743 (very late 15th Century)

and subsidiarily upon two copies of V:

Va = Vatican Library, Codex Palatinus Graecus 98 (14th Century)

Neap. = Naples, National Library II.5.9 (or no.165) (14th Century)

and upon a copy of a copy of Va:

Haun. = Copenhagen, Royal Library 417 (15th Century). V and P differ frequently. Q is a hybrid, related to both V and P, but with independent value; its text of lines 1-610 derives from the same source as P, but that of 611-1332, written a good deal later, most probably from a copy of Va, perhaps with influence from the tradition of P (on these manuscripts, and their relationships, see Diggle vi-viii). Sporadic checks on the manuscripts are afforded by variant readings in the ancient commentaries (scholia) on Euripides (for *Trojan Women* preserved in V and Neap.); and by quotations in other writers of all kinds, especially anthologists. In sum, the text of *Trojan Women* rests on a reasonably wide base, although there are many places of uncertainty or irrecoverable damage; in comparison, eight other plays of Euripides have a richer tradition, but the remaining ten rely upon only one medieval manuscript and a slightly divergent copy.

For accounts of the history of the text see the General Bibliography, at the end of Section I.

GENERAL BIBLIOGRAPHY

(This Bibliography has been compiled by the General Editor, and concentrates on works in English; a supplementary Bibliography for *Trojan Women* follows, compiled by the editor of this volume).

I : complete critical editions

The standard edition is by J. Diggle in the Oxford Classical Texts: Tomus I (1984) *Cyclops, Alcestis, Medea, Heraclidae, Hippolytus, Andromacha, Hecuba*; Tomus II (1981) *Supplices, Electra, Hercules, Troades, Iphigenia in Tauris, Ion*; until Tomus III is published, its predecessor, by G. Murray (1913[2]), will remain standard for *Helena, Phoenissae, Orestes, Bacchae, Iphigenia Aulidensis, Rhesus*.

The edition of R. Prinz and N. Wecklein (Leipzig, 1878-1902) is still useful for its *apparatus* and *appendices*. The 'Collection Budé' edition, by L. Méridier and others (Paris, 1923 onwards), still lacks *Rhesus*; it has French translation, introductory essays and some notes. The 'Bibliotheca Teubneriana' issues plays singly, each with bibliography and some with brief critical notes, by different editors (Leipzig, 1964 onwards).

Fragments: when it is published, Volume V of *Tragicorum Graecorum Fragmenta, Euripides*, ed. R. Kannicht, will at last unite in one book the many long-known and frequently re-edited fragments with modern finds. For the present, see *Hypsipyle*, ed. G.W. Bond (Oxford, 1963); *Phaethon*, ed. J. Diggle (Cambridge, 1970); A. Nauck, *Tragicorum Graecorum Fragmenta* (Leipzig, 1889[2], reprinted Hildesheim, 1964 with *Supplementum* by B. Snell); D.L. Page, *Greek Literary Papyri* ('Loeb', London, 1942); C. Austin, *Nova Fragmenta Euripidea in Papyris Reperta* (Berlin, 1967).

History of the text: W.S. Barrett, *Euripides: Hippolytos* (Oxford, 1964) 45-90; G. Zuntz, *An Inquiry into the Transmission of the Plays of Euripides* (Cambridge, 1965) esp. 249-88; J. Diggle, *Praefatio* to his *OCT* Tomus I, v-xiv.

II : complete commentaries

F.A. Paley (London, 1857[1]-1889[2]) (commonsensical and still useful).

E. Schwartz, *Scholia in Euripidem* (Berlin, 1887-91) (nine plays only; a more widely based edition of the ancient and medieval scholia is needed).

'Reference' commentaries on single plays are: W.S. Barrett, *Hippolytos* (Oxford, 1964); G.W. Bond, *Heracles* (Oxford, 1981); C. Collard, *Supplices* (Groningen, 1975); J.D. Denniston, *Electra* (Oxford, 1939); E.R. Dodds, *Bacchae* (Oxford, 1960); R. Kannicht, *Helena* (Heidelberg, 1969); U. von Wilamowitz-Moellendorff, *Herakles* (Berlin, 1895²; reprinted Bad Homburg 1959).

Commentaries on the other tragedians important for reference are: E. Fraenkel, *Aeschylus: Agamemnon* (Oxford, 1950); R.C. Jebb, *Sophocles* (7 vols., Cambridge, 1883¹-1903³); A.C. Pearson, *The Fragments of Sophocles* (3 vols., Cambridge, 1917).

III : complete English translations
D. Grene, R. Lattimore (eds.), *The Complete Greek Tragedies: Euripides* (2 vols., Chicago, 1958-9)
P. Vellacott, *Euripides* (4 vols., Harmondsworth, 1953-72) ('Penguin Classics')

IV : lexicography
J.T. Allen, G. Italie, *A Concordance to Euripides*, Berkeley/London 1954, reprinted Groningen 1970; *Supplement* by C. Collard, Groningen 1971.

V : bibliographical aids
L'Année Philologique has recorded publications since 1924.
Anzeiger für die Altertumswissenschaft has published occasional evaluative surveys since 1948.
From Section VI below, see Burian, *Cambridge History of Greek Literature, I*, Collard (evaluative), Lesky (1983; bibliography only till 1971) and Webster (esp. lost plays).

VI : general studies and handbooks (Greek Tragedy; Euripides)
A. Brown, *A New Companion to Greek Tragedy* (London, 1983) (a 'dictionary').
P. Burian (ed.), *Directions in Euripidean Criticism* (Durham, U.S.A., 1985).
A.P. Burnett, *Catastrophe Survived: Euripides' plays of mixed reversal* (Oxford, 1971).
Cambridge History of Classical Literature, Volume I: Greek Literature ed. P.E. Easterling, B.M.W. Knox, (Cambridge, 1985), 258-345, 758-73 (chapters by leading scholars).
C. Collard, *Euripides*, 'Greece and Rome' New Surveys in the Classics No. 14 (Oxford, 1981) (brief survey with bibliographical emphasis).

42

D.J. Conacher, *Euripidean Drama: Myth, Theme and Structure* (Toronto, 1967) (best general introduction of its kind).

A.M. Dale, *Collected Papers* (Cambridge, 1969) (on many aspects of drama).

K.J. Dover (ed.), *Ancient Greek Literature* (Oxford, 1980), 53-73 (Ch. 4, 'Tragedy', by K.J. Dover).

G.F. Else, *Aristotle's Poetics: the Argument* (Harvard, 1957).

Entretiens sur l'Antiquité Classique, VI: Euripide (Vandoeuvres-Genève, 1960) (seven papers, and transcribed discussion, by leading scholars).

L.H.G. Greenwood, *Aspects of Euripidean Drama* (Cambridge, 1953).

G.M. Grube, *The Drama of Euripides* (London, 1961^2) (handbook).

J. Jones, *On Aristotle and Greek Tragedy* (London, 1962).

H.D.F. Kitto, *Greek Tragedy: a Literary Study* (London, 1961^3).

B.M.W. Knox, *Word and Action* (Baltimore, 1979) (collected papers on drama).

W. Kranz, *Stasimon* (Berlin, 1933) (fundamental work on the Chorus).

R. Lattimore, *The Poetry of Greek Tragedy* (Oxford, 1958).

- *Story Patterns in Greek Tragedy* (London, 1964).

A. Lesky, *Greek Tragedy*, trans. H. Frankfort (London, 1967) (basic text-book).

- *Greek Tragic Poetry*, trans. M. Dillon (New Haven, 1983) (scholar's handbook).

D.W. Lucas, *Aristotle:Poetics* (Oxford, 1968) (commentary).

G. Murray, *Euripides and his Age* (London, 1946^2) (an 'evergreen').

A.W. Pickard-Cambridge, *Dithyramb, Tragedy and Comedy*, 2. ed. by T.B.L. Webster (Oxford, 1962).

A. Rivier, *Essai sur le tragique d'Euripide* (Paris, 1975^2).

L. Séchan, *Etudes sur la tragédie grecque dans ses rapports avec la céramique* (Paris, 1926).

E. Segal (ed.), *Oxford Readings in Greek Tragedy* (Oxford, 1984) (important essays by leading scholars reprinted).

W.B. Stanford, *Greek Tragedy and the Emotions* (London, 1983).

O. Taplin, *The Stagecraft of Aeschylus* (Oxford, 1977) (important for all Tragedy).

- *Greek Tragedy in Action* (London, 1978) (vigorous introduction).

A.D. Trendall, T.B.L. Webster, *Illustrations of Greek Drama* (London, 1971) (vase-paintings and the plays).

P. Vellacott, *Ironic Drama: a Study of Euripides' Method and Meaning* (Cambridge, 1976) (the plays as veiled social criticism).

J.P. Vernant, P. Vidal-Naquet, *Tragedy and Myth in Ancient Greece*, English trans. (Brighton, 1981).
B. Vickers, *Towards Greek Tragedy: Drama, Myth, Society* (London, 1973).
P. Walcot, *Greek Drama in its Theatrical and Social Context* (Cardiff, 1976).
T.B.L. Webster, *The Tragedies of Euripides* (London, 1967) (a profile of the dramatic and poetic career as it developed).
Yale Classical Studies 25 (1977): *Greek Tragedy* (papers invited from prominent scholars).

VII : Euripides and contemporary events and ideas
R.G. Buxton, *Persuasion in Greek Tragedy: a Study of 'Peitho'* (Cambridge, 1982).
K. Reinhardt, *Tradition und Geist* (Göttingen, 1960) 223-56 ('Die Sinneskrise bei Euripides': classic discussion of Euripides' intellectualism and its reflection in his dramaturgy).
P.T. Stevens, 'Euripides and the Athenians', *JHS* 76 (1976), 76-84 (contemporary reception).
R.P. Winnington-Ingram, 'Euripides: Poiētēs Sophos', *Arethusa* 2 (1969), 127-42 (need for balanced interpretation of Euripides' cleverness).
G. Zuntz, *The Political Plays of Euripides* (Manchester, 1963^2).
Cf. esp. Lesky (1983), Murray, Vellacott, Vernant, Vickers and Walcot from Section VI above.

VIII : theatre and production
P.D. Arnott, *Introduction to the Greek Theatre* (London, 1959).
- *Greek Scenic Conventions in the Fifth Century B.C.* (Oxford, 1962).
H.C. Baldry, *The Greek Tragic Theatre* (London, 1971).
M. Bieber, *The History of the Greek and Roman Theatre* (Princeton, 1961^2) (copious illustrations).
R.C. Flickinger, *The Greek Theater and its Drama* (Chicago. 1936^4).
A.W. Pickard-Cambridge, *The Theatre of Dionysus in Athens* (Oxford, 1946).
- *The Dramatic Festivals of Athens*, 2. ed. by J. Gould, D.M. Lewis (Oxford, 1968).
E. Simon, *The Ancient Theatre*, trans. C.E. Vafopoulo-Richardson (London, 1982).
T.B.L. Webster, *Greek Theatre Production* (London, 1970^2)
Cf. esp. Dale, Taplin (1978), Trendall and Walcot in Section VI above; Bain, Halleran, Hourmouziades, Jens and Mastronarde in Section IX below.

IX : dramatic form and theatrical technique
D. Bain, *Actors and Audience: a study of asides and related conventions in Greek drama* (Oxford, 1977).
M.R. Halleran, *Stagecraft in Euripides* (London, 1985).
N.C. Hourmouziades, *Production and Imagination in Euripides* (Athens, 1965).
W. Jens (ed.), *Die Bauformen der griechischen Tragödie* (München, 1971).
D.J. Mastronarde, *Contact and Discontinuity: Some Conventions of Speech and Action on the Greek Tragic Stage* (Berkeley, 1979).
W. Schadewaldt, *Monolog und Selbstgespräch* (Berlin, 1926).
W. Steidle, *Studien zum antiken Drama unter besonderer Berücksichtigung des Bühnenspiels* (München, 1968).
H. Strohm, *Euripides: Interpretationen zur dramatischen Form* (München, 1957).
Cf. esp. Burnett, Kranz, Lesky (1983) and Taplin (1977) from Section VI above.

X : language and style
S.A. Barlow, *The Imagery of Euripides* (London, 1971) (widest appreciative study).
W. Breitenbach, *Untersuchungen zur Sprache der euripideischen Lyrik* (Stuttgart, 1934) (*Index Locorum* by K.H. Lee, Amsterdam, 1979).
P.T. Stevens, *Colloquial Expressions in Euripides* (Wiesbaden, 1977).
Cf. Section IV above; Lattimore (1958), Lesky (1983) and Stanford from Section VI above; Buxton from Section VII above.

XI : verse and metre
A.M. Dale, *The Lyric Metres of Greek Drama* (Cambridge, 1968^2).
- *Metrical Analyses of Tragic Choruses*, *BICS* Supplement 21.1 (1971); 21.2 (1981); 21.3 (1983) (index of Choruses in 21.3)
D.S. Raven, *Greek Metre* (London, 1962) (analyses many complete odes).
M.L. West, *Greek Metre* (Oxford, 1982) (standard handbook).
U. von Wilamowitz-Moellendorff, *Griechische Verskunst* (Berlin, 1921) (analyses and interprets many complete odes).

BIBLIOGRAPHY TO *TROJAN WOMEN*

Editions with Commentary
Euripides, *Troades*, ed. R.Y. Tyrrell (London, 1897)
Euripide, *Le Troiane*, ed. G. Schiassi (Firenze, 1953)
Euripides, *Troades*, ed. K.H. Lee (London, 1976)

Translations
R. Lattimore, *Trojan Women*, in *The Complete Greek Tragedies: Euripides*, ed. D. Grene, R. Lattimore (Chicago, 1958-9)
P. Vellacott, *Trojan Women*, in *Euripides: the Bacchae and Other Plays*, (Harmondsworth, 1954)
N. Curry, *The Trojan Women* (London, 1966)
L. Parmentier, *Les Troyennes*, in *Euripide*, IV ('Bude' edition) (Paris, 1925)

General
(Note: works on Euripides cited in the General Bibliography are not repeated here)

R.S. Bluck, 'Euripides, *Troades* 636-40', *CQ* 11 (1961), 125-6
A.P. Burnett, '*Trojan Women* and the Ganymede Ode', *YCS* 25 (1977), 291-316
R. Coles, *A New Oxyrhynchus Papyrus. The Hypothesis of Euripides' Alexandros*, *BICS Supplement* 32 (1974)
C. Collard, 'Formal Debates in Euripides' Drama', *G&R* 22 (1975), 58-71
E. Delebecque, *Euripide et la Guerre du Péloponnèse* (Paris, 1951)
J. Diggle, Review of *Troades*, ed. K.H. Lee, in *Proceedings of the African Classical Association* 14 (1978), 27-32
J. Duchemin, L'Agon dans la tragédie grecque (Paris, 1968[2])
K. Gilmartin, 'Talthybius in the *Trojan Women*', *AJP* 91 (1970), 213-22
Gorgias, *Encomium on Helen*, ed. D.M. MacDowell (Bristol, 1982)
J.O. de G. Hanson, 'Reconstruction of Euripides' *Alexandros*', *Hermes* 92 (1964), 171-81
E.A. Havelock, 'Watching the *Trojan Women*', in Euripides, ed. E. Segal (Englewood Cliffs, 1968), 115-27
M. Kaimio, *The Chorus of Greek Drama* (Helsinki, 1970)
G.L. Koniaris, '*Alexander, Palamedes, Troades, Sisyphus*. A connected tetralogy? A connected trilogy?', *HSCP* 77 (1973), 85-124

*M. Lloyd, 'The Helen Scene in Euripides' *Trojan Women*', *CQ* 34 (1984), 303–13

G. Murray, 'Euripides' Tragedies of 415: the Deceitfulness of Life', in *Greek Studies* (Oxford, 1946), 128–48

– 'The Trojan Trilogy of Euripides (415 B.C.)', in *Mélanges Gustave Glotz*, II (Paris, 1932), 645–56

E. O'Neill, Jr., 'The Prologue of the *Troades* of Euripides', *TAPA* 72 (1941), 288–320

A. Poole, 'Total Disaster: Euripides' *The Trojan Women*', *Arion* 3 (1976), 257–87

R. Scodel, *The Trojan Trilogy of Euripides*, Hypomnemata 60 (Göttingen, 1980)

B. Seidensticker, *Palintonos Harmonia*, Hypomnemata 72 (Göttingen, 1982)

T. Sienkiewicz, 'Euripides' *Trojan Women*: an Interpretation', *Helios* 6 (1978), 81–95

B. Snell, *Euripides' Alexandros und andere Strassburger Papyri*, *Hermes Einzelschriften* V (1937)

T.C.W. Stinton, *Euripides and the Judgement of Paris* (London, 1965)

R.A.H. Waterfield, 'Double Standards in Euripides' *Troades*', *Maia* 34 (1982), 139–42

J.R. Wilson, 'The Etymology in Euripides' *Troades*', *AJP* 89 (1968), 66–71

* This article came to my notice only after the Commentary had been prepared for printing.

ABBREVIATIONS

Abbreviations follow the standard forms in Liddell and Scott's *Greek-English Lexicon*, 9th. Edition, rev. H. Stuart Jones (Oxford 1925-40) and *L'Année Philologique*.

A.R.V.   = **J.D. Beazley**, *Attic Red-figure Vase-painters* (Oxford, 1963)

G.P.   = **J.D. Denniston**, *The Greek Particles*[2] (Oxford, 1954)

Roscher, *Lex. Myth.*   = **W.H. Roscher**, *Ausführliches Lexikon der griechischen und römischen Mythologie* (Leipzig, 1884-)

SIGLA

V	Vaticanus gr. 909	saec. xiii ex.
V^{ac}	V ante correctionem	
V^{pc}	V post correctionem siue a prima siue ab alia manu	
P	Palatinus gr. 287	saec. xiv in.
p^{ac}	P ante correctionem	
p^{pc}	P post correctionem siue a prima siue ab alia manu	
p	codicis P corrector Italus	saec. xv ex.
Q	Harleianus 5743 (uu. 1–610)	saec. xv ex. uel xvi in.

Apographa codicis V

Neap.	Neapolitanus 165	saec. xiv
Va	Palatinus gr. 98	saec. xiv

Apographa apographi Va

Haun.	Hauniensis 417	saec. xv
q	Harleianus 5743 (uu. 611–1332)	saec. xv ex. uel xvi in.

Gnomologia

gB	Vaticanus Barberini gr. 4	c. 1300
gE	Escorialensis gr. 10.1.13	saec. xiv in.

Papyrus

Π	P. Oxy. 2455 fr. 13 col. xii: argumenti pars

Sigla et Notae

Σ	lectio quam disertim testatur scholiasta
Σ^{l}	lemma scholiastae
Σ^{i}	lectio quam in textu inuenisse scholiastam ex eius interpretatione intellegitur
~	testimonium cum codicibus consentit contra lectionem uel coniecturam modo memoratam
*	littera erasa uel obliterata

Dramatis Personae

Ποσειδῶν	Poseidon
᾽Αθηνᾶ	Athena
῾Εκάβη	Hecuba
Ταλθύβιος	Talthybius
Κασσάνδρα	Cassandra
᾽Ανδρομάχη	Andromache
Μενέλαος	Menelaus
῾Ελένη	Helen
χορὸς ἐξ αἰχμαλωτίδων Τρωιάδων	Chorus of Trojan captives

TROJAN WOMEN

With Prose Translation

ΥΠΟΘΕCΙC ΤΡΩΙΑΔΩΝ

Μετὰ τὴν Ἰλίου πόρθησιν ἔδοξεν Ἀθηνᾶι τε καὶ Πο-
σειδῶνι τὸ τῶν Ἀχαιῶν cτράτευμα διαφθεῖραι, τοῦ μὲν
εὐνοοῦντοc τῆι πόλει διὰ τὴν κτίcιν, τῆc δὲ μιcηcάcηc
τοὺc Ἕλληναc διὰ τὴν Αἴαντοc εἰc Καccάνδραν ὕβριν. οἱ
δὲ Ἕλληνεc κληρωcάμενοι περὶ τῶν αἰχμαλώτων γυναι-   5
κῶν τὰc ἐν ἀξιώμαcιν ἔδωκαν Ἀγαμέμνονι μὲν Καccάνδραν, Ἀνδρομάχην δὲ Νεοπτολέμωι, Πολυξένην δὲ Ἀχιλ-
λεῖ. ταύτην μὲν οὖν ἐπὶ τῆc τοῦ Ἀχιλλέωc ταφῆc ἔcφαξαν,
Ἀcτυάνακτα δὲ ἀπὸ τῶν τειχῶν ἔρριψαν. Ἑλένην δὲ ὡc
ἀποκτενῶν Μενέλαοc ἤγαγεν, Ἀγαμέμνων δὲ τὴν χρη-   10
cμωιδὸν ἐνυμφαγώγηcεν. Ἑκάβη δὲ τῆc μὲν Ἑλένηc
κατηγορήcαcα, τοὺc ἀναιρεθένταc δὲ κατοδυραμένη τε καὶ
κηδεύcαcα, πρὸc τὰc Ὀδυccέωc ἤχθη cκηνάc, τούτωι λα-
τρεύειν δοθεῖcα.

τὰ τοῦ δράματοc πρόcωπα· Ποcειδῶν, Ἀθηνᾶ, Ἑκάβη,   15
χορὸc ἐξ αἰχμαλωτίδων Τρωιάδων, Ταλθύβιοc, Καccάν-
δρα, Ἀνδρομάχη, Μενέλαοc, Ἑλένη.

---

argumentum habent VPQ, linearum 1–6 frustula P. Oxy. 2455
fr. 13 col. xii

2 διαφθεῖραι V: -φεῖραι P: -φθαρῆναι Q:]αϲαι Π

5 κληρωϲάμενοι ... γυναικῶν VQ: ἐκληρώϲαντο τὰc αἰχμαλωτίδαc τῶν
γυναικῶν P: κληρωϲαμεν]οι τῳ[ν] αιχμαλ[Π

10 ἀποκτενῶν uoluit Aldina: -κτείνων VPQ

12 τὸν ἀναιρεθέντα Diggle   δὲ PQ: μὲν V   τε καὶ PQ: καὶ V
καὶ ⟨τὸν Ἀcτυάνακτα⟩ Kirchhoff

13 κηδεύcαcα V: θρηνήcαcα P: θρηνήcαcα καὶ κηδεύcαcα Q

Hypothesis

After the sack of Troy, Athena and Poseidon decided to destroy the Greek army. Poseidon was well disposed to the city (of Troy) because he had had a rôle in founding it, Athena hated the Greeks because of the assault on Cassandra by Ajax. The Greeks drew lots for the women captives and according to rank allocated Cassandra to Agamemnon, Andromache to Neoptolemus and Polyxena to Achilles. They slaughtered Cassandra at Achilles' tomb and flung Astyanax from the walls. Menelaus brought Helen out with the intention of killing her, Agamemnon took the prophetess Cassandra home as his bride. After Hecuba had made accusations against Helen, and lamented over and seen to the burial of the dead, she was led to the tent of Odysseus to whom she had been given as a slave.

The persons of the drama are as follows: Poseidon, Athena, Hecuba, Chorus of Trojan women captives, Talthybius, Cassandra, Andromache, Menelaus, Helen.

ΤΡΩΙΑΔΕC

ΠΟCΕΙΔΩΝ

ἥκω λιπὼν Αἰγαῖον ἁλμυρὸν βάθος
πόντου Ποσειδῶν, ἔνθα Νηρήιδων χοροὶ
κάλλιστον ἴχνος ἐξελίccουcιν ποδός.
ἐξ οὗ γὰρ ἀμφὶ τήνδε Τρωϊκὴν χθόνα
Φοῖβόc τε κἀγὼ λαΐνους πύργους πέριξ   5
ὀρθοῖcιν ἔθεμεν κανόcιν, οὔποτ' ἐκ φρενῶν
εὔνοι' ἀπέcτη τῶν ἐμῶν Φρυγῶν πόλει·
ἢ νῦν καπνοῦται καὶ πρὸς Ἀργείου δορὸς
ὄλωλε πορθηθεῖc'. ὁ γὰρ Παρνάcιος
Φωκεὺς Ἐπειὸc μηχαναῖcι Παλλάδος   10
ἐγκύμον' ἵππον τευχέων cυναρμόcαc
πύργων ἔπεμψεν ἐντός, ὀλέθριον βάρος.
[ὅθεν πρὸς ἀνδρῶν ὑcτέρων κεκλήcεται
δούρειος ἵππος, κρυπτὸν ἀμπιcχὼν δόρυ.]
ἔρημα δ' ἄλcη καὶ θεῶν ἀνάκτορα   15
φόνωι καταρρεῖ· πρὸς δὲ κρηπίδων βάθροιc
πέπτωκε Πρίαμος Ζηνὸς ἑρκείου θανών.
πολὺς δὲ χρυσὸς Φρυγιά τε cκυλεύματα
πρὸς ναῦς Ἀχαιῶν πέμπεται· μένουcι δὲ
πρύμνηθεν οὖρον, ὡς δεκαcπόρωι χρόνωι   20
ἀλόχους τε καὶ τέκν' εἰcίδωcιν ἄcμενοι,
οἳ τήνδ' ἐπεcτράτευcαν Ἕλληνεc πόλιν.
ἐγὼ δέ (νικῶμαι γὰρ Ἀργείας θεοῦ
Ἥραc Ἀθάναc θ', αἳ cυνεξεῖλον Φρύγας)
λείπω τὸ κλεινὸν Ἴλιον βωμούς τ' ἐμούc·   25
ἐρημία γὰρ πόλιν ὅταν λάβηι κακή,
νοcεῖ τὰ τῶν θεῶν οὐδὲ τιμᾶcθαι θέλει.

2 χοροὶ .V et Aristid. 44. 9: -ὸc PQ
3 ποδί Aristid.
12 βρέταc V
13–14 del. Burges (ψυχρῶc ἠτυμολόγηcε Σ)
13 κληθήcεται PQ
14 ἀμπιcχὼν L. Dindorf: ἀμπίcχων V: ἀμφί- PQ
15 ἀγάλματα Σʸᵖ

54

Enter Poseidon

Poseidon I am Poseidon. I come from the salt depths of
the Aegean Sea where the dancing Nereids
circle with graceful steps. Ever since the
time when Phoebus and I built the encompassing
stone towers around this land of Troy with
straight rule, love for this city of Phrygians
has never left my heart. Now it is smouldering
and sacked, destroyed by the Argive spear.
By the designs of Pallas Athena, Epeius the   10
Parnassian from Phocis constructed a horse
pregnant with arms and sent it within the city's
walls, a burden that brought death. [As a
result it will be called by future generations
the Wooden Horse, the concealer of hidden
weapons.] The sacred groves are desolate and
the gods' shrines are running with blood. Near
the steps at the base of the altar of Zeus the
Protector, Priam has been fatally cut down.
A mass of gold and Trojan loot is being sent to
the Greek ships. They await a following wind,   20
so that after ten long years they may have
the pleasure of seeing their wives and children
again, the Greeks who made the expedition
against this city. For my own part I am leaving
this famed city of Troy and my altars in it,
since the Argive goddess Hera and Athena,
who together destroyed the Trojans, have got
the better of me. Whenever cruel desolation
takes hold of a city, religious worship suffers
and no longer receives its honour. The river

πολλοῖς δὲ κωκυτοῖσιν αἰχμαλωτίδων
βοᾶι Cκάμανδρος δεσπότας κληρουμένων.
καὶ τὰς μὲν Ἀρκάς, τὰς δὲ Θεςςαλὸς λεὼς   30
εἴληχ' Ἀθηναίων τε Θηςεῖδαι πρόμοι.
ὅςαι δ' ἄκληροι Τρωιάδων, ὑπὸ cτέγαις
ταῖςδ' εἰςί, τοῖς πρώτοιςιν ἐξηιρημέναι
cτρατοῦ, cὺν αὐταῖς δ' ἡ Λάκαινα Τυνδαρὶς
Ἑλένη, νομιςθεῖς' αἰχμάλωτος ἐνδίκως.   35
τὴν δ' ἀθλίαν τήνδ' εἴ τις εἰςορᾶν θέλει,
πάρεςτιν Ἑκάβη κειμένη πυλῶν πάρος,
δάκρυα χέουςα πολλὰ καὶ πολλῶν ὕπερ·
ἧι παῖς μὲν ἀμφὶ μνῆμ' Ἀχιλλείου τάφου
λάθραι τέθνηκε τλημόνως Πολυξένη·   40
φροῦδος δὲ Πρίαμος καὶ τέκν'· ἣν δὲ παρθένον
μεθῆκ' Ἀπόλλων δρομάδα Καςςάνδραν ἄναξ,
τὸ τοῦ θεοῦ τε παραλιπὼν τό τ' εὐcεβὲς
γαμεῖ βιαίως cκότιον Ἀγαμέμνων λέχος.
ἀλλ', ὦ ποτ' εὐτυχοῦςα, χαῖρέ μοι, πόλις   45
ξεστόν τε πύργωμ'· εἴ cε μὴ διώλεcεν
Παλλὰς Διὸς παῖς, ἦcθ' ἂν ἐν βάθροις ἔτι.

ΑΘΗΝΑ

ἔξεςτι τὸν γένει μὲν ἄγχιςτον πατρὸς
μέγαν τε δαίμον' ἐν θεοῖς τε τίμιον,
λύςαςαν ἔχθραν τὴν πάρος, προςεννέπειν;   50
Πο. ἔξεςτιν· αἱ γὰρ cυγγενεῖς ὁμιλίαι,
ἄναςς' Ἀθάνα, φίλτρον οὐ cμικρὸν φρενῶν.
Αθ. ἐπήινες' ὀργὰς ἠπίους· φέρω δὲ cοὶ
κοινοὺς ἐμαυτῆι τ' ἐς μέςον λόγους, ἄναξ.
Πο. μῶν ἐκ θεῶν του καινὸν ἀγγέλλεις ἔπος,   55
ἢ Ζηνὸς ἢ καὶ δαιμόνων τινὸς πάρα;

32 παρθένων Σγρ
37 ἑκάβην κειμένην V
38 δάκρυα χέουςα Scaliger: δακρυχέουςα PQ: δάκρυα χέουςαν V
40 λάθρα V: οἰκτρὰ PQΣγρ
49 μέγαν δὲ Elmsley
52 μικρὸν P
55 κοινὸν PQ   ἀγγελεῖς V   56

Scamander echoes with the incessant cries of women captives waiting to be allocated masters. Some the Arcadian people have won, some the Thessalian, and others the sons of Theseus, leaders of the Athenians. Those of the Trojan women who are still unallotted wait here in these tents. They are reserved for the chiefs of the army and with them is Helen of Sparta, Tyndareus' daughter, rightly classed as a prisoner. If anyone wishes to look on the unhappy woman here, this is Hecuba, lying in front of the entrance, weeping many tears for many people and many reasons. Unknown to her, her daughter Polyxena has been slaughtered in a pitiable death at Achilles' tomb. Priam and their children are dead. Cassandra, whom the lord Apollo left a crazed virgin, will be forced into an unlawful union with Agamemnon who has deserted piety and respect for the god. O city that was once so prosperous with your squared stone walls, farewell. If Pallas Athena, Zeus' daughter, had not destroyed you, you would still be strong on your foundations.

Enter Athena

Athena   May I relinquish my former enmity and speak to one who is closely related to my father and a greatly honoured power among the gods?

Poseidon   You may. Family ties, my lady Athena, are no small attraction to the mind.

Athena   I thank you for your kind attitude and I propose we discuss a subject of common interest to us both, my lord.

Poseidon   Is it a new word from one of the gods you are bringing? From Zeus for instance, or even some other deity?

Αθ. οὔκ, ἀλλὰ Τροίας οὕνεκ', ἔνθα βαίνομεν,
    πρὸς cὴν ἀφῖγμαι δύναμιν, ὡς κοινὴν λάβω.
Πο. οὔ πού νιν, ἔχθραν τὴν πρὶν ἐκβαλοῦca, νῦν
    ἐc οἶκτον ἦλθεc πυρὶ κατηιθαλωμένην;   60
Αθ. ἐκεῖcε πρῶτ' ἄνελθε· κοινώcηι λόγουc
    καὶ cυνθελήcειc ἂν ἐγὼ πρᾶξαι θέλω;
Πο. μάλιcτ'· ἀτὰρ δὴ καὶ τὸ còν θέλω μαθεῖν·
    πότερον Ἀχαιῶν ἦλθεc οὕνεκ' ἢ Φρυγῶν;
Αθ. τοὺc μὲν πρὶν ἐχθροὺc Τρῶαc εὐφρᾶναι θέλω,   65
    cτρατῶι δ' Ἀχαιῶν νόcτον ἐμβαλεῖν πικρόν.
Πο. τί δ' ὧδε πηδᾶιc ἄλλοτ' εἰc ἄλλουc τρόπουc
    μιcεῖc τε λίαν καὶ φιλεῖc ὃν ἂν τύχηιc;
Αθ. οὐκ οἶcθ' ὑβριcθεῖcάν με καὶ ναοὺc ἐμούc;
Πο. οἶδ'· ἡνίκ' Αἴαc εἷλκε Καccάνδραν βίαι.   70
Αθ. κοὐ δείν' Ἀχαιῶν ἔπαθεν οὐδ' ἤκουc' ὕπο.
Πο. καὶ μὴν ἔπερcάν γ' Ἴλιον τῶι cῶι cθένει.
Αθ. τοιγάρ cφε cὺν coὶ βούλομαι δρᾶcαι κακῶc.
Πο. ἕτοιμ' ἃ βούληι τἀπ' ἐμοῦ. δράcειc δὲ τί;
Αθ. δύcνοcτον αὐτοῖc νόcτον ἐμβαλεῖν θέλω.   75
Πο. ἐν γῆι μενόντων ἢ καθ' ἁλμυρὰν ἅλα;
Αθ. ὅταν πρὸc οἴκουc ναυcτολῶc' ἀπ' Ἰλίου.
    καὶ Ζεὺc μὲν ὄμβρον καὶ χάλαζαν ἄcπετον
    πέμψει δνοφώδη τ' αἰθέροc φυcήματα·
    ἐμοὶ δὲ δώcειν φηcὶ πῦρ κεραύνιον,   80
    βάλλειν Ἀχαιοὺc ναῦc τε πιμπράναι πυρί.
    cὺ δ' αὖ, τὸ cόν, παράcχεc Αἰγαῖον πόρον
    τρικυμίαιc βρέμοντα καὶ δίναιc ἁλόc,
    πλῆcον δὲ νεκρῶν κοῖλον Εὐβοίαc μυχόν,

59 οὔ Wecklein: ἢ VPQ
60 κατηιθαλωμένην Elmsley: -ηc VPQ
62 cυμπονήcειc PQ
68 τύχηc V· -η(ι) PQ (-ῆι Q) et gE et Cyrill. c. Iul. 175 B (PG 76.
   767 Migne)
70 εἷλε V et Cyrill.
71 κοὐ δείν' Nauck: κοὐδὲν V: κοὐδέν γ' PQ et Cyrill.
72 ἔπερcάν γ' Victorius: -cάν τ' VQ: ἔπερcατ' P
75 δύcτηνον V
76 μένουcιν PQ
79 πέμψειν Porson   58

Athena	No, it is for Troy's sake, where we are now walking, that I am approaching your power, to ally it with mine.
Poseidon	Surely you have not cast aside your former hostility and come to pity the city now that it is burnt to ashes?
Athena	Return to the point at issue. Will you take counsel with me and cooperate in what I wish to do?
Poseidon	Most certainly. But I want to know your interest in the matter too. Is it for the Greeks or the Trojans that you have come?
Athena	I want to bring heart to the Trojans whom I hated before, and to give the Greek army a painful journey home.
Poseidon	Why are you so fickle in your attitudes, hating too much and loving too much, just as chance dictates?
Athena	Are you not aware that I have been insulted and my temples too?
Poseidon	I am; it was when Ajax forcibly dragged off Cassandra.
Athena	And the Greeks neither punished nor reproached him.
Poseidon	Besides, it was by your strength that they sacked Troy.
Athena	That is exactly why I want, with your help, to do them some damage.
Poseidon	For my part I am ready for what you wish. But what are you going to do?
Athena	I want to make their return home an unhappy one.
Poseidon	While they stay here on land, or on the open sea?
Athena	As they are sailing for home from Troy. And Zeus will send rain, enormous hailstones and dark storm blasts. He promises he will give me for my use the fire of the thunderbolt to strike the Greek ships and to burn them. You, though, your part is to make the Aegean sea rage with huge waves and whirlpools, and fill the deep bay of Euboea with corpses so that

60

70

80

<pre>
            ὡς ἂν τὸ λοιπὸν τἄμ' ἀνάκτορ' εὐσεβεῖν   85
            εἰδῶσ' Ἀχαιοὶ θεούς τε τοὺς ἄλλους σέβειν.
    Πο.   ἔσται τάδ'· ἡ χάρις γὰρ οὐ μακρῶν λόγων
            δεῖται· ταράξω πέλαγος Αἰγαίας ἁλός.
            ἀκταὶ δὲ Μυκόνου Δήλιοί τε χοιράδες
            Σκῦρός τε Λῆμνός θ' αἱ Καφήρειοί τ' ἄκραι   90
            πολλῶν θανόντων σώμαθ' ἕξουσιν νεκρῶν.
            ἀλλ' ἕρπ' Ὄλυμπον καὶ κεραυνίους βολὰς
            λαβοῦσα πατρὸς ἐκ χερῶν καραδόκει,
            ὅταν στράτευμ' Ἀργεῖον ἐξιῆι κάλως.
            μῶρος δὲ θνητῶν ὅστις ἐκπορθεῖ πόλεις   95
            ναούς τε τύμβους θ', ἱερὰ τῶν κεκμηκότων·
            ἐρημίαι δούς ⟨σφ'⟩ αὐτὸς ὤλεθ' ὕστερον.
</pre>

ΕΚΑΒΗ

<pre>
            ἄνα, δύσδαιμον· πεδόθεν κεφαλὴν
            ἐπάειρε δέρην ⟨τ'⟩· οὐκέτι Τροία
            τάδε καὶ βασιλῆς ἐσμεν Τροίας.   100
            μεταβαλλομένου δαίμονος ἄνσχου.
            πλεῖ κατὰ πορθμόν, πλεῖ κατὰ δαίμονα,
            μηδὲ προσίστη πρῶιραν βιότου
            πρὸς κῦμα πλέουσα τύχαισιν.
            αἰαῖ αἰαῖ·   105
            τί γὰρ οὐ πάρα μοι μελέαι στενάχειν,
            ἧι πατρὶς ἔρρει καὶ τέκνα καὶ πόσις;
            ὦ πολὺς ὄγκος συστελλόμενος
            προγόνων, ὡς οὐδὲν ἄρ' ἦσθα.
</pre>

95 γε gB
96 δὲ Blomfield (∼gB), nulla in fine u. distinctione   post τύμβους
θ' dist. Σ
97 ⟨σφ'⟩ Page
98 Εκ. VQΣ: Χο. P (item 101-2 quos citat choro trib. Stob.
4. 44. 15)   κεφαλὴν PQ: -λὰ V: utrumque casum agnoscit Σ
99 ⟨τ'⟩ Musgrave
101 ἄνσχου Nauck: ἀνέχου VPQΣ et gE et Stob. 4. 44. 15
103 προσίστη PQ: -ίστω VΣ‖ et gE
105 Εκ. praescr. P
108 συστελλόμενος Victorius: -μένων VPQΣ‖

	in future the Greeks will learn to respect my
	power and worship the other gods.
Poseidon	It shall be so. The favour you are asking does
	not need any long speeches. I shall stir up the
	water of the Aegean sea. The shores of Mykonos,
	the rocky reefs of Delos, Skyros, Lemnos, and
	the promontories of Caphereus shall be filled with

Poseidon It shall be so. The favour you are asking does
not need any long speeches. I shall stir up the
water of the Aegean sea. The shores of Mykonos,
the rocky reefs of Delos, Skyros, Lemnos, and
the promontories of Caphereus shall be filled with   90
the bodies of many dead. Go to Olympus and when
you have taken your father's thunderbolts, watch
for the moment the Greek fleet lets out its sails.
The man who sacks cities, temples and graves, the
sacred places of the dead, is a fool. Having given
them over to devastation, he himself perishes
later.

Poseidon and Athena leave the stage
Hecuba raises her head to sing

Hecuba Up, you poor one: lift your head and neck from
the ground. This is no longer Troy nor we the   100
Queen of Troy. Bear with your fortune as it
changes. Sail according to the strait's current,
sail in accordance with destiny and do not turn
life's prow against the waves' swell, sailing as
you do on the winds of chance. Ai-ai. Ai-ai.
What is there that I do not mourn in my wretchedness, I for whom country, children and
husband are all gone? All that wealth which
belonged to my ancestors reduced - you came to

τί με χρὴ ςιγᾶν; τί δὲ μὴ ςιγᾶν;   110
τί δὲ θρηνῆςαι;
δύςτηνος ἐγὼ τῆς βαρυδαίμονος
ἄρθρων κλίςεως, ὡς διάκειμαι,
νῶτ᾽ ἐν ςτερροῖς λέκτροιςι ταθεῖς᾽.
οἴμοι κεφαλῆς, οἴμοι κροτάφων   115
πλευρῶν θ᾽, ὥς μοι πόθος εἱλίξαι
καὶ διαδοῦναι νῶτον ἄκανθάν τ᾽
εἰς ἀμφοτέρους τοίχους μελέων,
ἐπιοῦς᾽ αἰεὶ δακρύων ἐλέγους.
μοῦςα δὲ χαΰτη τοῖς δυςτήνοις   120
ἄτας κελαδεῖν ἀχορεύτους.

πρῶιραι ναῶν, ὠκείαις
Ἴλιον ἱερὰν αἳ κώπαις
δι᾽ ἅλα πορφυροειδῆ καὶ
λιμένας Ἑλλάδος εὐόρμους   125
αὐλῶν παιᾶνι ςτυγνῶι
ςυρίγγων τ᾽ εὐφθόγγων φωνᾶι
βαίνουςαι †πλεκτὰν Αἰγύπτου
παιδείαν ἐξηρτήςαςθ᾽†,
αἰαῖ, Τροίας ἐν κόλποις   130
τὰν Μενελάου μετανιςόμεναι
ςτυγνὰν ἄλοχον, Κάςτορι λώβαν
τῶι τ᾽ Εὐρώται δύςκλειαν,

111 μὴ θρηνῆςαι V   τί δὲ θρηνῆςαι del. Tyrrell
113 κλίςεως Musgrave: κλίςιος PQ: -ςίας V: τῆς ἀνακλίςεως Σ
114 ςτερροῖς Haun. (sec. Kirchhoff): ςτεροῖς V: ςτέρνοις PQ: Va non
legibilis   ταθεῖς᾽ Aldina: -εῖςα VPQ
119 ἐπιοῦς᾽ Musgrave   ἐπὶ τοὺς VPRQΣ
122 ὠκείαις Tyrrell: ὠκεῖαι VPRQΣΙ
124 πορφυροειδῆ Hesych. (i. 435 Latte): -δέα VPQ (-ρείδεα Q, -ρίδεα P)
126 ⟨cὺν⟩ παιᾶνι Page
127 φωνᾶ(ι) PQ: -αῖς V
128–9 λεκτὰν Q fort.   πλεκτάς (Musgrave), Αἰγύπτου / παίδευμ᾽
(Tyrrell), ἐξηρτήκαςθ᾽ ⟨αἰαῖ⟩ (Page)

62

nothing after all! Why should I be silent? Or
why not be silent? Why should I sing a lament?   110
How unhappy I am in the cruel destiny which
forces me to lay down my limbs here in this state,
stretched out on my back on this hard bed. Oh,
my head and temples and ribs, how I long to rock
my body, to shift my back and spine to either side,
in my endless tearful laments. Yet even this is   120
music to the wretched, to sing of joyless troubles.
You ships' prows who sailed with swift oars to
holy Troy across the purple sea and by way of
the fair harbours of Greece, to the accompaniment
of a hateful paean of flutes and to the hateful
voice of tuneful pipes, you hung from your sterns
the Egyptian rope cables when you went to find
in the Gulfs of Troy the hateful wife of Menelaus, 130
Castor's blight and a disgrace to the Eurotas, she

ἃ σφάζει μὲν
τὸν πεντήκοντ᾽ ἀροτῆρα τέκνων 135
†Πρίαμον, ἐμέ τε μελέαν Ἑκάβαν†
ἐς τάνδ᾽ ἐξώκειλ᾽ ἄταν.
ὤμοι, θάκους οἵους θάσσω,
σκηναῖς ἐφέδρους Ἀγαμεμνονίαις.
δούλα δ᾽ ἄγομαι 140
γραῦς ἐξ οἴκων πενθήρη
κρᾶτ᾽ ἐκπορθηθεῖσ᾽ οἰκτρῶς.
ἀλλ᾽ ὦ τῶν χαλκεγχέων Τρώων
ἄλοχοι μέλεαι
†καὶ κόραι δύσνυμφαι†,
τύφεται Ἴλιον, αἰάζωμεν. 145
μάτηρ δ᾽ ὡσεὶ πτανοῖς κλαγγὰν
†ὄρνισιν ὅπως ἐξάρξω ᾽γὼ
μολπὰν οὐ τὰν αὐτὰν†
οἵαν ποτὲ δὴ
σκήπτρωι Πριάμου διερειδομένου 150
ποδὸς ἀρχεχόρου πλαγαῖς Φρυγίους
εὐκόμποις ἐξῆρχον θεούς.

135–6 τε ⟨τὰν⟩ Seidler (iam Burges, sed Πρίαμον del.), κἄμ᾽ αὖ μ-
Paley, ἐμὲ δ᾽ αὖ μ- deletis Πρίαμον et Ἑκάβαν Lenting
139 ἐφέδρους Bothe: -ος VPQ
141 ante πενθήρη (-ει) uocabula κουρᾶ(ι) ξυρήκει (Alc. 427) quae
habent VPQΣ del. Murray
144 καὶ κοῦραι δύσνυμφοι Aldina, καὶ κοῦραι δυcνυμφ⟨ότατ⟩αι uel ἄλοχοι
μέλεαι δύσνυμφοι (κόραι iam del. Kirchhoff) Diggle, ⟨μέλεαι⟩ κοῦραι
δύσνυμφοι Page
145 αἰάζωμεν Aldina: -ζομεν VPQΣⁱ
146 ὡσεὶ VQΣⁱ: ὡσεί τις P   πτανοῖς VPᶜQΣⁱ: παν- V: πτην- P
147 ὄρνις (del. ὅπως) Dindorf
148 οὐ ⟨μὰν⟩ Hermann, ⟨ἀλλ᾽⟩ οὐ Seidler, μολπᾶν οὐ τὰν αὐτὰν
⟨ἀχὰν⟩ Jackson   incertum quid legerit Σ
150 διερειδομένου Herwerden: -μένα VP(δ᾽ ἐρ- P)QΣ
151 πλαγαῖς Seidler: πλαγγ- V: πληγ- PQ   Φρυγίους Wilamowitz:
-ίαις VPQ et Σ ut uid.

64

who is the murderer of Priam, father of fifty
children, she who has run me, wretched Hecuba,
aground into this destruction. Alas, what a
place this is where now I sit, close by the tents
of Agamemnon. I am being led away from my   140
home, a slave, an old woman with her head
drastically, pitifully shorn in her mourning.
Troy is burning, let us lament it, you wretched
wives of Trojan bronze-speared warriors, and
you ill-wedded daughters. Like a mother bird
for her young, I shall lead the crying, but it
will not be the same song as once I led in honour
of Troy's gods with the confident ringing beat
of the footsteps that began the dance while
Priam leant on his sceptre.   150

Ἑκάβη, τί θροεῖς; τί δὲ θωΰςςεις;   [ςτρ. α
ποῖ λόγος ἥκει; διὰ γὰρ μελάθρων
ἄιον οἴκτους οὓς οἰκτίζηι.   155
διὰ δὲ ςτέρνων φόβος ἀίςςει
Τρωιάςιν, αἳ τῶνδ' οἴκων εἴςω
δουλείαν αἰάζουςιν.

Εκ. ὦ τέκν', Ἀχαιῶν πρὸς ναῦς ἤδη
κινεῖται κωπήρης χείρ.   160

Ημ. οἲ 'γώ, τί θέλους'; ἦ πού μ' ἤδη
ναυςθλώςουςιν πατρίας ἐκ γᾶς;

Εκ. οὐκ οἶδ', εἰκάζω δ' ἄταν.

Ημ. ἰὼ ἰώ.
μέλεαι, μόχθων ἐπακουςόμεναι,   165
Τρωιάδες, ἐξορμίζεςθ' οἴκων·
ςτέλλους' Ἀργεῖοι νόςτον.

Εκ. ἒ ἔ.
μή νύν μοι τὰν
ἐκβακχεύουςαν Καςςάνδραν,
αἰςχύναν Ἀργείοιςιν,   171
πέμψητ' ἔξω,   170
μαινάδ', ἐπ' ἄλγεςι δ' ἀλγυνθῶ.
ἰὼ ἰώ.
Τροία Τροία δύςταν', ἔρρεις,
δύςτανοι δ' οἵ ς' ἐκλείποντες
καὶ ζῶντες καὶ δμαθέντες.   175

---

153 *HMIXOPION A'* Musgrave: Χο. VPQ: uide VQ ad 164, Σ ad 176
154–5 ποῖ λόγος ἥκει et ἄιον οἴκ om. P et primitus Q (suppl. q)
159 Ἀχαιῶν Schroeder: ἀργείων VPQ
161 *Ημ.* Musgrave: Χο. VQ: om. P   οἲ 'γώ Kirchhoff: οἱ ἐγώ
μελέα V: οἲ 'γὼ (οἲ ἐγὼ Q) τλάμων PQ
163 *Εκ.* Musgrave: om. VPQ
164 *Ημ.* VQ: Χο. P
166 ἐξορμίζεςθ' Headlam: ἔξω κομίζεςθ' VPQΣ¹: ἔξω κομίςαςθ'
Aldina: quid legerit Σ incertum
171 et 170 inter se trai. Murray
172 ἄλγει V
173 ἰὼ ἰώ V: ἰώ PQ: del. Seidler:
174 ς' ἐκλείποντες Burges: ς' ἐκλιπόντες VQ: ςε λιπ- P

First Half-Chorus enters

First Half-Chorus Hecuba, what are you crying aloud?
What are you calling out? What is the drift of
what you have said? I heard your pitiful
laments from indoors. Fear stabs the hearts
of the Trojan women mourning their slavery
inside.

Hecuba The oarsmen of the Greeks are already moving 160
to the ships.

First Half-Chorus Ah, what is their will? The time has
already come then for them to take me from my
own home country?

Hecuba I have no knowledge. I can only guess at our
ruin.

First Half-Chorus Alas, you unhappy Trojans, come out
and hear of the drudgery you must do. The
Greeks are preparing their return.

Hecuba Alas, do not let Cassandra come out in her
delirious, mad state to be degraded by the
Argives and bring me even more pain. Ah, 170
Troy, unhappy Troy, you are gone and those
who leave you, are unhappy too, both the
surviving and the dead.

οἴμοι. τρομερὰ cκηνὰc ἔλιπον   [ἀντ. α
τάcδ' 'Αγαμέμνονοc ἐπακουcομένα,
βαcίλεια, cέθεν· μή με κτείνειν
δόξ' 'Αργείων κεῖται μελέαν;
ἢ κατὰ πρύμναc ἤδη ναῦται   180
cτέλλονται κινεῖν κώπαc;

Εκ. ὦ τέκνον, ὀρθρεύουcαν ψυχὰν
ἐκπληχθεῖc' ἦλθον φρίκαι.

Ημ. ἤδη τιc ἔβα Δαναῶν κῆρυξ;
τῶι πρόcκειμαι δούλα τλάμων;   185

Εκ. ἐγγύc που κεῖcαι κλήρου.

Ημ. ἰὼ ἰώ.
τίc μ' 'Αργείων ἢ Φθιωτᾶν
ἢ νηcαίαν ἄξει χώραν
δύcτανον πόρcω Τροίαc;

Εκ. φεῦ φεῦ.   190

τῶι δ' ἁ τλάμων
ποῦ παῖ γαίαc δουλεύcω γραῦc,
ὡc κηφήν, ἁ δειλαία,
νεκροῦ μορφά,
νεκύων ἀμενηνὸν ἄγαλμα,
αἰαῖ αἰαῖ,
τὰν παρὰ προθύροιc φυλακὰν κατέχουc'
ἢ παίδων θρέπτειρ', ἃ Τροίαc   195
ἀρχαγοὺc εἶχον τιμάc;

176 *HMIXOPION B'* Musgrave cum Σ: *Xo.* VPQ
182 ὀρθρεύουcαν Aldina: ὀρθρεύου cὰν VPQΣli
183 Hecubae contin. Aldina: choro trib. VPQ
184 *Ημ.* Seidler: om. VPQ
187 *Ημ.* Musgrave: *Xo.* VP: om. Q·   φθιωτᾶν Q: -ὰν P: -ῶν V
188 νηcαίαc ... χώραc Wecklein   ἄξει Brodaeus: μ' ἄξει V: ἤξει PQ
189 πόρcω Dindorf: πρόcω VΣ: πόρρω PQΣγρ
190 *Εκ.* Seidler: *Xo.* P: om. VQ
193-5 sic mutilos exhibent PQ: νεκύων ἀμενηνὰ (ἀμενη Q) / παρὰ
προθύροιc / ἢ (c' ἢ Q) παίδων θρέπτηραc (θρέπτειν Q)
193-4 ἄγαλμα, / αἰαῖ αἰαῖ post Hermann Diggle : ἄγαλμ'· ἢ VΣl
(desunt PQ): ἄγαλμα (del. ἢ) Lachmann   δειλαία ... ἄγαλμα
habent gB et gE
194 παρὰ PQ: παρά τε VΣl

Second Half-Chorus enters

Second Half-Chorus Shivering with fear, I have left the
        tents of Agamemnon to listen to you, my Queen.
        Have the Argives decided to kill me in all my
        misery, or are the Greek seamen now ready   180
        to set their oars in motion at the sterns?

Hecuba   My child, I came in terror, my spirit, awake
        since dawn, struck by panic.

Second Half-Chorus Has a herald come from the Greeks
        yet? Whom have they assigned me to as a
        slave, wretched that I am?

Hecuba   You are near that assignment now.

Second Half-Chorus What Argive or Phthian will take me,
        poor creature, far away from Troy? Or will
        it be to an island home?

Hecuba   Alas, alas, whose slave shall I be? Where on
        earth shall I live my life as a servant, an old   190
        woman, I the wretched one, the unhappy one,
        drone-like, corpse-like, a feeble adornment
        of the dead? Shall I stand guard at their
        doors, or nurse their children, I who once
        held a ruler's honour in Troy?

Χο. αἰαῖ αἰαῖ, ποίοις δ' οἴκτοις   [στρ. β
τάνδ' ἂν λύμαν ἐξαιάζοις;
οὐκ Ἰδαίοις ἱστοῖς κερκίδα
δινεύους' ἐξαλλάξω.   200
νέατον τοκέων δώματα λεύσσω,
νέατον· μόχθους ⟨δ'⟩ ἔξω κρείσσους,
ἢ λέκτροις πλαθεῖς' Ἑλλάνων
(ἔρροι νὺξ αὗτα καὶ δαίμων)
ἢ Πειρήνας ὑδρευομένα   205
πρόσπολος οἰκτρὰ σεμνῶν ὑδάτων.
τὰν κλεινὰν εἴθ' ἔλθοιμεν
Θησέως εὐδαίμονα χώραν.
μὴ γὰρ δὴ δίναν γ' Εὐρώτα   210
τάν ⟨τ'⟩ ἐχθίσταν θεράπναν Ἑλένας,
ἔνθ' ἀντάσω Μενέλαι δούλα,
τῶι τᾶς Τροίας πορθητᾶι.

τὰν Πηνειοῦ σεμνὰν χώραν,   [ἀντ. β
κρηπῖδ' Οὐλύμπου καλλίσταν,   215
ὄλβωι βρίθειν φάμαν ἤκους'
εὐθαλεῖ τ' εὐκαρπείαι·
τὰ δὲ δεύτερά μοι μετὰ τὰν ἱερὰν
Θησέως ζαθέαν ἐλθεῖν χώραν.

197 Χο. ΡΣ: Εκ. VQ
198 τάνδ' ἂν Wilamowitz: τὰν σὰν VPQ   ἐξαιάζοις Wilamowitz: -αιάζεις V: -ετάζεις PQ
199 Χο. praescr. VQ: Εκ. P
201 Εκ. praescr. V   νέατον Seidler: -τοι V (νεάτοι) PQΣ¹ τοκέων δώματα Parmentier cl. 602: τεκέων σώματα VPQ: τοκέων σήματα Wilamowitz
202 νέατον Seidler: -τοι VPQ   ⟨δ'⟩ Seidler
205 ὑδρευομένα Heiland: -σομένα V (-α cum ι subscr.) PQ
206 οἰκτρὰ om. VQ   ὑδάτων Hermann: ὑδάτων ἔσομαι VPQ πρόπολος σεμνῶν ὑδάτων ἔσομαι Dindorf
207 Χο. praescr. P
210 Εκ. praescr. P   δὴ δίναν VΣ¹: ἐν δίνα(ι) PQ
211 ⟨τ'⟩ Musgrave
218 τὰ δὲ Diggle: τάδε VQΣ¹¹: τὰ P

Chorus Aiai, aiai, think of the lamentations with which
you could bewail this degrading ruin of ours.
No longer shall I move the whirling shuttle
back and forth at Trojan looms. This is the   200
last time I shall look on the home of my parents,
the very last time. I shall have trials greater
than this, for either I shall be brought to the
bed of Greeks (may that night and the destiny
which brings it be accursed!) or as a pitiful
servant I shall draw water at the sacred fountain
of Peirene. I would prefer to come to the famed
and favoured land of Theseus. But I wish I
may never set eyes on the swirling river
Eurotas, hated home of Helen, where as a   210
slave I should meet Menelaus, the sacker of
Troy.
I have heard that the hallowed land of Peneus,
beautiful foundation of Mount Olympus, is
teeming with wealth and fertile fruitfulness.
This is second choice for me after going to
Theseus' sacrosanct, holy country. The land

καὶ τὰν Αἰτναίαν Ἡφαίστου   220
Φοινίκας ἀντήρη χώραν,
Cικελῶν ὀρέων ματέρ᾽, ἀκούω
καρύccεcθαι cτεφάνοιc ἀρετᾶc,
τάν τ᾽ ἀγχιcτεύουcαν γᾶν
†᾽Ιονίωι ναύται πόντωι†,   225
ἃν ὑγραίνει καλλιcτεύων
ὁ ξανθὰν χαίταν πυρcαίνων
Κρᾶθιc ζαθέαιc παγαῖcι τρέφων
εὔανδρόν τ᾽ ὀλβίζων γᾶν.

καὶ μὴν Δαναῶν ὅδ᾽ ἀπὸ cτρατιᾶc   230
κῆρυξ, νεοχμῶν μύθων ταμίαc,
cτείχει ταχύπουν ἴχνοc ἐξανύτων.
τί φέρει; τί λέγει; δοῦλαι γὰρ δὴ
Δωρίδοc ἐcμὲν χθονὸc ἤδη.

ΤΑΛΘΥΒΙΟC

Ἑκάβη, πυκνὰc γὰρ οἶcθά μ᾽ ἐc Τροίαν ὁδοὺc   235
ἐλθόντα κήρυκ᾽ ἐξ Ἀχαιικοῦ cτρατοῦ,
ἐγνωcμένοc δὴ καὶ πάροιθέ cοι, γύναι,
Ταλθύβιοc ἥκω καινὸν ἀγγελῶν λόγον.
Εκ. †τόδε τόδε φίλαι γυναῖκεc† ὁ φόβοc ἦν πάλαι.
Τα. ἤδη κεκλήρωcθ᾽, εἰ τόδ᾽ ἦν ὑμῖν φόβοc.   240
Εκ. αἰαῖ, τίν᾽ ἢ
    Θεccαλίαc πόλιν Φθιάδοc εἶπαc ἢ
    Καδμείαc χθονόc;
Τα. κατ᾽ ἄνδρ᾽ ἑκάcτη κοὐχ ὁμοῦ λελόγχατε.
Εκ. τίν᾽ ἄρα τίc ἔλαχε; τίνα πότμοc εὐτυχὴc

225 ναύται (ι adscr.) PQ: -τα V
227 πυρcαίνων V et Σ Lycoph. 1021: πυρcεύων VslQ (nisi -cαύων Q): πυρδεύων P
237 δὴ Mistchenko: δὲ VPQ﹡ u. del. Dobree
238 κοινὸν PQ   ἀγγελῶν Q: -έλων VPac: -έλλων Ppc
239 τόδε alterum del. Matthiae   γυναῖκεc V: τρω(ι)άδεc PQ
τόδε, φίλαι γυναῖκεc, τόδε, Τρωϊάδεc Diggle
242 πόλιν Hartung: πόλιν ἢ VPQ
244 Εκ. PQ: Χο. V

of Etna and of Hephaestus, opposite Carthage,   220
mother of the Sicilian mountains, is extolled
far and wide for its garlands of valour, so I
hear, and the country near the Ionian Sea
which the beautiful river Crathis waters and
cherishes with its hallowed streams that tint
hair to red-gold with their dye, and bless the
land to make it happy in its men.
Here comes a herald, hurrying from the Greek   230
army, bringing more news. What is it he brings?
What has he got to say? For we know we are
already enslaved to Greece.

    Talthybius enters

Talthybius   Hecuba – I can call you by your name
        because you know that I have come on frequent
        journeys from the Greek camp to Troy as a
        herald. I am Talthybius – you know me from
        earlier times, and now I have come to bring
        you new messages.

Hecuba   This is what I have long since been afraid of,
        my dear friends.

Talthybius   You have now been assigned by lot – if   240
        this was your fear.

Hecuba   Alas, is it a city in Phthian Thessaly, or in the
        land of Cadmus?

Talthybius   You have been allotted separately, each to
        a man.

Hecuba   To whom has each been allotted? Which of the

'Ιλιάδων μένει; 245

Τα. οἶδ'· ἀλλ' ἕκαστα πυνθάνου, μὴ πάνθ' ὁμοῦ.

Εκ. τοὐμὸν τίς ἄρ'
ἔλαχε τέκος, ἔνεπε, τλάμονα Κασσάνδραν;

Τα. ἐξαίρετόν νιν ἔλαβεν 'Αγαμέμνων ἄναξ.

Εκ. ἦ τᾶι Λακεδαιμονίαι νύμφαι 250
δούλαν; ὤμοι μοι.

Τα. οὔκ, ἀλλὰ λέκτρων σκότια νυμφευτήρια.

Εκ. ἦ τὰν τοῦ Φοίβου παρθένον, ἆι γέρας ὁ
χρυσοκόμας ἔδωκ' ἄλεκτρον ζόαν;

Τα. ἔρως ἐτόξευς' αὐτὸν ἐνθέου κόρης. 255

Εκ. ῥῖπτε, τέκνον, ζαθέους κλάδας καὶ ἀπὸ χροὸς ἐνδυ-
τῶν στεφέων ἱεροὺς στολμούς.

Τα. οὐ γὰρ μέγ' αὐτῆι βασιλικῶν λέκτρων τυχεῖν;

Εκ. τί δ' ὁ νεοχμὸν ἀπ' ἐμέθεν ἐλάβετε τέκος, 260
†ποῦ μοι†;

Τα. Πολυξένην ἔλεξας ἢ τίν' ἱστορεῖς;

Εκ. ταύταν· τῶι πάλος ἔζευξεν;

Τα. τύμβωι τέτακται προσπολεῖν 'Αχιλλέως.

Εκ. ὤμοι ἐγώ· τάφωι πρόσπολον ἐτεκόμαν. 265
ἀτὰρ τίς ὅδ' ἦν νόμος ἢ τί
θέσμιον, ὦ φίλος, 'Ελλάνων;

Τα. εὐδαιμόνιζε παῖδα σήν· ἔχει καλῶς.

Εκ. τί τόδ' ἔλακες;
ἀρά μοι ἀέλιον λεύσσει; 270

Τα. ἔχει πότμος νιν, ὥστ' ἀπηλλάχθαι. πόνων.

245 μένει Hermann: -νεῖ VPQ
247 ἄρ' Kirchhoff: ἄρ' PQ: om. V
248 τέκνον Q   ἔνεπε Seidler: ἔνν- VPQ
249 ἔλαχεν Q
251 ὤμοι μοι Hermann: ἰώ μοι (μοί V) μοι VPQ: ὤμοι Diggle:
cf. 578
254 ζόαν Dindorf : ζωάν VPQ
256 κλάδας J. Stanley : κληίδας PQ: κλειίδας V
260 δ' ὁ Tyrwhitt: δὲ τὸ VQ: δὲ τὸν P   ποῦ μοι del. Dindorf
ποῦ μοι ⟨νῦν κυρεῖ⟩; Diggle
271 πόνων V et gB: κακῶν PQ

74

Trojan women has happiness in store for her?

Talthybius   I know, but ask questions one by one, not all at the same time.

Hecuba   My poor daughter Cassandra – tell me – who has been allotted her?

Talthybius   King Agamemnon took her as a special prize.

Hecuba   To be a slave to that Spartan wife. How wretched that makes me!   250

Talthybius   No, not so, but as concubine to share his bed.

Hecuba   This for the virgin of Apollo to whom the golden haired god gave the gift of an unwedded life?

Talthybius   Passion for the god-possessed girl struck him hard.

Hecuba   Throw away, my child, your consecrated laurel branches, and put from your body the sacred wreaths you wear.

Talthybius   Yes, for isn't it a great thing for her to win a King's bed?

Hecuba   And what of her you took from me, my youngest child, where is she?   260

Talthybius   Do you mean Polyxena? Or who is it you ask about?

Hecuba   Polyxena. To whom has her lot bound her?

Talthybius   It has been decreed that she attend Achilles' tomb.

Hecuba   Alas, that I bore a daughter to be an attendant at a tomb! But what established custom or law among the Greeks is this, my friend?

Talthybius   Consider your daughter happy. All is well with her.

Hecuba   What did I hear you say? Does she still *live*?   270

Talthybius   She is in the hands of her fate: her cares are over.

75

Εκ.   τί δ' ἀ τοῦ χαλκεομήςτορος "Εκτορος δάμαρ,
      'Ανδρομάχα τάλαινα, τίν' ἔχει τύχαν;
Τα.   καὶ τήνδ' 'Αχιλλέως ἔλαβε παῖς ἐξαίρετον.
Εκ.   ἐγὼ δὲ τῶι πρόσπολος ἀ τριτοβάμονος   275
      δευομένα βάκτρου γεραιᾶι χερί;
Τα.   'Ιθάκης 'Οδυccεὺς ἔλαχ' ἄναξ δούλην c' ἔχειν.
Εκ.   ἒ ἔ.

      ἄραccε κρᾶτα κούριμον,
      ἕλκ' ὀνύχεccι δίπτυχον παρειάν.   280
      ἰώ μοί μοι.

      μυcαρῶι δολίωι λέλογχα
      φωτὶ δουλεύειν,
      πολεμίωι δίκας, παρανόμωι δάκει,
      ὃc πάντα τἀκεῖθεν ἐνθάδ⟨ε cτρέφει,   285
      τὰ δ'⟩ ἀντίπαλ' αὖθιc ἐκεῖcε
      διπτύχωι γλώccαι,
      φίλα τὰ πρότερ' ἄφιλα τιθέμενοc πάλιν.
      †γοᾶcθ', ὦ Τρωιάδεc, με.
      βέβακα δύcποτμοc οἴχομαι ἀ†   290
      τάλαινα δυcτυχεcτάτωι
      προcέπεcον κλήρωι.

Χο.   τὸ μὲν còν οἶcθα, πότνια· τὰc δ' ἐμὰc τύχαc
      τίc ἄρ' 'Αχαιῶν ἢ τίc 'Ελλήνων ἔχει;

272 χαλκεομήcτοροc Burges: -μήτοροc V: -μίτοροc PQ: cf. Hesych.
χαλκεομήcτοροc· ἰcχυρόφρονοc (Kirchhoff: χαλκεομίcτωρ· ἰcχυροφόροc
cod.)   δάμαρ del. Page
275 τριτοβάμονος PQ et gB: τριβάμ- VΣ
276 δευομένα ... γεραιᾶι χερί Wilamowitz: χειρὶ δευομένα (-α cum ι
subscr. V, -η Σ) ... γεραιῶ(ι) κάρα(ι) VPQ et gB
285 τἀκεῖθεν V et gB: τἀκεῖc' PQΣ: κεῖθεν Σl   ⟨cτρέφει, τὰ δ'⟩
Wilamowitz (cτρέφει post γλώccαι iam add. Musgrave) ⟨ἀνcτρέφει,
τὰ δ'⟩ Diggle
288 φίλα ... ἄφιλα Seidler: ἄφιλα ... φίλα VPQ et gB   πάλιν
praeeunte Seidler Wilamowitz: πάντων VPQ
289 γοᾶcθέ μ', ὦ   Τ- Hartung, γ- ὦ Τ- με δύcποτμον Wilamowitz
με del. Stinton
290 βέβακ', οἴχομαι. / δύcποτμοc ἀ   , τ- uel β- οἴ- / τάλαινα κτλ.
(ἀ iam del. Seidler) Wilamowitz οἴχομαι del. Murray
291 τάλαινα V et gE: τάλαινα ἂ PQ

Hecuba   And what of the wife of Hector, skilled in arms,
           wretched Andromache, what is to happen to her?
Talthybius   Achilles' son chose her as his prize.
Hecuba   And whom shall I serve, I who need for my
           elderly hand the help of a stick to walk with?
Talthybius   Odysseus, the lord of Ithaca, has drawn you
           to be his slave.
Hecuba   Ah, tear your shorn head, score your cheeks   280
           with your nails – cry out! It is my lot to serve
           a foul man of treachery, the enemy of justice,
           a lawless monster who, with his double talk,
           twists everything from one extreme to the other
           and back again, turning love into hate. Weep
           for me, you Trojan women. With this ill fate I   290
           am ruined, lost – I poor wretch have fallen on
           the worst lot.
Chorus   You know your fate, my lady. But which
           Achaean or Greek is master of mine?

Τα.　ἴτ', ἐκκομίζειν δεῦρο Κασσάνδραν χρεὼν
　　　ὅσον τάχιστα, δμῶες, ὡς στρατηλάτηι
　　　ἐς χεῖρα δούς νιν εἶτα τὰς εἰληγμένας
　　　καὶ τοῖσιν ἄλλοις αἰχμαλωτίδων ἄγω.
　　　ἔα· τί πεύκης ἔνδον αἴθεται σέλας;
　　　πιμπρᾶσιν, ἢ τί δρῶσι, Τρωιάδες μυχούς,
　　　ὡς ἐξάγεσθαι τῆσδε μέλλουσαι χθονὸς
　　　πρὸς Ἄργος, αὑτῶν τ' ἐκπυροῦσι σώματα
　　　θανεῖν θέλουσαι; κάρτα τοι τοὐλεύθερον
　　　ἐν τοῖς τοιούτοις δυσλόφως φέρει κακά.
　　　ἄνοιγ' ἄνοιγε, μὴ τὸ ταῖσδε πρόσφορον
　　　ἐχθρὸν δ' Ἀχαιοῖς εἰς ἔμ' αἰτίαν βάληι.
Εκ.　οὐκ ἔστιν· οὐ πιμπρᾶσιν, ἀλλὰ παῖς ἐμὴ
　　　μαινὰς θοάζει δεῦρο Κασσάνδρα δρόμωι.

ΚΑΣΣΑΝΔΡΑ

　　　ἄνεχε, πάρεχε, φῶς φέρε· σέβω φλέγω —　　　　[στρ.
　　　ἰδοὺ ἰδού —
　　　λαμπάσι τόδ' ἱερόν. ὦ Ὑμέναι' ἄναξ·
　　　μακάριος ὁ γαμέτας,
　　　μακαρία δ' ἐγὼ βασιλικοῖς λέκτροις
　　　κατ' Ἄργος ἁ γαμουμένα.
　　　Ὑμὴν ὦ Ὑμέναι' ἄναξ.
　　　ἐπεὶ σύ, μᾶτερ, †ἐπὶ δάκρυσι καὶ†

295

300

305

310

315

296 δούς νιν PQ: δῶμεν V　　εἰληγμένας Heath: εἰλεγ- VPQ
Σˡ: utrumque Σˡ
297 αἰχμαλωτίδας λέγω P(-ώτ-)Q
298 αἴθεται PQ: ἵσταται V
308 φέρε Bothe, Seidler e Σ Ar. Au. 1720: φέρω VPQ et Σ Ar.
Vesp. 1326　　φλέγω σέβω Σ alter Ar. Vesp.
309 ἰδοὺ ἰδού quae post ἄναξ 310 habent VPQ huc trai. Hermann
310 ὦ PQ: ὦ ὑμὴν VΣˡ
311 ⟨∪—⟩ μακάριος et 328 ὅσιος ⟨ὅσιος⟩ Diggle
312 βασιλικοῖς λέκτροις om. PQ
313 ἁ γαμουμένα p: ἀγα**μένα P ut uid.: ἁ γαμημένα Q: ἀγουμένα Vᵖᶜ:
ἀ***μένα V
314 ὦ om. PQ　　ἄναξ] Ὑμήν Hermann: cf. 331
315 hic et 332 lectio una cum numeris incerta est
δακρύοισι Wecklein olim

Talthybius   You servants, go and bring Cassandra out
            here as quickly as you can, so that I can hand
            her over to the commander, and then distribute
            to the rest also the women prisoners who have
            been drawn by lot. Ah! What's this burst of
            torch flame inside? Are the Trojan women
            setting fire to their rooms because they are on
            the point of being taken from here to Argos?   300
            Or what are they doing? Are they burning
            themselves to death in their search for suicide?
            It is true that in such circumstances a free
            spirit takes its misfortune hard. Open the
            doors, open them up! I'm afraid that what is
            in their interest may be so resented by the
            Greeks that it brings blame upon me.
Hecuba   There is no fire. They are not burning the
            place, it is my daughter Cassandra running
            out here in a frenzied rush.
    Cassandra enters brandishing flaming torches
Cassandra   Hold up the torch, show it, bring it on.
            See how I reverence this temple. I make it
            blaze with light. O Lord Hymenaeus! Blessed   310
            the bridegroom, blessed am I, to be married
            in a royal wedding at Argos. O Hymen, Lord
            Hymenaeus! Since you, mother, continually

79

γόοιϲι τὸν θανόντα πατέρα πατρίδα τε
φίλαν καταϲτένουϲ' ἔχειϲ,
ἐγὼ δ' ἐπὶ γάμοιϲ ἐμοῖϲ
ἀναφλέγω πυρὸϲ φῶϲ   320
ἐϲ αὐγάν, ἐϲ αἴγλαν,
διδοῦϲ', ὦ Ὑμέναιε, ϲοί,
διδοῦϲ', ὦ Ἑκάτα, φάοϲ
παρθένων ἐπὶ λέκτροιϲ
ᾇ νόμοϲ ἔχει.

πάλλε πόδ' αἰθέριον, ⟨ἄναγ'⟩ ἄναγε χορόν —   [ἀντ.
εὐὰν εὐοῖ —   326
ὡϲ ἐπὶ πατρὸϲ ἐμοῦ μακαριωτάταιϲ
τύχαιϲ. ὁ χορὸϲ ὅϲιοϲ.
ἄγε ϲὺ Φοῖβέ νιν· κατὰ ϲὸν ἐν δάφναιϲ
ἀνάκτορον θυηπολῶ.   330
Ὑμὴν ὦ Ὑμέναι Ὑμήν.
χόρευε, μᾶτερ, χόρευμ' ἄναγε, πόδα ϲὸν
ἕλιϲϲε τᾷδ' ἐκεῖϲε μετ' ἐμέθεν ποδῶν
φέρουϲα φιλτάταν βάϲιν.
βόαϲον ὑμέναιον ὦ   335
μακαρίαιϲ ἀοιδαῖϲ
ἰαχαῖϲ τε νύμφαν.
ἴτ', ὦ καλλίπεπλοι Φρυγῶν
κόραι, μέλπετ' ἐμῶν γάμων
τὸν πεπρωμένον εὐνᾶι   340
πόϲιν ἐμέθεν.

322 διδοῦϲ' om. PQ   ϲοι PQΣ: ϲύ V
324 ᾇ(ι) PQΣⁱ: ᾇ V
325 ⟨ἄναγ'⟩ Hermann   ἄναγε PQ: ἄνεχε V
328 uide ad 311
329 νιν Musgrave: νῦν VPQ
330 θυηπόλωι ut uid. Σⁱ, sicut coni. Musgrave
331 ὑμέναι Pᵃᶜ ut uid.: ὑμὴν VPᵖᶜQ
332 χόρευμ' ἄναγε, πόδα ϲὸν Diggle: χόρευ' (-ευε Q) ἄναγε πόδα ϲὸν
PQ: ἀναγέλαϲον V
333 τᾷδ' Q: τάδ' VP
335 βόαϲον Diggle: βοάϲατε τὸν V: βοάϲατ' (βάϲατ' P) εὖ τὸν PQ:
βοάϲαθ' Burges
339 ἐμῶν γάμων VP: -ὸν -ον   Q: ἐμοῖϲ γάμοιϲ Diggle

weep and lament, mourning my father who died,
and our cherished country, it is I who make
the torch fire blaze out at my own wedding,
blaze into bright rays, into radiance, making   320
light for you, Hymenaeus, making it for you,
Hecate, as is customary at the marriages of
young girls.
Poise your foot high: lead on the dance –
Euhan Euhoi – just as we did when times were
happiest in my father's lifetime. There is
sacredness in the dance. Lead it yourself,
Apollo. It is in your temple that I, crowned   330
with bay leaves, offer sacrifice. Hymen, O
Hymenaeus! Dance, mother, lead the dance,
join in most gladly and turn your steps with
mine, now here and now there. Cry out the
wedding song and celebrate the bride with
songs of happiness and acclamation. Come,
you beautifully dressed daughters of Trojans,
sing for the husband destiny has decreed I
should lie beside.   340

Χο. βασίλεια, βακχεύουσαν οὐ λήψηι κόρην,
     μὴ κοῦφον ἄρηι βῆμ' ἐς Ἀργείων στρατόν;
Εκ. Ἥφαιστε, δαιδουχεῖς μὲν ἐν γάμοις βροτῶν,
     ἀτὰρ λυγράν γε τήνδ' ἀναιθύσσεις φλόγα
     ἔξω τε μεγάλων ἐλπίδων. οἴμοι, τέκνον,   345
     ὡς οὐχ ὑπ' αἰχμῆς ⟨σ'⟩ οὐδ' ὑπ' Ἀργείου δορὸς
     γάμους γαμεῖσθαι τούσδ' ἐδόξαζόν ποτε.
     παράδος ἐμοὶ φῶς· οὐ γὰρ ὀρθὰ πυρφορεῖς
     μαινὰς θοάζους', οὐδὲ σαῖς τύχαις, τέκνον,
     σεσωφρόνηκας ἀλλ' ἔτ' ἐν ταὐτῶι μένεις.   350
     ἐσφέρετε πεύκας δάκρυά τ' ἀνταλλάσσετε
     τοῖς τῆσδε μέλεσι, Τρωιάδες, γαμηλίοις.
Κα. μῆτερ, πύκαζε κρᾶτ' ἐμὸν νικηφόρον
     καὶ χαῖρε τοῖς ἐμοῖσι βασιλικοῖς γάμοις·
     καὶ πέμπε, κἂν μὴ τἀμά σοι πρόθυμά γ' ἦι   355
     ὤθει βιαίως· εἰ γὰρ ἔστι Λοξίας,
     Ἑλένης γαμεῖ με δυσχερέστερον γάμον
     ὁ τῶν Ἀχαιῶν κλεινὸς Ἀγαμέμνων ἄναξ.
     κτενῶ γὰρ αὐτὸν κἀντιπορθήσω δόμους
     ποινὰς ἀδελφῶν καὶ πατρὸς λαβοῦσ' ἐμοῦ.   360
     ἀλλ' αὔτ' ἐάσω· πέλεκυν οὐχ ὑμνήσομεν,
     ὃς ἐς τράχηλον τὸν ἐμὸν εἶσι χἀτέρων,
     μητροκτόνους τ' ἀγῶνας, οὓς οὑμοὶ γάμοι
     θήσουσιν, οἴκων τ' Ἀτρέως ἀνάστασιν.
     πόλιν δὲ δείξω τήνδε μακαριωτέραν   365
     ἢ τοὺς Ἀχαιούς, ἔνθεος μέν, ἀλλ' ὅμως

341 Χο. VP: om. Q: Τα. 'quidam' apud Σ
342 ἄρηι Wecklein: αἴρη(ι) PQ: αἴρε V
344 λυγράν V: λυπράν Q: πικράν P
346 ⟨σ'⟩ Musgrave
349 σαῖς τύχαις Heath: σ' αἱ τύχαι VPQΣˡ
350 σεσωφρόνηκας Nauck: -ήκας gE: ἐσωφρονήκασ' VPQΣˡ: σεσωφρονί-
κασ' Σˡ (σώφρονα πεποιήκασι): ἐσωφρόνησας idem Nauck   σαὶ τύχαι ... σεσωφρονήκασ' Seidler
351 ἀνταλλάσσετε VPQΣˡ: -άξατε Σ
357 δυστυχέστερον PQ
361 ἀλλ' αὔτ' Musgrave: ἄλλα (ἀλλά V)   τ' VPQΣˡ
ὑμνήσομαι PQ

Chorus   Will you not stop your daughter in her delirium,
          my Queen, in case she blithely rushes down to
          the Greek camp?
Hecuba   O Hephaistus, you are the torch-bearer at
          people's weddings, but the torch you burn here
          is one of painful misery and a long way from what
          my high hopes were. I never imagined, my
          child, you would contract a marriage at spear-
          point under force of Greek arms. Give the torch
          to me. You are not carrying it straight in your
          frenzied rush. Your plight has not given you
          sanity, but you remain in the same state. Take   350
          in the torches, women of Troy; let tears be
          exchanged for her wedding songs.
Cassandra   Mother, crown my triumphant head with
          wreaths and be glad at my royal marriage.
          Escort me, and if I seem, to say the least,
          unwilling, send me, forcibly. If Loxias is
          Loxias still, the renowned lord of the Greeks,
          Agamemnon, will in marrying me, make a more
          disastrous marriage than Helen's. For I will
          kill him and make his house desolate in revenge
          for my brothers' and my father's blood. But   360
          I shall pass over this. I shall not sing of the
          axe which will fall on my throat and that of
          others, nor the struggles of matricide which my
          marriage will bring about, nor the overthrow
          of the house of Atreus. I shall show that this
          city of ours is more blessed than the Greeks
          are. I may be possessed by god, but to this

τοσόνδε γ᾽ ἔξω στήσομαι βακχευμάτων·
οἳ διὰ μίαν γυναῖκα καὶ μίαν Κύπριν,
θηρῶντες Ἑλένην, μυρίους ἀπώλεσαν.
ὁ δὲ στρατηγὸς ὁ σοφὸς ἐχθίστων ὕπερ   370
τὰ φίλτατ᾽ ὤλες᾽, ἡδονὰς τὰς οἴκοθεν
τέκνων ἀδελφῶι δοὺς γυναικὸς οὕνεκα,
καὶ ταῦθ᾽ ἑκούσης κοὐ βίαι λεληισμένης.
ἐπεὶ δ᾽ ἐπ᾽ ἀκτὰς ἤλυθον Cκαμανδρίους,
ἔθνηισκον, οὐ γῆς ὅρι᾽ ἀποστερούμενοι   375
οὐδ᾽ ὑψίπυργον πατρίδ᾽· οὓς δ᾽ Ἄρης ἕλοι,
οὐ παῖδας εἶδον, οὐ δάμαρτος ἐν χεροῖν
πέπλοις συνεστάλησαν, ἐν ξένηι δὲ γῆι
κεῖνται. τὰ δ᾽ οἴκοι τοῖσδ᾽ ὅμοι᾽ ἐγίγνετο·
χῆραί γ᾽ ἔθνηισκον, οἱ δ᾽ ἄπαιδες ἐν δόμοις   380
ἄλλως τέκν᾽ ἐκθρέψαντες· οὐδὲ πρὸς τάφοις
ἔσθ᾽ ὅστις αὐτῶν αἷμα γῆι δωρήσεται.
[ἦ τοῦδ᾽ ἐπαίνου τὸ στράτευμ᾽ ἐπάξιον.
cιγᾶν ἄμεινον τἀισχρά, μηδὲ μοῦcά μοι
γένοιτ᾽ ἀοιδὸς ἥτις ὑμνήσει κακά.]   385
Τρῶες δὲ πρῶτον μέν, τὸ κάλλιστον κλέος,
ὑπὲρ πάτρας ἔθνηισκον· οὓς δ᾽ ἕλοι δόρυ,
νεκροί γ᾽ ἐς οἴκους φερόμενοι φίλων ὕπο
ἐν γῆι πατρώιαι περιβολὰς εἶχον χθονός,
χερσὶν περισταλέντες ὧν ἐχρῆν ὕπο·   390
ὅσοι δὲ μὴ θάνοιεν ἐν μάχηι Φρυγῶν,
ἀεὶ κατ᾽ ἦμαρ σὺν δάμαρτι καὶ τέκνοις
ὤικουν, Ἀχαιοῖς ὧν ἀπῆσαν ἡδοναί.

---

367 τοσόνδε δ᾽ ἐκτὸς Σ Or. 268
368 κύπριν V et gE: πόλιν PQ
376 ὑψίπυργον πατρίδ᾽ Lenting: -γου -ίδος VPQ
380 γ᾽ Diggle: τ᾽ VPQ
381 ἄλλως Tyrwhitt: -οις VPQ
382 αὐτῶν PQ: -οῖς V
383 del. Wilamowitz   ἦ Va: ἦι Q: ἦ VP   ἦ τοῦδ᾽] τοιοῦδ᾽
Dobree
384-5 (quos habet gE) del. Reichenberger, eosdem post 364 trai. Weil
cιγᾶν ⟨δ᾽⟩ Dobree
387 ἕλοι δόρυ PQ: ἄρης ἕλοι V e 376
388 u. del. Dobree   84

extent I shall stand outside my madness. For
one woman's sake and for one act of love, the
Greeks hunted down Helen and destroyed
thousands, while this clever general killed what   370
he loved for the sake of what he hated, giving
up for a brother the pleasures of children at
home, all for the sake of a woman, and that of
one who had gone off willingly and not been
abducted by force. And when they came to the
banks of the Scamander, they died one after
another, though they were not being robbed of
their own boundaries, nor of their high-towered
fatherland. Those whom the War God caught,
never saw their children again, nor were they
wrapped up in winding sheets by their wives'
hands, but instead lie buried in a foreign country.
Similar things happened to those at home. For
they died widows and others died childless at   380
home, since they had reared their children in
vain. There is no-one to attend their tombs
with a blood offering. [This is the praise the
army deserves! Better to keep silent about
shameful events. Let not my inspiration become
a singer only of disasters.]
Now the Trojans. First they have the greatest
glory - they died for their country. And those
whom the spear took, were carried home as
corpses by their dear ones and found earth's
embrace in their native land, and were laid out
for burial by those who had the right to bury   390
them. And those Trojans who did not die in
battle, lived day after day in the company of
their wives and children, pleasures denied to

τὰ δ' Ἕκτορός coι λύπρ' ἄκουcον ὡς ἔχει·
δόξαc ἀνὴρ ἄριcτοc οἴχεται θανών,   395
καὶ τοῦτ' Ἀχαιῶν ἴξιc ἐξεργάζεται·
εἰ δ' ἦcαν οἴκοι, χρηcτὸc ὢν ἐλάνθαν' ἄν.
Πάριc δ' ἔγημε τὴν Διόc· γήμαc δὲ μή,
cιγώμενον τὸ κῆδοc εἶχ' ἂν ἐν δόμοιc.
φεύγειν μὲν οὖν χρὴ πόλεμον ὅcτιc εὖ φρονεῖ· 400
εἰ δ' ἐc τόδ' ἔλθοι, cτέφανοc οὐκ αἰcχρὸc πόλει
καλῶc ὀλέcθαι, μὴ καλῶc δὲ δυcκλεέc.
ὧν οὕνεκ' οὐ χρή, μῆτερ, οἰκτίρειν cε γῆν,
οὐ τἀμὰ λέκτρα· τοὺc γὰρ ἐχθίcτουc ἐμοὶ
καὶ coὶ γάμοιcι τοῖc ἐμοῖc διαφθερῶ.   405
Χο. ὡc ἡδέωc κακοῖcιν οἰκείοιc γελᾶιc
μέλπειc θ' ἃ μέλπουc' οὐ cαφῆ δείξειc ἴcωc.
Τα. εἰ μή c' Ἀπόλλων ἐξεβάκχευcεν φρέναc,
οὔ τἂν ἀμιcθὶ τοὺc ἐμοὺc cτρατηλάταc
τοιαῖcδε φήμαιc ἐξέπεμπεc ἂν χθονόc.   410
ἀτὰρ τὰ cεμνὰ καὶ δοκήμαcιν cοφὰ
οὐδέν τι κρείccω τῶν τὸ μηδὲν ἦν ἄρα.
ὁ γὰρ μέγιcτοc τῶν Πανελλήνων ἄναξ,
Ἀτρέωc φίλοc παῖc, τῆcδ' ἔρωτ' ἐξαίρετον
μαινάδοc ὑπέcτη· καὶ πένηc μέν εἰμ' ἐγώ,   415
ἀτὰρ λέχοc γε τῆcδ' ἂν οὐκ ἠιτηcάμην.
καὶ coῦ μέν (οὐ γὰρ ἀρτίαc ἔχειc φρέναc)

395 δόξαc] φανεὶc Chr. Pat. 1656
396 τοῦτ' PQ: ταῦτ' V et Chr. Pat. 1652   ἴξιc Va^pc: ἴξιc VPQΣ^l: ἡ 'ρξιc
uoluit Σ^yp (ἤρξιc), item ἡ ἔρξιc Q^yp: ἴξιc Hesych. s.u. sine nom.
auct.: ἤξιc Bekker Anecd. 1. 99. 4
397 ὧν ἐλάνθαν' ἄν Burges, Schaefer: ὧν ἐλάνθαν∈ν PQ et Chr. Pat. 1658:
ἔλαθεν ἂν γεγώc VΣ^l
398 δ' PQ: τ' VΣ^l
399 κῆδοc PQ: κῦδοc VΣ^l et Chr. Pat. 1660   εἶχ' ἂν Burges,
Schaefer: εἶχεν PQ et Chr. Pat.: εἶδεν V: ἔcχε Σ
402 δυcκλεήc V et gE
404 οὐ V: ἢ PQ
408 ἐξεβάκχευcε VQ: -χευε PΣ^l
409 οὔ τἂν Lenting: οὐκ ἂν V: οὔκουν P: οὐκοῦν Q .
416 ἠιτηcάμην Naber: ἐκτηc- VPQ
417 coῦ Hermann: coὶ VPQ (coι Q)

the Greeks. As for Hector's fate, so cruel in
your eyes, listen to the truth. He may be dead
and gone, but he has the very greatest
reputation and the coming of the Greeks is the
cause of this. If they had stayed at home, his
valour would never have been revealed. Paris
too. He married the daughter of Zeus. Had
he not married her, he would have had at home
a bride whom no one talked about. The man of   400
sense should avoid war, but, if it comes to it,
a glorious death is not an accolade the city
should despise, whereas an inglorious death
brings it into bad repute. It's for this, mother,
that you should not pity our country or my
union. For by my marriage I shall destroy those
you and I hate the most.

Chorus   You laugh with gladness at your own misfortunes
and you sing things which your song perhaps
leaves obscure.

Talthybius   Were it not that Apollo had maddened your mind,
you would have had to pay for sending my
commanders from this country with such ill-
omened words. But those that are grand and   410
wise by repute, are no better after all than those
who count for nothing. For the most powerful
King of the Greeks, the beloved son of Atreus,
is saddled with a passion of his own choosing
for this mad woman, whereas I, poor man though
I am, would never have wanted her bed. As for

87

'Αργεῖ' ὀνείδη καὶ Φρυγῶν ἐπαινέσεις
ἀνέμοις φέρεσθαι παραδίδωμ'· ἕπου δέ μοι
πρὸς ναῦς, καλὸν νύμφευμα τῶι στρατηλάτηι.   420
cù δ', ἡνίκ' ἄν cε Λαρτίου χρήζηι τόκος
ἄγειν, ἕπεcθαι· cώφρονος δ' ἔcηι λάτρις
γυναικός, ὥc φαc' οἱ μολόντες Ἴλιον.

Κα. ἦ δεινὸς ὁ λάτρις. τί ποτ' ἔχουcι τοὔνομα
κήρυκες, ἓν ἀπέχθημα πάγκοινον βροτοῖς,   425
οἱ περὶ τυράννους καὶ πόλεις ὑπηρέται;
cù τὴν ἐμὴν φὴιc μητέρ' εἰς 'Οδυccέως
ἥξειν μέλαθρα; ποῦ δ' 'Απόλλωνος λόγοι,
οἳ φαcιν αὐτὴν εἰς ἔμ' ἡρμηνευμένοι
αὐτοῦ θανεῖcθαι; τἄλλα δ' οὐκ ὀνειδιῶ.   430
δύcτηνος, οὐκ οἶδ' οἷά νιν μένει παθεῖν·
ὡc χρυcὸς αὐτῶι τἀμὰ καὶ Φρυγῶν κακὰ
δόξει ποτ' εἶναι. δέκα γὰρ ἐκπλήcας ἔτη
πρὸς τοῖcιν ἐνθάδ' ἵξεται μόνος πάτραν
⟨   ⟩
†οῦ δὴ cτενὸν δίαυλον ὤικιcται πέτραc†   435
δεινὴ Χάρυβδιc ὠμοβρώc τ' ὀρειβάτης
Κύκλωψ Λιγυcτίc θ' ἡ cυῶν μορφώτρια
Κίρκη θαλάccης θ' ἁλμυρᾶc ναυάγια
λωτοῦ τ' ἔρωτες 'Ηλίου θ' ἁγναὶ βόες,
αἱ cαρξὶ φοινίαιcιν ἥcουcίν ποτε   440
πικρὰν 'Οδυccεῖ γῆρυν. ὡc δὲ cυντέμω,
ζῶν εἶc' ἐς "Αιδου κἀκφυγὼν λίμνης ὕδωρ
κάκ' ἐν δόμοιcι μυρί' εὑρήcει μολών.

422 ἕπεcθαι V: φέρεcθαι PQ (ἕπου Qˢˡ)
433 ἀντλήcac PQ
434 post h.u. lac. indic. Heath
435–43 del. Tyrrell
435 ὤκιcτα Vᵃᶜ ut uid. (ὤκ∗cτα Vᵖᶜ)   πέρας P   cτενὸc
δίαυλοc ὤριcται πέτραις Diggle
436 ὠμοβρώc τ' ὀρειβάτης Scaliger: ὠμόβροcτορ- P: ὠμόβοροc τ' ὀρ- Q:
ὠμόφρων ἐπιcτάτης VQʸʳ: cf. Hesych. (iv. 276 Schmidt) Χάρυβδιc
ὠμόβροτος
440 cαρξὶ φοινίαιcιν Bothe: cάρκα φωνήεccαν V(-εcαν)P
(fort. φον- Pᵃᶜ) Q

your criticism of the Greeks and praise of the Trojans, I consign them to the winds, for you are not in your right mind. Follow me now to the ships, a good match for our general. And you, Hecuba, when Laertes' son seeks to lead you away, follow him. The woman whose slave you will be, is a good person, so those who come to Troy say. 420

Cassandra He has clever pretensions this servant. Why do they have the honourable name of herald when they are universally hated by all men, attendants at the beck and call of tyrants and states? You tell me that my mother will come to Odysseus's palace. What about the words of Apollo which were communicated to me, that she should die here? I will not reproach her by mentioning the rest. Odysseus, 430 poor wretch, little knows what he still must go through. My troubles and those of Troy will seem to him positively golden beside his own. After spending ten full years, on top of those he spent here, he will arrive alone in his own country, ... where terrible Charybdis inhabits the narrow strait of rock and the mountain dwelling Cyclops who eats raw flesh, the Ligurian witch Circe who changes men into swine, the shipwreck on the salt sea and the desire for the lotus and the sacred oxen of the sun, whose bloody flesh will emit a bitter sound for Odysseus. To cut the story short, he will go 440 down to Hades alive and after escaping the (perils of) the sea he will find innumerable troubles in his home when he gets there.

ἀλλὰ γὰρ τί τοὺς Ὀδυccέωc ἐξακοντίζω πόνουc;
cτεῖχ' ὅπωc τάχιcτ'· ἐν Ἅιδου νυμφίωι γημώμεθα.   445
ἢ κακὸc κακῶc ταφήcηι νυκτόc, οὐκ ἐν ἡμέραι,
ὦ δοκῶν cεμνόν τι πράccειν, Δαναϊδῶν ἀρχηγέτα.
κἀμέ τοι νεκρὸν φάραγγεc γυμνάδ' ἐκβεβλημένην
ὕδατι χειμάρρωι ῥέουcαι νυμφίου πέλαc τάφου
θηρcὶ δώcουcιν δάcαcθαι, τὴν Ἀπόλλωνοc λάτριν.   450
ὦ cτέφη τοῦ φιλτάτου μοι θεῶν, ἀγάλματ' εὔια,
χαίρετ'· ἐκλέλοιφ' ἑορτὰc αἷc πάροιθ' ἠγαλλόμην.
ἴτ' ἀπ' ἐμοῦ χρωτὸc cπαραγμοῖc, ὡc ἔτ' οὖc' ἁγνὴ χρόα
δῶ θοαῖc αὔραιc φέρεcθαι cοὶ τάδ', ὦ μαντεῖ' ἄναξ.
ποῦ cκάφοc τὸ τοῦ cτρατηγοῦ; ποῖ πόδ' ἐμβαίνειν
      με χρή;   455
οὐκέτ' ἂν φθάνοιc ἂν αὔραν ἱcτίοιc καραδοκῶν,
ὡc μίαν τριῶν Ἐρινὺν τῆcδέ μ' ἐξάξων χθονόc.
χαῖρέ μοι, μῆτερ· δακρύcηιc μηδέν· ὦ φίλη πατρίc,
οἵ τε γῆc ἔνερθ' ἀδελφοὶ χὠ τεκὼν ἡμᾶc πατήρ,
οὐ μακρὰν δέξεcθέ μ'· ἥξω δ' ἐc νεκροὺc νικηφόροc   460
καὶ δόμουc πέρcαc' Ἀτρειδῶν, ὧν ἀπωλόμεcθ' ὕπο.

Χο. Ἑκάβηc γεραιᾶc φύλακεc, οὐ δεδόρκατε
      δέcποιναν ὡc ἄναυδοc ἐκτάδην πίτνει;
      οὐκ ἀντιλήψεcθ'; ἢ μεθήcετ', ὦ κακαί,
      γραῖαν πεcοῦcαν; αἴρετ' εἰc ὀρθὸν δέμαc.   465

Εκ. ἐᾶτέ μ' (οὔτοι φίλα τὰ μὴ φίλ', ὦ κόραι)
      κεῖcθαι πεcοῦcαν· πτωμάτων γὰρ ἄξια
      πάcχω τε καὶ πέπονθα κἄτι πείcομαι.
      ὦ θεοί· κακοὺc μὲν ἀνακαλῶ τοὺc cυμμάχουc,

445 ἐν Heiland: ἐc VPQ   γημώμεθα PQ: γαμ- V: γαμούμεθα Porson
447 ἀρχηγέτα V: cτρατηλάτα PQ (-α cum ι subscr. Q)
454 cοὶ Page : cοὶ VPQ: cοῦ Burges
455 τὸ τῶν Ἀτρειδῶν Cic. ad Att. 7. 3. 5   πόδ' Elmsley: πότ' VPQ
457 ἐρινύων Burges
460 ἥξω PQᵖᶜ (ἄξω Qᵃᶜ ut uid.): ἥκω V
463 ἐκτάδην Verrall: εἰc ἄδην P: εἰc ἄιδου Q: ἐc πέδον V
464 ἢ Musgrave: ἦ VPQ
465 δέμαc V: πάλιν PQ
466 οὔτι fere codd. Chr. Pat. 1034 (∼gB)

90

But why do I hurl prophecies of Odysseus'
trials at him? Go quickly on, and let me marry
my bridegroom in the house of Death. A
dishonourable man, you shall be buried dishonourably, not by day but by night, you
leader of the Greeks who think you have
accomplished something great. Myself they
will cast out as a naked corpse, and the ravines
flowing with storm water shall give me to wild
beasts to feed on near the grave of my bridegroom, me, the servant of Apollo. Farewell   450
you garlands of the god I loved so dearly,
mystic marks of honour. I have already left
those festivals I once so delighted in. Go, I
tear you from my flesh and give you, while my
body is still untainted, to the swift winds to
carry away for you, O lord of prophecy.
Where is the general's ship? Where must I get
on board? You cannot be too quick in waiting
for a wind for the sails, yet it is one of the three
Furies you will be taking when you take me from
this land. I bid you goodbye, Mother. Do not
weep. O my beloved country, and my brothers
beneath the ground and our father, in a short
time you will welcome me. I shall come triumphant
to the dead below when I have wrecked the house   460
of Atreus which ruined us.

*Cassandra is taken away by Talthybius
and Hecuba falls to the ground*

Chorus   You attendants of the old lady, Hecuba, do you
not see that your mistress has fallen outstretched
on the ground without a word? Will you not take
hold of her? Will you let an old lady lie fallen,
you wretches? Lift her up.

Hecuba   No, let me lie where I have fallen – kind acts
one does not want are not kind acts at all, my
women. It is not surprising I should faint at
what I suffer and have suffered and shall go
on suffering. Oh, you gods! They make poor
allies for me to call on, yet there's something

91

ὅμως δ' ἔχει τι cχῆμα κικλήcκειν θεούς,   470
ὅταν τιc ἡμῶν δυcτυχῇ λάβηι τύχην.
πρῶτον μὲν οὖν μοι τἀγάθ' ἐξᾶιcαι φίλον·
τοῖc γὰρ κακοῖcι πλείον' οἶκτον ἐμβαλῶ.
ἡ μὲν τύραννοc κἀc τύρανν' ἐγημάμην,
κἀνταῦθ' ἀριcτεύοντ' ἐγεινάμην τέκνα,   475
οὐκ ἀριθμὸν ἄλλωc ἀλλ' ὑπερτάτουc Φρυγῶν·
οὓc Τρωιὰc οὐδ' Ἑλληνὶc οὐδὲ βάρβαροc
γυνὴ τεκοῦcα κομπάcειεν ἄν ποτε.
κἀκεῖνά τ' εἶδον δορὶ πεcόνθ' Ἑλληνικῶι
τρίχαc τ' ἐτμήθην τάcδε πρὸc τύμβοιc νεκρῶν,   480
καὶ τὸν φυτουργὸν Πρίαμον οὐκ ἄλλων πάρα
κλύουc' ἔκλαυcα, τοῖcδε δ' εἶδον ὄμμαcιν
αὐτὴ καταcφαγέντ' ἐφ' ἑρκείωι πυρᾶι,
πόλιν θ' ἁλοῦcαν. ἃc δ' ἔθρεψα παρθένουc
ἐc ἀξίωμα νυμφίων ἐξαίρετον,   485
ἄλλοιcι θρέψαc' ἐκ χερῶν ἀφηιρέθην·
κοὔτ' ἐξ ἐκείνων ἐλπὶc ὡc ὀφθήcομαι
αὐτή τ' ἐκείναc οὐκέτ' ὄψομαί ποτε.
τὸ λοίcθιον δέ, θριγκὸc ἀθλίων κακῶν,
δούλη γυνὴ γραῦc Ἑλλάδ' εἰcαφίξομαι.   490
ἃ δ' ἐcτὶ γήραι τῶιδ' ἀcυμφορώτατα,
τούτοιc με προcθήcουcιν, ἢ θυρῶν λάτριν
κλῆιδαc φυλάccειν, τὴν τεκοῦcαν Ἕκτορα,
ἢ cιτοποιεῖν κἀν πέδωι κοίταc ἔχειν
ῥυcοῖcι νώτοιc, βαcιλικῶν ἐκ δεμνίων,   495
τρυχηρὰ περὶ τρυχηρὸν εἱμένην χρόα
πέπλων λακίcματ', ἀδόκιμ' ὀλβίοιc ἔχειν.
οἲ 'γὼ τάλαινα, διὰ γάμον μιᾶc ἕνα
γυναικὸc οἵων ἔτυχον ὧν τε τεύξομαι.

474 ἢ μὲν τύραννοc Elmsley: ἦμεν τύραννοι VPQ: ἤμην τύραννοc
Apsines p. 311: ἤμην (ἀνανδροc) Chr. Pat. 537
477 οὓc Stephanus: οὐ VPQ et Aps.
480 om. Aps. (qui 472-9 et 481-3 citat)
483 ἑρκείω p: -ίω(ι) V (ἐφερκίω) Q et Aps. (-ίου Διὸc pars codd.):
-ίο P ut uid.
486 Ἕλληcι Wilamowitz
490 Ἑλλάδ' om. PQ

to be said for invoking them whenever one of
us is in trouble. In view of this I want first to 470
sing of my good fortune one last time. For then
I shall inspire more pity for my bad fortune. I
was royal, and I married into a royal house, and
then I had pre-eminent children, not as mere
ciphers, but to be lords of the Phrygians. They
were such sons as no Trojan or Greek woman or
foreigner could boast of having. And I both
saw them fall beneath the Greek spear, and had
this hair of mine cut in mourning at their tombs. 480
I wept for Priam, their father, and I did not
hear from others, but saw with my own eyes
his butchery at the household altar and the
capture of the city. The girls I brought up to
marry carefully selected bridegrooms, I really
brought up for others, and had them taken out
of my hands. And just as there is no hope that I
shall again be seen by them, so I myself will no
longer see them. Finally, to crown my abject
misery it will be as a slave I shall come to Greece,
a female slave and old. They will put upon me 490
tasks quite unfitting to this old age of mine. I
shall have to be servant at the door and guard
the keys, I the mother of Hector, or make bread,
or lay my poor decrepit back on the ground after
a royal couch, my tattered flesh dressed in
tattered rags, unseemly for the prosperous to
wear. Alas, I am wretched! Just because of
one marriage of one woman, look at the unhappiness I have encountered, and will go on
encountering.

ὦ τέκνον, ὦ cύμβακχε Κασσάνδρα θεοῖς,   500
οἵαις ἔλυσας cυμφοραῖς ἄγνευμα cόν.
cύ τ', ὦ τάλαινα, ποῦ ποτ' εἶ, Πολυξένη;
ὡς οὔτε μ' ἄρςην οὔτε θήλεια cπορὰ
πολλῶν γενομένων τὴν τάλαιναν ὠφελεῖ.
τί δῆτά μ' ὀρθοῦτ'; ἐλπίδων ποίων ὕπο;   505
ἄγετε τὸν ἁβρὸν δή ποτ' ἐν Τροίαι πόδα,
νῦν δ' ὄντα δοῦλον, cτιβάδα πρὸς χαμαιπετῆ
πέτρινά τε κρήδεμν', ὡς πεcοῦc' ἀποφθαρῶ
δακρύοις καταξανθεῖcα. τῶν δ' εὐδαιμόνων
μηδένα νομίζετ' εὐτυχεῖν, πρὶν ἂν θάνηι.   510

Χο. ἀμφί μοι Ἴλιον, ὦ   [cτρ.
      Μοῦcα, καινῶν ὕμνων
      ἆιcον cὺν δακρύοις ὠιδὰν ἐπικήδειον·
      νῦν γὰρ μέλος ἐc Τροίαν ἰαχήcω,   515
      τετραβάμονος ὡς ὑπ' ἀπήνας
      Ἀργείων ὀλόμαν τάλαινα δοριάλωτος,
      ὅτ' ἔλιπον ἵππον οὐράνια
      βρέμοντα χρυcεοφάλαρον ἔνο-   520
          πλον ἐν πύλαις Ἀχαιοί·
      ἀνὰ δ' ἐβόαcεν λεὼς
      Τρωϊάδος ἀπὸ πέτρας cταθείc·
      Ἴτ', ὦ πεπαυμένοι πόνων,
      τόδ' ἱερὸν ἀνάγετε ξόανον   525
      Ἰλιάδι Διογενεῖ κόραι.
      τίc οὐκ ἔβα νεανίδων,
      τίc οὐ γεραιὸc ἐκ δόμων;
      κεχαρμένοι δ' ἀοιδαῖc
      δόλιον ἔcχον ἄταν.   530

513 ἆιcον cὺν Burges (cὺν) et Seidler: ἄειcον ἐν VPQ
514 ἐπικήδειον Σ: ἐπιτήδ-. VPQ
517 ὀλόμαν Musgrave: ὀλοίμ- VPQ
520 χρυcοφάλαρον Seidler
522 ἐβόαcεν Aldina: -cε VPQ: -c' ὁ Hesych. (i. 149 Latte)
523 Τρωϊάδος Dobree: τρω(ι)άδος VP (ὁ τ- P) Q

My daughter, Cassandra, you who shared your   500
inspiration with the gods, in what miserable
circumstances have you lost your chaste life
now. And you, my poor Polyxena, where are
you? So many children, and yet no son or
daughter can help me now in pain. Why then
raise me from the ground? What do you hope for?
Guide the steps which once went so daintily in
Troy but are now enslaved, take me to the straw
pallet on the ground and the stony head-rest, that
I may cast myself down and be worn to destruction
by crying. . Call no one who prospers fortunate
until he is dead.   510

Chorus   Sing, Muse, of Ilium; sing with tears a song of
death in strange new strain. For I shall sing an
ode for Troy, how I perished, an unhappy captive,
because of the four-wheeled horse when the
Achaeans left it at the gates, rattling to high
heaven with its arms, and magnificently decked   520
out in gold trappings.
The people stood on the Trojan rock and
shouted aloud. "Our troubles are over, go
down and bring in the image sacred to the Trojan
goddess, Zeus' daughter". What young girl
then, what old person, did not run from their
houses? Happy in their songs they took to their
hearts death in disguise.   530

πᾶca δὲ γέννα Φρυγῶν   [ἀντ.
πρὸc πύλαc ὡρμάθη,
πεύκαν οὐρεῖαν, ξεcτὸν λόχον Ἀργείων,
καὶ Δαρδανίαc ἄταν θεᾶι δώcων,
χάριν ἄζυγοc ἀμβροτοπώλου·   535
κλωcτοῦ δ' ἀμφιβόλοιc λίνοιο ναὸc ὡcεὶ
cκάφοc κελαινὸν εἰc ἕδρανα
λάϊνα δάπεδά τε, φονέα πατρί-   540
δι, Παλλάδοc θέcαν θεᾶc.
ἐπὶ δὲ πόνωι καὶ χαρᾶι
νύχιον ἐπεὶ κνέφαc παρῆν,
Λίβυc τε λωτὸc ἐκτύπει
Φρύγιά τε μέλεα, παρθένοι δ'   545
ἄειρον ἅμα κρότον ποδῶν
βοάν τ' ἔμελπον εὔφρον', ἐν
δόμοιc δὲ παμφαὲc cέλαc
πυρὸc μέλαιναν αἴγλαν
†ἔδωκεν ὕπνωι†.   550

ἐγὼ δὲ τὰν ὀρεcτέραν   [ἐπωιδ.
τότ' ἀμφὶ μέλαθρα παρθένον
Διὸc κόραν ἐμελπόμαν
χοροῖcι· φοινία δ' ἀνὰ   555

533 πεύκαν οὐρεῖαν Dobree: πεύκα(ι) ἐν οὐρεία(ι) VPQΣⁱ
535 Δαρδανίδαc Σⁱ   θεᾶι Aldina: θέα VPQ: θέαι Σⁱ
536 χάριν Aldina : καὶ χάριν VPQΣ   ἀμβροτοπώλου post Barnes
(ἀμβροτα-) Musgrave: ἀμβρότα πώλου VΣ: ἀμβρῶτα πώλου P (πόλ-) Q
538 λίνοιο Bothe e Σ (λίνου): λίνοιcι VPQ   ὡcεὶ Matthiae e Σ
(καθάπερ): ὡc εἰc V: ὡc PQ
540 φονέα Diggle: φοίνια PQ: φοίνιά τε V: φονία (φόνια uel φοίνια Σⁱ)
τε Σⁱ: φόνια Aldina
542 ἐπὶ PQ: ἐν VΣⁱ
543 ἐπεὶ Reiske: ἐπὶ VPQ
546 ἄειρον ἅμα Diggle: ἀέριον ἀνὰ VPQ et gE, quibus seruatis τ' 547
(quod habet etiam gE) del. Burges: αἰθέριον ἀνὰ Wecklein cl. 325
554 κόραν Seidler: κόραν ἄρτεμιν VPQ

The whole race of Trojans rushed to the gates
to give to the goddess the mountain pinewood,
polished ambush of the Argives which was to be
the destruction of Troy. It was a gift to the
virgin goddess of the immortal steeds.
They brought it like the dark hull of a ship,
with encircling ropes of spun flax, to the stone
floor of the temple of the goddess Pallas. It was
death to our country. And when the darkness   540
of night came upon their exertion and their exhil-
aration, the Libyan pipe sounded and Phrygian
strains, and young girls lifted pulsing feet as
they sang lighthearted songs. Inside the houses
the shining brightness of torch flares gave a
dark flickering gleam amid sleep.   550
I for my part at that time was singing and
dancing in the palace in honour of the mountain-
dwelling daughter of Zeus. A bloody shout went

πτόλιν βοὰ κατέσχε Περ-
γάμων ἕδρας· βρέφη δὲ φίλι-
α περὶ πέπλους ἔβαλλε μα-
τρὶ χεῖρας ἐπτοημένας.
λόχου δ' ἐξέβαιν' Ἄρης,   560
κόρας ἔργα Παλλάδος.
σφαγαὶ δ' ἀμφιβώμιοι
Φρυγῶν ἔν τε δεμνίοις
καράτομος ἐρημία
νεανίδων στέφανον ἔφερεν   565
Ἑλλάδι κουροτρόφον,
Φρυγῶν δὲ πατρίδι πένθος.

Ἑκάβη, λεύσσεις τήνδ' Ἀνδρομάχην
ξενικοῖς ἐπ' ὄχοις πορθμευομένην;
παρὰ δ' εἰρεσίαι μαστῶν ἕπεται   570
φίλος Ἀστυάναξ, Ἕκτορος ἶνις.
ποῖ ποτ' ἀπήνης νώτοισι φέρηι,
δύστηνε γύναι,
πάρεδρος χαλκέοις Ἕκτορος ὅπλοις
σκύλοις τε Φρυγῶν δοριθηράτοις,
οἷσιν Ἀχιλλέως παῖς Φθιώτας   575
στέψει ναούς, ἀπὸ Τροίας;

ΑΝΔΡΟΜΑΧΗ

    Ἀχαιοὶ δεσπόται μ' ἄγουσιν.   [στρ. α
Εκ. οἴμοι. Αν. τί παιᾶν' ἐμὸν στενάζεις;
Εκ. αἰαῖ Αν. τῶνδ' ἀλγέων
Εκ. ὦ Ζεῦ Αν. καὶ συμφορᾶς.   580
Εκ. τέκεα Αν. πρίν ποτ' ἦμεν.

556 κατέσχε Wilamowitz: κατεῖχε(ν) VPQΣ
558 ἔβαλλε Vsl: ἔβαλε VPQ
562 ἀμφὶ βώμιοι VΣl: ἀμφὶ βωμοῖσι(ν) PQ
566 κουροτρόφον V: -ω(ι) PQ: -ων Diggle
567 δὲ πατρίδι πενθος VΣl: πατρίδι πένθη PQ
572–6 choro contin. Kirchhoff: Hecubae trib. VPQ
578 οἴμοι Σ sicut coni. Burges: ἰώ μοι (ἰὼ μοί V) μοὶ VPQ: ὤμοι Seidler
579 αἰαῖ Burges: αι αι αι αι VPQ
580 ὦ Seidler: ἰὼ VPQ

through the city and possessed the site of Troy.
Beloved children clutched their mothers' dress
with trembling hands. War was stalking from   560
his hiding place. This was the work of Pallas.
And at the altars there was the murder of
Trojans, and on the beds headless desolation
yielded a prize of young women who would bear
sons for Greece, and bring pain to the homeland
of the Trojans.

*Andromache with her son Astyanax enters
on a cart piled high with Trojan spoils*
    Hecuba, you see Andromache over here being
borne along in a wagon belonging to the enemy.
Her beloved Astyanax, Hector's son, is close
to her heaving breast. Where are they taking   570
you in the cart, poor woman, next to the bronze
weapons of Hector and the Trojan spoils captured
by the spear with which, now that they are
taken from Troy, Achilles' son will deck Phthian
temples?

Andromache   The Greeks who have become our masters
    are taking me away.

Hecuba   Oimoi.

Andromache   Your lament is the same as mine....

Hecuba   Ai-ai . . .

Andromache   . . . for these troubles . . .

Hecuba   O Zeus!   580

Andromache   . . . and for this unhappiness.

Hecuba   Oh, my children . . .

Andromache   . . . as we once were . . .

Εκ. βέβακ' ὄλβος, βέβακε Τροία [ἀντ. α
Αν. τλάμων. Εκ. ἐμῶν τ' εὐγένεια παίδων.
Αν. φεῦ φεῦ Εκ. φεῦ δῆτ' ἐμῶν
Αν. κακῶν. Εκ. οἰκτρὰ τύχα
Αν. πόλεος Εκ. ἃ καπνοῦται. 585

Αν. μόλοις, ὦ πόcιc μοι
Εκ. βοᾶιc τὸν παρ' "Αιδαι [cτρ. β
παῖδ' ἐμόν, ὦ μελέα.
Αν. cᾶc δάμαρτοc ἄλκαρ.
Αν. †cύ τ'†, ὦ λῦμ' 'Αχαιῶν 590
Εκ. τέκνων δή ποθ' ἁμῶν [ἀντ. β
πρεcβυγενὲc Πριάμωι.
Αν. κοιμίcαι μ' ἐc "Αιδου.

[cτρ. γ
Αν. οἵδε πόθοι μεγάλοι Εκ. cχετλία, τάδε πάcχομεν ἄλγη 595
Αν. οἰχομέναc πόλεωc Εκ. ἐπὶ δ' ἄλγεcιν ἄλγεα κεῖται.
Αν. δυcφροcύναιcι θεῶν, ὅτε cὸc γόνοc ἔκφυγεν "Αιδαν,
ὃc λεχέων cτυγερῶν χάριν ὤλεcε πέργαμα Τροίαc·
αἱματόεντα δὲ θεᾶι παρὰ Παλλάδι cώματα νεκρῶν
γυψὶ φέρειν τέταται· ζυγὰ δ' ἤνυcε δούλια Τροίαι. 600

582 βέβακ' Burges: -κεν VPQ et gB
585 Αν. P: om. V et spat. uac. relicto Q   Εκ. P: Αν. VQ
οἰκτρὰ Burges: οἰκτρά γε VPQ
586 Αν. ... Εκ. P: Εκ. ... Αν. VQ   πόλεοc Burges: -εωc VPQ
587 Αν. P: om. VQ   πόcιc Burges: πόcι V (ποcί) PQΣ
591 Αν. Hermann: Εκ. P: om. VQ   cύ τ' P: cύ τε VQΣ: cὐ
δ' Page, εἶθ' (et 594 κοιμίcαιc) Dawe
592 Εκ. Hermann: om VPQ   δή ποθ' Seidler: δέcποθ' VP
(δέπ- P) Q
593 Πριάμωι Musgrave: -αμε VPQΣ
594 Αν. Hermann: om. VPQ   κοιμίcαι Burges: κόμιcαί VP
(-cέ P) Q: κοίμιcαί Seidler
595 Αν. Murray: Χο. VPQ   Εκ. P: Αν. V: om. Q
cχέτλιαι Scaliger
596 Αν. Murray: Χο. P· om. VQ   Εκ. P: om. VQ
597 Αν. Murray: Χο. P: om. VQ   ὅτε V: ὁ δὲ PQ   ἔκφυγεν
Aldina: ἔφυγ- VPQ

100

Hecuba   Troy lost, our power lost . . .
Andromache   . . . unhappy!
Hecuba   . . . and my royal children.
Andromache   Alas, alas . . .
Hecuba   Yes, and alas for my own . . .
Andromache   . . . sorrows.
Hecuba   Pitiable is the destiny . . .
Andromache   . . . of our city . . .
Hecuba   . . . which is engulfed in smoke.
Andromache   Come back, my husband . . .
Hecuba   My son, to whom you cry, is in Hades, poor child.
Andromache   . . . to defend your wife.   590
        You destroyer of the Greeks . . .
Hecuba   First born of the children to Priam, who once
        were mine.
Andromache   . . . take me to Hades.
        These longings are strong . . .
Hecuba   These are the troubles we experience, unhappy one.
Andromache   . . . for my lost city . . .
Hecuba   Pain weighs heavily upon pain.
Andromache   . . . because of the hatred of the gods, when
        your son escaped death and brought down the
        towers of Troy all for the sake of an accursed
        marriage. The bloodstained bodies are stretched
        out at the feet of Pallas Athene for the vultures
        to carry away. He brought the yoke of slavery   600
        upon Troy.

Εκ. ὦ πατρίς, ὦ μελέα Αν. καταλειπομέναν ϲε δακρύω [ἀντ. γ
Εκ. νῦν τέλος οἰκτρὸν ὁρᾶις. Αν. καὶ ἐμὸν δόμον ἐνθ᾽ ἐλοχεύθην.
Εκ. ὦ τέκν᾽, ἐρημόπολις μάτηρ ἀπολείπεται ὑμῶν.
    †οἷος ἰάλεμος οἷά τε πένθη†
    δάκρυά τ᾽ ἐκ δακρύων καταλείβεται ⟨   ⟩   605
    ἁμετέροιϲι δόμοιϲ· ὁ θανὼν δ᾽ ἐπιλάθεται ἀλγέων.

Χο. ὡς ἡδὺ δάκρυα τοῖς κακῶς πεπραγόϲιν
    θρήνων τ᾽ ὀδυρμοὶ μοῦϲά θ᾽ ἣ λύπας ἔχει.
Αν. ὦ μῆτερ ἀνδρὸς ὅς ποτ᾽ Ἀργείων δορὶ   610
    πλείϲτους διώλεϲ᾽ Ἕκτορος, τάδ᾽ εἰϲορᾶις;
Εκ. ὁρῶ τὰ τῶν θεῶν, ὡς τὰ μὲν πυργοῦϲ᾽ ἄνω
    τὸ μηδὲν ὄντα, τὰ δὲ δοκοῦντ᾽ ἀπώλεϲαν.
Αν. ἀγόμεθα λεία ϲὺν τέκνωι· τὸ δ᾽ εὐγενὲς
    ἐς δοῦλον ἥκει, μεταβολὰς τοϲάϲδ᾽ ἔχον.   615
Εκ. τὸ τῆς ἀνάγκης δεινόν· ἄρτι κἀπ᾽ ἐμοῦ
    βέβηκ᾽ ἀποϲπαϲθεῖϲα Καϲϲάνδρα βίαι.
Αν. φεῦ φεῦ·
    ἄλλος τις Αἴας, ὡς ἔοικε, δεύτερος
    παιδὸς πέφηνε ϲῆς· νοϲεῖς δὲ χἄτερα.
Εκ. ὧν γ᾽ οὔτε μέτρον οὔτ᾽ ἀριθμός ἐϲτί μοι·   620
    κακῶι κακὸν γὰρ εἰς ἄμιλλαν ἔρχεται.
Αν. τέθνηκέ ϲοι παῖς πρὸς τάφωι Πολυξένη
    ϲφαγεῖϲ᾽ Ἀχιλλέως, δῶρον ἀψύχωι νεκρῶι.
Εκ. οἲ ᾽γὼ τάλαινα· τοῦτ᾽ ἐκεῖν᾽ ὅ μοι πάλαι
    Ταλθύβιος αἴνιγμ᾽ οὐ ϲαφῶς εἶπεν ϲαφές.   625
Αν. εἶδόν νιν αὐτὴ κἀποβᾶϲα τῶνδ᾽ ὄχων
    ἔκρυψα πέπλοις κἀπεκοψάμην νεκρόν.

601 Αν. Murray: om. VPQ   κατερειπομέναν Jacobs
602 Εκ. Murray: Χο. VPQ   Αν. Murray: Εκ. VPQ
603 Εκ. Murray: Αν. P: om. VQ   ἐρημόπολις Seidler: ἔρημος πόλις VPQ
604 Εκ. praescr. P   ante οἷος lac. indic. Seidler   οἷα δὲ Blaydes
605 lac. indic. Seidler   ⟨οἰκτρὰ κατ᾽ ὄϲϲων⟩ Heinsch
607 ἀλγέων post Seidler Dobree: ἀλγέων ἀδάκρυτος VPQ
608 πεπραγόϲι V et gB: πεπονθόϲι PQ et gE et Stob. 4. 54. 4
610 δορὶ om. Q, qui post h.u. explicit
613 τὸ Elmsley: τὰ VP et gE
615 τοιάϲδ᾽ V
624 ἐκεῖν᾽ ὅ Fix: ἐκεῖνό VP (-ο P)

Hecuba   Oh my country, my unhappy country . . .

Andromache   I am weeping for you even as you are being abandoned.

Hecuba   . . . now you see your miserable end.

Andromache   . . . and I weep for my house where I bore my children.

Hecuba   Children, your mother who has lost her city, is deprived of you. What lamentation and sorrow, tears shed upon tears in our house! The dead man is at least oblivious of grief.

Chorus   Those who are in trouble find relief in tears and songs of lamentation and the music of grief.

Andromache   You are the mother of the man who once 610 killed so many Greeks with his spear – do you see this?

Hecuba   I see the work of the gods, how they build tower-high that which is nothing, and destroy that which merely appears powerful.

Andromache   My child and I are being taken away as spoils – nobility reduced to slavery in these great changes of circumstance.

Hecuba   The power of necessity is terrifying. Just now Cassandra was forcibly torn from me.

Andromache   Alas, alas, it seems a second Ajax has appeared a second time to threaten your child. There is another way too in which you must suffer.

Hecuba   Yes, there is no counting or limit to my 620 sufferings. Evil contends with evil.

Andromache   Your daughter is dead. Polyxena was murdered at Achilles' grave, a gift to him in death – to a corpse.

Εκ. αἰαῖ, τέκνον, cῶν ἀνοcίων προcφαγμάτων·
    αἰαῖ μάλ' αὖθιc, ὡc κακῶc διόλλυcαι.

Αν. ὄλωλεν ὡc ὄλωλεν· ἀλλ' ὅμωc ἐμοῦ   630
    ζώcηc γ' ὄλωλεν εὐτυχεcτέρωι πότμωι.

Εκ. οὐ ταὐτόν, ὦ παῖ, τῶι βλέπειν τὸ κατθανεῖν·
    τὸ μὲν γὰρ οὐδέν, τῶι δ' ἔνειcιν ἐλπίδεc.

Αν. [ὦ μῆτερ, ὦ τεκοῦcα, κάλλιcτον λόγον
    ἄκουcον, ὥc cοι τέρψιν ἐμβάλω φρενί.]   635
    τὸ μὴ γενέcθαι τῶι θανεῖν ἴcον λέγω,
    τοῦ ζῆν δὲ λυπρῶc κρεῖccόν ἐcτι κατθανεῖν.
    †ἀλγεῖ γὰρ οὐδὲν τῶν κακῶν ἠιcθημένοc·†
    ὁ δ' εὐτυχήcαc ἐc τὸ δυcτυχὲc πεcὼν
    ψυχὴν ἀλᾶται τῆc πάροιθ' εὐπραξίαc.   640
    κείνη δ', ὁμοίωc ὥcπερ οὐκ ἰδοῦcα φῶc,
    τέθνηκε κοὐδὲν οἶδε τῶν αὑτῆc κακῶν.
    ἐγὼ δὲ τοξεύcαcα τῆc εὐδοξίαc
    λαχοῦcα πλεῖcτον τῆc τύχηc ἡμάρτανον.
    ἃ γὰρ γυναιξὶ cώφρον' ἔcθ' ηὕρημένα,   645
    ταῦτ' ἐξεμόχθουν Ἕκτοροc κατὰ cτέγαc.
    πρῶτον μέν, ἔνθα (κἂν προcῆι κἂν μὴ προcῆι
    ψόγοc γυναιξίν) αὐτὸ τοῦτ' ἐφέλκεται
    κακῶc ἀκούειν, ἥτιc οὐκ ἔνδον μένει,
    τούτου παρεῖcα πόθον ἔμιμνον ἐν δόμοιc·   650
    ἔcω τε μελάθρων κομψὰ θηλειῶν ἔπη
    οὐκ εἰcεφρούμην, τὸν δὲ νοῦν διδάcκαλον
    οἴκοθεν ἔχουcα χρηcτὸν ἐξήρκουν ἐμοί.
    γλώccηc τε cιγὴν ὄμμα θ' ἥcυχον πόcει

633 τῶι μὲν Stob. cod. Sᵖᶜ sicut coni. Burges (∼gB et Stob. codd.
A et Sᵃᶜ)

634 om. P neque habet Stob. (qui 632-3 et 635-6 separatim
citat): habent VΣ

634-5 del. Dindorf.

638 lac. (οὐδὲν ⟨ ... οὐδὲν⟩ τῶν) indic. Seidler   ⟨ὅcτιc οὐκ ἔβλεψέ
πω / τὸ φέγγοc, οὐδὲν⟩ e.g. Diggle   ἠcθημένοc P u. del. Wecklein
u. del. Wecklein

644 πλεῖcτον Hartung et Σⁱ: πλεῖον VP   πλέον λαχοῦcα Wilamowitz
645 γυναικὶ Chr. Pat. 538

649 εἴ τιc Chr. Pat. 543 pars codd.

Hecuba   Oh, the cruel misery I feel! That is what
          Talthybius meant when he spoke obscurely and
          in riddles – but clear now.
Andromache   I saw her myself, and got down from this
          cart to cover her body with garments and
          beat my breast in mourning for her.
Hecuba   Oh my child what an unholy sacrifice, I cry
          out yet again – how viciously you were killed!
Andromache   Her death is a fact now. Yet in her death   630
          she fared better than I who am still alive.
Hecuba   You must not confuse life and death, for the one
          means hope, the other nothing.
Andromache   [Mother, mother, listen to an argument
          well reasoned enough to comfort your mind.]
          In my opinion, death is the same as not being
          born, and death better (by far) than living
          a painful life. For the dead man after experienc-
          ing the ills of life does not suffer. One who
          falls from happiness to unhappiness is mentally
          bewildered because of former prosperity.   640
          Polyxena is dead: it is as if she had never
          seen the light of day and she knows nothing of
          what she suffered. As for me, I aimed at high
          repute and then having for the most part
          achieved it, failed to gain happiness. I worked
          hard in Hector's house at all the things that are
          considered right for women. First of all, whether
          blame already attaches to women or not, I put
          aside my longing for the very thing that brings
          the most scandal, namely staying outside, and I   650
          stayed in the house. I didn't let into my house
          the clever talk of women but I was content with
          having in my own mind a sound teacher from my
          own resources. I kept before my husband a
          quiet tongue and tranquil look. I knew where

παρεῖχον· ἤιδη δ' ἅμ' ἐχρῆν νικᾶν πόσιν   655
κείνωι τε νίκην ὧν ἐχρῆν παριέναι.
καὶ τῶνδε κληδὼν ἐς ϲτράτευμ' Ἀχαιικὸν
ἐλθοῦϲ' ἀπώλεϲέν μ'· ἐπεὶ γὰρ ἡιρέθην,
Ἀχιλλέωϲ με παῖϲ ἐβουλήθη λαβεῖν
δάμαρτα· δουλεύϲω δ' ἐν αὐθεντῶν δόμοιϲ.   660
κεἰ μὲν παρώϲαϲ' Ἕκτοροϲ φίλον κάρα
πρὸϲ τὸν παρόντα πόϲιν ἀναπτύξω φρένα,
κακὴ φανοῦμαι τῶι θανόντι· τόνδε δ' αὖ
ϲτυγοῦϲ' ἐμαυτῆϲ δεϲπόταιϲ μιϲήϲομαι.
καίτοι λέγουϲιν ὡϲ μί' εὐφρόνη χαλᾶι   665
τὸ δυϲμενὲϲ γυναικὸϲ εἰϲ ἀνδρὸϲ λέχοϲ·
ἀπέπτυϲ' αὐτὴν ἥτιϲ ἄνδρα τὸν πάροϲ
καινοῖϲι λέκτροιϲ ἀποβαλοῦϲ' ἄλλον φιλεῖ.
ἀλλ' οὐδὲ πῶλοϲ ἥτιϲ ἂν διαζυγῆι
τῆϲ ϲυντραφείϲηϲ ῥαιδίωϲ ἕλκει ζυγόν.   670
καίτοι τὸ θηριῶδεϲ ἄφθογγόν τ' ἔφυ
ξυνέϲει τ' ἄχρηϲτον τῆι φύϲει τε λείπεται.
ϲὲ δ', ὦ φίλ' Ἕκτορ, εἶχον ἄνδρ' ἀρκοῦντά μοι
ξυνέϲει γένει πλούτωι τε κἀνδρείαι μέγαν·
ἀκήρατον δέ μ' ἐκ πατρὸϲ λαβὼν δόμων   675
πρῶτοϲ τὸ παρθένειον ἐζεύξω λέχοϲ.
καὶ νῦν ὄλωλαϲ μὲν ϲύ, ναυϲθλοῦμαι δ' ἐγὼ
πρὸϲ Ἑλλάδ' αἰχμάλωτοϲ ἐϲ δοῦλον ζυγόν.
ἆρ' οὐκ ἐλάϲϲω τῶν ἐμῶν ἔχει κακῶν
Πολυξένηϲ ὄλεθροϲ, ἣν καταϲτένειϲ;   680
ἐμοὶ γὰρ οὐδ' ὃ πᾶϲι λείπεται βροτοῖϲ
ξύνεϲτιν ἐλπίϲ, οὐδὲ κλέπτομαι φρέναϲ
πράξειν τι κεδνόν· ἡδὺ δ' ἐϲτὶ καὶ δοκεῖν.
Χο. ἐϲ ταὐτὸν ἥκειϲ ϲυμφορᾶϲ· θρηνοῦϲα δὲ
τὸ ϲὸν διδάϲκειϲ μ' ἔνθα πημάτων κυρῶ.   685

655 ἤιδη Heath: ἤ(ι)δειν VPΣ¹ et gE et Chr. Pat. 551
ἅμ' ἐχρῆν P: ἅμε χρή VΣ¹ (ἐχρῆν Σ): ὥϲ μ' ἐχρῆν gE: οἷϲ μ' ἐχρῆν
Chr. Pat.
670 ἕλκει gE et Ppc (ἕλκ ει· P): ἕλξει V
681 φαίνεται gB et gE (∼Chr. Pat. 591)
683 ἕξειν Chr. Pat. 593 (∼gB et gE)

it was proper for me to have my way and where
it was right for me to give in to him. Report
of this reached the Greek camp and was my
undoing. For when I was captured, Achilles'
son wanted me for his wife. I shall be a slave   660
in the house of murderers. If I push aside the
memory of my dearest Hector and open my heart
to my new husband, I shall appear a traitor to
the dead. But if I show hostility to my present
husband, I shall be hated by him who is my
master. And yet they say that one night is
enough to dispel the antipathy of a woman to a
man's bed. I loathe the woman who casts out
her previous husband and loves another in a
new relationship. Not even a horse when
separated from its mate will easily bear the yoke.   670
Yet an animal is dumb, unreasoning and lower
in nature than man. In you, my dearest Hector,
I had everything I wanted in a husband, for you
were strong in understanding, rank, wealth and
courage. You took me untouched from my father's
house and first joined marriage with me, a virgin.
Now *you* are dead and I shall be taken in a ship
to Greece to enter as a prisoner upon a yoke of
slavery. Is not the death of Polyxena, for whom
you weep, less than what I have to suffer? For   680
me there is not even that which is all people's
refuge – hope, nor do I delude myself that I
shall fare at all well – however pleasant such
delusions.

Chorus   Your suffering is the same as ours. In lamenting
your own lot, you teach me to know the depths
of my own troubles.

Εκ. αὐτὴ μὲν οὔπω ναὸς εἰσέβην σκάφος,
   γραφῆι δ' ἰδοῦσα καὶ κλύουσ' ἐπίσταμαι.
   ναύταις γὰρ ἦν μὲν μέτριος ἦι χειμὼν φέρειν,
   προθυμίαν ἔχουσι σωθῆναι πόνων,
   ὁ μὲν παρ' οἴαχ', ὁ δ' ἐπὶ λαίφεσιν βεβώς,   690
   ὁ δ' ἄντλον εἴργων ναός· ἢν δ' ὑπερβάληι
   πολὺς ταραχθεὶς πόντος, ἐνδόντες τύχηι
   παρεῖσαν αὑτοὺς κυμάτων δραμήμασιν.
   οὕτω δὲ κἀγὼ πόλλ' ἔχουσα πήματα
   ἄφθογγός εἰμι καὶ παρεῖσ' ἔχω στόμα·   695
   νικᾶι γὰρ οὐκ θεῶν με δύστηνος κλύδων.
   ἀλλ', ὦ φίλη παῖ, τὰς μὲν Ἕκτορος τύχας
   ἔασον· οὐ μὴ δάκρυά νιν σώσηι τὰ σά.
   τίμα δὲ τὸν παρόντα δεσπότην σέθεν,
   φίλον διδοῦσα δέλεαρ ἀνδρὶ σῶν τρόπων.   700
   κἂν δρᾶις τάδ', ἐς τὸ κοινὸν εὐφρανεῖς φίλους
   καὶ παῖδα τόνδε παιδὸς ἐκθρέψειας ἂν
   Τροίαι μέγιστον ὠφέλημ', ἵν' οἱ ποτε
   ἐκ σοῦ γενόμενοι παῖδες Ἴλιον πάλιν
   κατοικίσειαν καὶ πόλις γένοιτ' ἔτι.   705
   ἀλλ' ἐκ λόγου γὰρ ἄλλος ἐκβαίνει λόγος,
   τίν' αὖ δέδορκα τόνδ' Ἀχαιικὸν λάτριν·
   στείχοντα καινῶν ἄγγελον βουλευμάτων;
Τα. Φρυγῶν ἀρίστου πρίν ποθ' Ἕκτορος δάμαρ,
   μή με στυγήσηισ· οὐχ ἑκὼν γὰρ ἀγγελῶ   710
   Δαναῶν τε κοινὰ Πελοπιδῶν τ' ἀγγέλματα.

687 γραφῆ(ι) ΡΣ et Chr. Pat. 623: -ήν V
688 ναῦται Diggle
692 τύχηι] φορᾶι Chr. Pat. 628 (~gB)
693 παρῆκαν gB et Chr. Pat. 629   δραμήμασιν Cobet: δρομ- VP et gB et Chr. Pat.
695 ἔχω Burges: ἐῶ VP et gB et Chr. Pat. 631
698 οὐ μὴ ... σώσῃ P: οὐ γὰρ ... σώσει V
700 φίλων gE
703 τροίας P   οἱ Aldina: εἰ VP
704 ἐκ σοῦ V: ἐξ οὗ P, quibus acceptis εἶναι pro ἵν' εἰ 703 Nauck
ἴλιον P: ὕστερον V, quo accepto εἰ νιν pro ἵν' εἰ 703 Kirchhoff
709 ΑΓΓΕΛΟΣ Elmsley propter Σ

Hecuba   I myself have never been on a ship but I have
seen them in painting and I know about them
from hearing people talk. If the wind is moderate
enough for the crew to brave it, they are all
eagerness to escape trouble. One man stands at
the helm, another at the sails, another keeps the   690
bilge in check. But if the sea is very heavy and
too much for them, then they give in to hap-
hazardness and let themselves go with the run
of the waves. It's like that with me. I have so
many troubles that I don't have any words to
say. I let them be and hold my tongue, so
powerful is the terrible wave the gods have
sent. But, my dear child, stop mourning now
for Hector. Your tears cannot save him.
Honour your new master and give your husband
incentive to love you for your conduct. If you   700
do this you will please your loved ones all
together, and may bring up my grandson here
to help Troy in the best way possible, so that
one day your children might settle Troy again
and the city still exist. However another
However another subject takes us away from
this one, for who is this I see – a servant of
the Greeks coming again? Will he announce
new decisions?

Talthybius enters

Talthybius   Wife of Hector, once the bravest man in Troy,
do not hate me. It is with reluctance that I   710
shall announce these unanimous words from the
Greeks and the grandsons of Pelops.

Αν. τί δ' ἔστιν; ὥς μοι φροιμίων ἄρχηι κακῶν.
Τα. ἔδοξε τόνδε παῖδα ... πῶς εἴπω λόγον;
Αν. μῶν οὐ τὸν αὐτὸν δεσπότην ἡμῖν ἔχειν;
Τα. οὐδεὶς Ἀχαιῶν τοῦδε δεσπόσει ποτέ.   715
Αν. ἀλλ' ἐνθάδ' αὐτὸν λείψανον Φρυγῶν λιπεῖν;
Τα. οὐκ οἶδ' ὅπως coι ῥαιδίως εἴπω κακά.
Αν. ἐπήινεc' αἰδῶ, πλὴν ἐὰν λέγηιc κακά.
Τα. κτενοῦcι còν παῖδ', ὡς πύθηι κακὸν μέγα.
Αν. οἴμοι, γάμων τόδ' ὡς κλύω μεῖζον κακόν.   720
Τα. νικᾶι δ' Ὀδυccεὺc ἐν Πανέλληcιν λέγων
Αν. αἰαῖ μάλ'· οὐ γὰρ μέτρια πάcχομεν κακά.
Τα. λέξαc ἀρίcτου παῖδα μὴ τρέφειν πατρόc
Αν. τοιαῦτα νικήcειε τῶν αὑτοῦ πέρι.
Τα. ῥῖψαι δὲ πύργων δεῖν cφε Τρωϊκῶν ἄπο.   725
    ἀλλ' ὡς γενέcθω καὶ cοφωτέρα φανῆι·
    μήτ' ἀντέχου τοῦδ', εὐγενῶς δ' ἄλγει κακοῖc,
    μήτε cθένουcα μηδὲν ἰcχύειν δόκει.
    ἔχειc γὰρ ἀλκὴν οὐδαμῆι· cκοπεῖν δὲ χρή·
    πόλιc τ' ὄλωλε καὶ πόcιc, κρατῆι δὲ cύ,   730
    ἡμεῖc δὲ πρὸc γυναῖκα μάρναcθαι μίαν
    οἷοί τε. τούτων οὕνεκ' οὐ μάχηc ἐρᾶν
    οὐδ' αἰcχρὸν οὐδὲν οὐδ' ἐπίφθονόν cε δρᾶν
    οὐδ' αὖ c' Ἀχαιοῖc βούλομαι ῥίπτειν ἀράc.
    εἰ γάρ τι λέξειc ὧν χολώcεται cτρατόc,   735
    οὔτ' ἂν ταφείη παῖc ὅδ' οὔτ' οἴκτου τύχοι.
    cιγῶcα δ' εὖ τε τὰc τύχαc κεκτημένη
    τὸν τοῦδε νεκρὸν οὐκ ἄθαπτον ἂν λίποιc
    αὐτή τ' Ἀχαιῶν πρευμενεcτέρων τύχοιc.

712 ἄρχη(ι) P et Chr. Pat. 642 pars codd.: -ῆ V et Chr. Pat.
pars codd.: -ῆι gE
718 καλά p, quo accepto τάδε pro κακά 717 Wecklein et Jackson
721 λόγωι West
725 δεῖν Jacobs: δεῖ VP
731 δὲ V: τε P
731-2 ἡμῖν τε πῶc ... οἷόν τε; Nauck
734 οὐδ' Hartung: οὔτ' VP
736 οἴκτου τύχοι p: -ου τύχη V: οἰκτοc ἔχοι P
737 ταῖc τύχαιc κεχρημένη Hartung

Andromache   What can this mean? The hint of hateful
              news to come?
Talthybius   It has been resolved for your son here . . .
              How can I say this?
Andromache   Surely not that he shall have a different
              master from me?
Talthybius   No Greek shall ever rule this one.
Andromache   Is he to be left behind here, the last
              remaining trace of the Trojan people?
Talthybius   I do not know how I may easily tell you this
              bad news.
Andromache   Thank you for your scruple, unless the
              news you are going to tell me is really bad.
Talthybius   They are going to kill your son. Now you know
              the hard truth.
Andromache   Alas, what you tell me is far worse than my   720
              marriage.
Talthybius   Odysseus spoke in the Greek assembly and won
              his motion.
Andromache   Aiai. This is grief beyond all measure.
Talthybius   He told them not to allow the son of a hero
              to live.
Andromache   May it be the same for his own children!
Talthybius   He said he should be flung from the Trojan
              walls. But let it be so and you will show more
              wisdom. Do not cling on to your son here, but
              grieve over your troubles as befits your birth,
              and do not think you are strong when you have
              no strength at all. For you are powerless. You
              must look at the circumstances. Your city and
              your husband are destroyed – you are beaten and 730
              we are well able to contend with one woman!
              Therefore I wish you to give up struggling and
              not do anything provocative that will bring shame,
              nor hurl curses at the Greeks. For if you say
              anything to make the army angry, this son of
              yours will not be buried or find any compassion.
              But if you are quiet and bear your misfortunes
              as you should, you will not have your dead
              child unburied and you will find the Greeks
              more amenable.

Αν. ὦ φίλτατ', ὦ περισσὰ τιμηθεὶς τέκνον,   740
    θανῆι πρὸς ἐχθρῶν μητέρ' ἀθλίαν λιπών,
    [ἣ τοῦ πατρὸς δέ c' εὐγένει' ἀποκτενεῖ,
    ἢ τοῖςιν ἄλλοις γίγνεται ςωτηρία,]
    τὸ δ' ἐςθλὸν οὐκ ἐς καιρὸν ἦλθέ cοι πατρός.
    ὦ λέκτρα τἀμὰ δυςτυχῆ τε καὶ γάμοι,   745
    οἷς ἦλθον ἐς μέλαθρον Ἕκτορός ποτε,
    οὐ ςφάγιον ⟨υἱὸν⟩ Δαναΐδαις τέξους' ἐμόν,
    ἀλλ' ὡς τύραννον Ἀςιάδος πολυςπόρου.
    ὦ παῖ, δακρύεις; αἰςθάνηι κακῶν ςέθεν;
    τί μου δέδραξαι χερςὶ κἀντέχηι πέπλων,   750
    νεοςςὸς ὡςεὶ πτέρυγας ἐςπίτνων ἐμάς;
    οὐκ εἶςιν Ἕκτωρ κλεινὸν ἁρπάςας δόρυ
    γῆς ἐξανελθὼν ςοὶ φέρων ςωτηρίαν,
    οὐ ςυγγένεια πατρός, οὐκ ἰςχὺς Φρυγῶν·
    λυγρὸν δὲ πήδημ' ἐς τράχηλον ὑψόθεν   755
    πεςὼν ἀνοίκτως πνεῦμ' ἀπορρήξεις ςέθεν.
    ὦ νέον ὑπαγκάλιςμα μητρὶ φίλτατον,
    ὦ χρωτὸς ἡδὺ πνεῦμα· διὰ κενῆς ἄρα
    ἐν ςπαργάνοις ςε μαςτὸς ἐξέθρεψ' ὅδε,
    μάτην δ' ἐμόχθουν καὶ κατεξάνθην πόνοις.   760
    νῦν, οὔποτ' αὖθις, μητέρ' ἀςπάζου ςέθεν,
    πρόςπιτνε τὴν τεκοῦςαν, ἀμφὶ δ' ὠλένας
    ἕλιςς' ἐμοῖς νώτοιςι καὶ ςτόμ' ἅρμοςον.
    ὦ βάρβαρ' ἐξευρόντες Ἕλληνες κακά,
    τί τόνδε παῖδα κτείνετ' οὐδὲν αἴτιον;   765
    ὦ Τυνδάρειον ἔρνος, οὔποτ' εἶ Διός,

742–3 (quos una cum 744 habent gB et gE et testatur Chr. Pat.
1515–16) del. Nauck.
742 ἀποκτενεῖ P et gE et (-κτένει) Chr. Pat. 1515: ἀπώλεςεν V et gB
744 τ' gE et Chr. Pat. 1517 (~gB)
745–8 del. West (747–8 iam del. Paley)
745 γε Reiske
747 οὐ ςφάγιον ⟨υἱὸν⟩ Nauck: οὐχ' ὡς ςφάγιον VP: οὐχὶ ςφάγιον Chr.
Pat. 77
752 κλεινὸν P: -ὸς V et gE et Chr. Pat. 1534
760 del. Valckenaer: cf. Med. 1030
761 οὔποτ' Stephanus: εἴ ποτ' VP

Andromache   O my dearest child, too much honoured,
you will die at your enemies' hands and leave
your mother forlorn. [A father's high birth,
a salvation to others, will mean your death]
and your father's nobility has not turned out
to your advantage. Unhappy marriage bed
and the nuptials by which I came once to
Hector's house, I did not think I would bear
a son to be a sacrificial victim for the Greeks,
but to be a king of fruitful Asia. Are you
crying, my son? Do you perceive the troubles
that beset you? Why are you clutching and   750
clinging to my dress like a young bird coming
to nestle under my wings? Hector will not
return from the earth with his famed spear
in his hand to save you, nor his kinsmen,
nor those who made up the strength of the
Trojans. You will break your neck in a deathly
fall from a great height with none to pity you,
and cut short your life's breath. O my young
beloved one, so dear to your mother, O the
sweet scent of your skin! It was all for nothing
then that this breast nursed you when you were
in swaddling clothes, in vain that I laboured
(for you) and became worn out with my pains.   760
Now kiss your mother, embrace her who gave
you birth, for the last time, put your arms
round my neck and your lips to mine. O Greeks
who have devised atrocities worthy of barbarians,
why are you killing this child who is in no way
responsible? You scion of Tyndareus' house,
you were never born from Zeus, but I declare

πολλῶν δὲ πατέρων φημί c' ἐκπεφυκέναι,
'Αλάστορος μὲν πρῶτον, εἶτα δὲ Φθόνου
Φόνου τε Θανάτου θ' ὅσα τε γῆ τρέφει κακά.
οὐ γάρ ποτ' αὐχῶ Ζῆνά γ' ἐκφῦσαί c' ἐγώ,   770
πολλοῖcι κῆρα βαρβάροιc Ἕλληcί τε.
ὅλοιο· καλλίcτων γὰρ ὀμμάτων ἄπο
αἰcχρῶc τὰ κλεινὰ πεδί' ἀπώλεcαc Φρυγῶν.
⟨ἀλλ'⟩ ἄγετε φέρετε ῥίπτετ', εἰ ῥίπτειν δοκεῖ·
δαίνυcθε τοῦδε cάρκαc. ἔκ τε γὰρ θεῶν   775
διολλύμεcθα παιδί τ' οὐ δυναίμεθ' ἂν
θάνατον ἀρῆξαι. κρύπτετ' ἄθλιον δέμαc
καὶ ῥίπτετ' ἐc ναῦc· ἐπὶ καλὸν γὰρ ἔρχομαι
ὑμέναιον, ἀπολέcαcα τοὐμαυτῆc τέκνον.

Χο.   τάλαινα Τροία, μυρίουc ἀπώλεcαc   780
μιᾶc γυναικὸc καὶ λέχουc cτυγνοῦ χάριν.

Τα.   ἄγε, παῖ, φίλιον πρόcπτυγμα μεθεὶc
μητρὸc μογερᾶc, βαῖνε πατρώιων
πύργων ἐπ' ἄκραc cτεφάναc, ὅθι cοι
πνεῦμα μεθεῖναι ψῆφοc ἐκράνθη.   785
λαμβάνετ' αὐτόν. τὰ δὲ τοιάδε χρὴ
κηρυκεύειν ὅcτιc ἄνοικτοc
καὶ ἀναιδείαι τῆc ἡμετέραc
γνώμηc μᾶλλον φίλοc ἐcτίν.

Εκ.   ὦ τέκνον, ὦ παῖ παιδὸc μογεροῦ,   790
cυλώμεθα cὴν ψυχὴν ἀδίκωc
μήτηρ κἀγώ. τί πάθω; τί c' ἐγώ,
δύcμορε, δράcω; τάδε cοι δίδομεν
πλήγματα κρατὸc cτέρνων τε κόπουc·
τῶνδε γὰρ ἄρχομεν. οἳ 'γὼ πόλεωc,   795
οἴμοι δὲ cέθεν· τί γὰρ οὐκ ἔχομεν;

770 ἐκφῦcαι V: -φῦναι Ppc et gE   Ζηνὸc ἐκφῦναί Reiske
774 ⟨ἀλλ'⟩ Hermann
782 Τα. Tyrwhitt: Αν. VP
783 om. V
786 τοιάδε VΣ¹: τοιαῦτα PΣ
788 ἀναιδείαc P   ἡμετέραc Tyrwhitt: ὑμ- VP
794 κόπουc Seidler: κτύπουc VP
114

you are the child of many fathers, of the
Avenging Curse, of Envy, of Murder and
Death and all the plagues the Earth breeds!
Zeus never begot you, I am certain, you who   770
are a pestilence to countless Greeks and
barbarians alike. May you die! With your
lovely eyes you have brought ugly death to
the famed plains of Troy. But take him, carry
him away, fling him to his death if that is
your will. Feast on his flesh! The gods are
destroying me and I cannot keep my child
from death. Cover my wretched body and throw
me into the ships. It is a fine marriage indeed
I come to, when I have lost my very own child.

Talthybius takes the child from the cart
which then leaves the stage carrying
Andromache away

Chorus   Unhappy Troy, you have lost tens of thousands   780
           for the sake of one woman and her hateful
           marriage.

Talthybius   Come child, and now that you have left the
           loving embrace of your wretched mother, go to
           the topmost crown of the ancestral walls where
           it has been decreed your life shall end. (*to*
           the Guards) Take him. The man to announce
           such things is one without pity, someone who
           is more of a friend to heartlessness than is my
           nature.

Talthybius goes out

Hecuba   O child, child of my own unhappy child, your   790
           mother and I are being unjustly robbed of your
           life. What will happen to me? What can I do
           for you, so ill fated? I can beat my head and
           my breast like this – for over this at least I
           have control. Alas for the city and for you!
           What have we left to suffer? What prevents

115

τίνος ἐνδέομεν μὴ οὐ πανςυδίαι
χωρεῖν ὀλέθρου διὰ παντός;

Χο. μελιссοτρόφου Cαλαμῖνος ὦ βαcιλεῦ Τελαμών,   [cτρ. α
νάcου περικύμονος οἰκήcας ἕδραν   800
τᾶς ἐπικεκλιμένας ὄχθοις ἱεροῖς, ἵν' ἐλαίας
πρῶτον ἔδειξε κλάδον γλαυκᾶς 'Αθάνα,
οὐράνιον cτέφανον λιπαραῖcί ⟨τε⟩ κόcμον 'Αθάναις,
ἔβας ἔβας τῶι τοξοφόρωι cυναρι-
    cτεύων ἅμ' 'Αλκμήνας γόνωι   805
"Ιλιον "Ιλιον ἐκπέρcων πόλιν
ἁμετέραν τὸ πάροιθεν ⟨   ⟩
[ὅτ' ἔβας ἀφ' 'Ελλάδος]·

ὅθ' 'Ελλάδος ἄγαγε πρῶτον ἄνθος ἀτιζόμενος   [ἀντ. α
πώλων, Cιμόεντι δ' ἐπ' εὑρείται πλάταν   810
ἔσχαcε ποντοπόρον καὶ ναύδετ' ἀνήψατο πρυμνᾶν
καὶ χερὸς εὐcτοχίαν ἐξεῖλε ναῶν,
Λαομέδοντι φόνον· κανόνων δὲ τυκίcματα Φοίβου
πυρὸς ⟨πυρὸς⟩ φοίνικι πνοᾶι καθελὼν   815
    Τροίας ἐπόρθηcε χθόνα.
δὶς δὲ δυοῖν πιτύλοιν τείχη πέρι
Δαρδανίδας φονία κατέλυcεν αἰχμά.

μάταν ἄρ', ὦ χρυcέαις ἐν οἰνοχόαις ἁβρὰ βαίνων,   [cτρ. β
Λαομεδόντιε παῖ,   822
Ζηνὸς ἔχεις κυλίκων πλήρωμα, καλλίcταν λατρείαν.

801 ἱεροῖc ἵν' VΣ¹: ἱεροῖcιν P
802 'Αθάνα Σ¹ sicut coni. Aldina: -ναc VP
803 λιπαραῖc V   ⟨τε⟩ Seidler
807 πάροιθ' P   ὅτ'... 'Ελλάδος del. Dindorf
809 ἀτιζόμενος Jackson: ἀτυζ- VPΣ¹
810 δ**ευρείταο V (δ' ἐπ' εὐ- Va)
812 πρύμναν V
814 τυκίcματα Aldina: τεκ- P: τυκτ- V: τυχ- Maas
815 ⟨πυρὸς⟩ Meineke   πνοᾶ P: βοᾶ V
817 πέρι Diggle: περὶ V: παρὰ P
818 Δαρδανίδας Diggle: -δανίας V: -δάναc P   φονία Aldina: φοιν- VP
820 cὺν Wecklein

us from instant total destruction?

Chorus Telamon, King of Salamis, where the bees thrive,
who made his home on that wave-washed island   800
lying opposite the sacred hill where Athena first
revealed the branch of the grey olive to be a
heavenly crown and an adornment to shining
Athens, you went with Alcmena's son, the archer,
in bravery to sack the city of Troy that was ours
but a short time ago. [When you left Greece]
That was when Heracles, cheated of the reward
of the mares, led out the foremost flower of Greece,
slackened his seagoing oars by the fairflowing
river Simois, made fast the cables from the sterns, 810
and took from his ships his well-aimed bow that
would bring death to Laomedon. With the red
blast of fire he destroyed the hewn stone workings
of Apollo and sacked the land of Troy. Twice in
two battering attacks the bloody spear destroyed
the Dardanians around their walls.
In vain then, son of Laomedon, as you tread   820
delicately among golden wine jugs, do you have
the task of filling Zeus' cups in glorious servitude

ἁ δέ ϲε γειναμένα πυρὶ δαίεται, 825
ἠϊόνεϲ δ' ἅλιαι
ἴακχον οἰωνὸϲ οἶ-
    ον τέκνων ὕπερ βοῶϲ', 830
ἁι μὲν εὐνάϲ, ἁι δὲ παῖδαϲ,
ἁι δὲ ματέραϲ γεραιάϲ.
τὰ δὲ ϲὰ δροϲόεντα λουτρὰ
γυμναϲίων τε δρόμοι
βεβᾶϲι, ϲὺ δὲ πρόϲωπα νεα- 835
    ρὰ χάριϲι παρὰ Διὸϲ θρόνοιϲ
καλλιγάλανα τρέφειϲ. Πριάμοιο δὲ γαῖαν
Ἑλλὰϲ ὤλεϲ' αἰχμά.

Ἔρωϲ Ἔρωϲ, ὃϲ τὰ Δαρδάνεια μέλαθρά ποτ' ἦλθεϲ [ἀντ. β
οὐρανίδαιϲι μέλων, 842
ὡϲ τότε μὲν μεγάλωϲ Τροίαν ἐπύργωϲαϲ, θεοῖϲι
κῆδοϲ ἀναψάμενοϲ. τὸ μὲν οὖν Διὸϲ 845
οὐκέτ' ὄνειδοϲ ἐρῶ·
τὸ τᾶϲ δὲ λευκοπτέρου
    φίλιον Ἀμέραϲ βροτοῖϲ
φέγγοϲ ὀλοὸν εἶδε γαίαϲ, 850
εἶδε Περγάμων ὄλεθρον,
τεκνοποιὸν ἔχουϲα τᾶϲδε
γᾶϲ πόϲιν ἐν θαλάμοιϲ,
ὃν ἀϲτέρων τέθριπποϲ ἔλα- 855
    βε χρύϲεοϲ ὄχοϲ ἀναρπάϲαϲ,
ἐλπίδα γᾶι πατρίαι μεγάλαν. τὰ θεῶν δὲ
φίλτρα φροῦδα Τροίαι.

825 γειναμένα Musgrave: γ- τροία VP
829 ἴακχον Hartung: ἴαχον VΣ¹ (ἐβόηϲαν): ἴϲχον P
οἰωνὸϲ οἰον Hermann: οἰον οἰ- VP
830 τέκνων ὕπερ post Bothe (τεκέων cum Stephano) Diggle: ὑπὲρ τέκνων V:
ὑ- τοκέων P   βοῶϲ' Wecklein: βοᾶ(ι) VP
831-2 ἁι ter Wilamowitz: ἁ ... ἁ ... αἱ P: αἱ ter V   εὐνάϲ Seidler:
εὐνάτοραϲ VP: ἄνδραϲ Beyer
840 τὰ V: παρὰ P
848 τᾶϲ δὲ Victorius: τᾶϲδε VP
849 φίλιον Ἀμέραϲ Murray: ἀμ- φίλιον V: ἀμ- φίλαϲ P
850 γαίαϲ Lenting, Bothe et fort. Σ¹: γαῖαν VP

while the city which bore you blazes with fire,
and like a bird crying for its young, the sea   830
beaches groan, in one place for husbands, in
another for children, and in another for aged
mothers. Your dewy bathing places and the
courses where you exercised are gone, yet
beside Zeus' throne, your face is serene in its
youthful charm. The Greek spear has destroyed
the land of Priam.
Love, who once came to the halls of Dardanus,   840
Love, well established in the thoughts of the
heavenly ones, how mightily you built up Troy
then, joining her in marriage to the gods! But
I shall no longer reproach Zeus with that. The
light of white winged Dawn, friendly to mortals,
looked on the deathly destruction of the land,   850
looked on the ruin of Pergamum, although she
had a husband from this country in the marriage-
chamber as begetter of her children, he whom a
four-horse golden chariot from the stars bore
away to be a strong hope for our native land.
But the gods' love is lost to Troy.

ὦ καλλιφεγγὲς ἡλίου cέλας τόδε,   860
ἐν ὧι δάμαρτα τὴν ἐμὴν χειρώcομαι
['Ελένην· ὁ γὰρ δὴ πολλὰ μοχθήcας ἐγὼ
Μενέλαός εἰμι καὶ cτράτευμ' 'Αχαικόν].
ἦλθον δὲ Τροίαν οὐχ ὅcον δοκοῦcί με
γυναικὸς οὕνεκ', ἀλλ' ἐπ' ἄνδρ' ὃc ἐξ ἐμῶν   865
δόμων δάμαρτα ξεναπάτης ἐλήιcατο.
κεῖνος μὲν οὖν δέδωκε cὺν θεοῖc δίκην
αὐτός τε καὶ γῆ δορὶ πεcοῦc' 'Ελληνικῶι.
ἥκω δὲ τὴν Λάκαιναν (οὐ γὰρ ἡδέως
ὄνομα δάμαρτος ἥ ποτ' ἦν ἐμὴ λέγω)   870
ἄξων· δόμοις γὰρ τοῖcδ' ἐν αἰχμαλωτικοῖc⁻
κατηρίθμηται Τρωιάδων ἄλλων μέτα.
οἵπερ γὰρ αὐτὴν ἐξεμόχθηcαν δορὶ
κτανεῖν ἐμοί νιν ἔδοcαν, εἴτε μὴ κτανὼν
θέλοιμ' ἄγεcθαι πάλιν ἐc 'Αργείαν χθόνα.   875
ἐμοὶ δ' ἔδοξε τὸν μὲν ἐν Τροίαι μόρον
'Ελένης ἐᾶcαι, ναυπόρωι δ' ἄγειν πλάτηι
'Ελληνίδ' ἐc γῆν κᾆτ' ἐκεῖ δοῦναι κτανεῖν,
ποινὰς ὅcων τεθνᾶc' ἐν 'Ιλίωι φίλοι.
ἀλλ' εἶα χωρεῖτ' ἐc δόμους, ὀπάονες,   880
κομίζετ' αὐτὴν τῆc μιαιφονωτάτης
κόμης ἐπιcπάcαντεc· οὔριοι δ' ὅταν
πνοαὶ μόλωcι, πέμψομέν νιν 'Ελλάδα.

Εκ.   ὦ γῆς ὄχημα κἀπὶ γῆς ἔχων ἕδραν,
ὅcτις ποτ' εἶ cύ, δυcτόπαcτοc εἰδέναι,   885

862–3 del. Herwerden cl. Σ περιccὸν τὸ Μενέλαός εἰμι· αὔταρκες γὰρ
τὸ δάμαρτα τὴν ἐμὴν χειρώcομαι   lac. post 863 indic. Porson
869 λάκαιναν P: τάλαιναν V
876 δ' V et tabula Berolinensis [Pack² 430]: γ' P
879 ὅcων V: ὅcοι P: ωcων pot. quam εοcων tab. sec. edd. pr.: ὅcοιc Canter
τεθνᾶc' Heath: -ᾶcιν VP: τεθν[tab.
881 τὴν μιαιφονωτάτην Paley
885 εἰcιδεῖν Clem. Alex. protr. 2. 25. 3 et Sext. Emp. adu. math.
1. 288 et 7. 128

Enter Menelaus

Menelaus How bright the splendour of the sun is on this   860
day when I shall lay hands on my wife [Helen.
For I am Menelaus who with the Greek army
underwent so much.] I came to Troy not so
much, as people think, for the woman's sake,
but against the man who betrayed me, his host,
and stole my wife away from my palace. Now
he has, thanks to the gods, paid the price,
both he and his country which have fallen to
the Greek spear. And I have come for her the
Spartan (I cannot easily say the name of the
woman who was once my wife). She is numbered   870
with the other Trojan women in this place for
prisoners. The very men who have fought to
get her back, have handed her over to me to
kill, or, if I wish, to take her back alive to the
land of Argos. I have decided not to worry
about Helen's fate in Troy, but to take her
back to Greece in a sea-faring ship and there
put her to death as a retribution for all those
friends who fell in Troy.
Attendants there! Go inside and bring her out –   880
drag her by her murderous hair. When the
winds are favourable, we will take her to Greece.

Hecuba   O you who support the earth and who have
your seat upon earth, whoever you are, difficult

121

Ζεύς, εἴτ' ἀνάγκη φύσεος εἴτε νοῦς βροτῶν,
προσηυξάμην σε· πάντα γὰρ δι' ἀψόφου
βαίνων κελεύθου κατὰ δίκην τὰ θνήτ' ἄγεις.
Με. τί δ' ἔστιν; εὐχὰς ὡς ἐκαίνισας θεῶν.
Εκ. αἰνῶ σε, Μενέλα', εἰ κτενεῖς δάμαρτα σήν.   890
        ὁρᾶν δὲ τήνδε φεῦγε, μή σ' ἕλῃ πόθωι.
        αἱρεῖ γὰρ ἀνδρῶν ὄμματ', ἐξαιρεῖ πόλεις,
        πίμπρησιν οἴκους· ὧδ' ἔχει κηλήματα.
        ἐγώ νιν οἶδα καὶ σὺ χοἰ πεπονθότες.

ΕΛΕΝΗ

        Μενέλαε, φροίμιον μὲν ἄξιον φόβου   895
        τόδ' ἐστίν· ἐν γὰρ χερσὶ προσπόλων σέθεν
        βίαι πρὸ τῶνδε δωμάτων ἐκπέμπομαι.
        ἀτὰρ σχεδὸν μὲν οἶδά σοι στυγουμένη,
        ὅμως δ' ἐρέσθαι βούλομαι· γνῶμαι τίνες
        Ἕλλησι καὶ σοὶ τῆς ἐμῆς ψυχῆς πέρι;   900
Με. οὐκ εἰς ἀκριβὲς ἦλθεν ἀλλ' ἅπας στρατὸς
        κτανεῖν ἐμοί σ' ἔδωκεν, ὅνπερ ἠδίκεις.
Ελ. ἔξεστιν οὖν πρὸς ταῦτ' ἀμείψασθαι λόγωι,
        ὡς οὐ δικαίως, ἢν θάνω, θανούμεθα;
Με. οὐκ ἐς λόγους ἐλήλυθ' ἀλλά σε κτενῶν.   905
Εκ. ἄκουσον αὐτῆς, μὴ θάνηι τοῦδ' ἐνδεής,
        Μενέλαε, καὶ δὸς τοὺς ἐναντίους λόγους
        ἡμῖν κατ' αὐτῆς· τῶν γὰρ ἐν Τροίαι κακῶν
        οὐδὲν κάτοισθα. συντεθεὶς δ' ὁ πᾶς λόγος
        κτενεῖ νιν οὕτως ὥστε μηδαμοῦ φυγεῖν.   910

886 φύσεος Aldina: -εως VP et Plut. mor. 1026 B et Sext. Emp.
utrobique et ps.-Iustin. de mon. 5
887 ἐπευξάμην Sext. Emp. adu. math. 7. 128 (∼1. 288 et ps.-Iustin.)
891 ὁρᾶν Stanley, Reiske: -ῶν VP et gE   πόθος Pac ut uid.
sicut coni. Heiland
893 πίμπρησιν Dobree: -σι δ' V et gE: -σι δι' P
898 στυγουμένη V: μισουμένη P
901 ἦλθεν Σ: -ες VP et gB   ἀλλὰ πᾶς V
905 κτενῶν Stephanus: κτανών P: κτενῶ V
910 μηδαμῶς P

	to fathom and to understand, Zeus, whether	
	inflexible law of nature or man's mind, I call	
	upon you. Following your path soundlessly	
	you direct the affairs of men in accord with	
	justice.	
Menelaus	What's this? How strange and new these prayers	
	to the gods!	
Hecuba	Menelaus, I approve of your intention to kill	890
	your wife. But avoid setting eyes on her, in	
	case you are seized with desire for her. For	
	she captures the eyes of men, she ruins	
	cities and she burns homes. Such is the power	
	of her bewitchment. You and I have had	
	experience and we have suffered, as have others.	

Helen is brought out by Guards

Helen	Menelaus, this is a frightening beginning.	
	For I am being forcibly dragged out here at	
	the hands of your servants. I am almost	
	certain that you hate me – none the less I	
	wish to ask you a question. What decisions	
	have you and the Greeks made about my life?	900
Menelaus	No precise decision, but the whole army handed	
	you over to me, (I am the one you wronged,	
	after all) to put you to death.	
Helen	May I then contend in argument against that,	
	that it would be an injustice to put me to death?	
Menelaus	It was not for arguments I came, but for your	
	death.	
Hecuba	Listen to her, Menelaus – let her not die deprived	
	of this chance. Give me the opportunity to reply	
	to her. You know nothing of the wrongs she	
	has wrought in Troy. A full debate will mean	
	her inevitable death.	910

123

Με. ϲχολῆϲ τὸ δῶρον· εἰ δὲ βούλεται λέγειν,
  ἔξεϲτι. τῶν ϲῶν δ' οὕνεχ', ὡϲ μάθηιϲ, λόγων
  δώϲω τόδ' αὐτῆι· τῆϲδε δ' οὐ δώϲω χάριν.
Ελ. ἴϲωϲ με, κἂν εὖ κἂν κακῶϲ δόξω λέγειν,
  οὐκ ἀνταμείψηι πολεμίαν ἡγούμενοϲ.   915
  ἐγὼ δ', ἅ ϲ' οἶμαι διὰ λόγων ἰόντ' ἐμοῦ
  κατηγορήϲειν, ἀντιθεῖϲ' ἀμείψομαι
  [τοῖϲ ϲοῖϲι τἀμὰ καὶ τὰ ϲ' αἰτιάματα].
  πρῶτον μὲν ἀρχὰϲ ἔτεκεν ἥδε τῶν κακῶν,
  Πάριν τεκοῦϲα· δεύτερον δ' ἀπώλεϲεν   920
  Τροίαν τε κἄμ' ὁ πρέϲβυϲ οὐ κτανὼν βρέφοϲ,
  δαλοῦ πικρὸν μίμημ', Ἀλέξανδρον τότε.
  ἐνθένδε τἀπίλοιπ' ἄκουϲον ὡϲ ἔχει.
  ἔκρινε τριϲϲὸν ζεῦγοϲ ὅδε τριῶν θεῶν·
  καὶ Παλλάδοϲ μὲν ἦν Ἀλεξάνδρωι δόϲιϲ   925
  Φρυξὶ ϲτρατηγοῦνθ' Ἑλλάδ' ἐξανιϲτάναι·
  Ἥρα δ' ὑπέϲχετ' Ἀϲιάδ' Εὐρώπηϲ θ' ὅρουϲ
  τυραννίδ' ἕξειν, εἴ ϲφε κρίνειεν Πάριϲ·
  Κύπριϲ δὲ τοὐμὸν εἶδοϲ ἐκπαγλουμένη
  δώϲειν ὑπέϲχετ', εἰ θεὰϲ ὑπερδράμοι   930
  κάλλει. τὸν ἔνθεν δ' ὡϲ ἔχει ϲκέψαι λόγον·
  νικᾶι Κύπριϲ θεάϲ, καὶ τοϲόνδ' οὑμοὶ γάμοι
  ὤνηϲαν Ἑλλάδ'· οὐ κρατεῖϲθ' ἐκ βαρβάρων,
  οὔτ' ἐϲ δόρυ ϲταθέντεϲ, οὐ τυραννίδι.
  ἃ δ' εὐτύχηϲεν Ἑλλάϲ, ὠλόμην ἐγὼ   935
  εὐμορφίαι πραθεῖϲα, κὠνειδίζομαι
  ἐξ ὧν ἐχρῆν με ϲτέφανον ἐπὶ κάραι λαβεῖν.

912 μάθηιϲ q (-ηϲ Va): -η VP
913 τῆιδε P
918 del. Paley, neque agnoscit Σ ut uid.
921 κἄμ' ὁ Burges: κἀμὲ.VP
922 τότε Lenting: ποτε VP
924 τριῶν Wunder: τριϲϲῶν VP
927 δ' P et Tzetzes exeg. in Il. p. 39 Hermann : θ' V
928 om. Tzetzes (qui 925-7 et 929-31a citat)
930 ὑπερδράμοι Tzetzae cod. Lips. (sec. Hermann) sicut coni. Canter:
ὑπεκδ- VP et Tzetzae cod. Cantab. S. Trin. Coll. 981
931 ἔνθεν δ' q sicut coni. Tyrrell: ἐνθένδ' VP
932 οὑμοὶ p: οὔ μοι P: οἱμοὶ VΣˡ

Menelaus   This will require time, but I grant it. If she
wishes to speak, let her. But it is because of
what *you* say, understand, that I grant her
this privilege, not for her sake.

Helen   Perhaps you will not reply to me, irrespective
of whether I speak well or badly, because you
consider me an enemy. None the less in relation
to what your accusations will be if you enter into
discussion with me, I will set my arguments point
for point   [mine in response to yours and your
charges against me]. In the first place this
woman by giving birth to Paris, gave birth to
the beginning of our troubles. Secondly the old   920
King ruined Troy and me by not destroying the
infant, then called Alexander, fatal semblance of
the firebrand. Listen to what followed next.
Paris judged a group of three goddesses.
Pallas' gift to Alexander was that he should
destroy Greece at the head of the Trojan army.
Hera promised that he should have rule over
Asia and the boundaries of Europe if he judged
in her favour. Cypris, in great admiration of
my appearance, promised she would give me to
him if she outstripped the other goddesses in
the contest of beauty. Consider the logical   930
consequences which follow. Cypris won, and
to this extent my union benefited Greece. You
are not under the control of the barbarians,
either because of a battle or through tyranny.
But that which has given Greece happiness has
destroyed me. I was sold for my beauty and I
am reviled by those from whose hands I ought
to have received a crown for my head. You

125

οὔπω με φήςεις αὐτὰ τἀν ποςὶν λέγειν,
ὅπως ἀφώρμης' ἐκ δόμων τῶν ςῶν λάθραι.
ἦλθ' οὐχὶ μικρὰν θεὸν ἔχων αὑτοῦ μέτα   940
ὁ τῆςδ' ἀλάςτωρ, εἴτ' Ἀλέξανδρον θέλεις
ὀνόματι προςφωνεῖν νιν εἴτε καὶ Πάριν·
ὅν, ὦ κάκιςτε, ςοῖςιν ἐν δόμοις λιπὼν
Cπάρτης ἀπῆρας νηὶ Κρηςίαν χθόνα.
εἶέν.

οὐ ς', ἀλλ' ἐμαυτὴν τοὐπὶ τῶιδ' ἐρήςομαι·   945
τί δὴ φρονοῦςά γ' ἐκ δόμων ἅμ' ἑςπόμην
ξένωι, προδοῦςα πατρίδα καὶ δόμους ἐμούς;
τὴν θεὸν κόλαζε καὶ Διὸς κρείςςων γενοῦ,
ὃς τῶν μὲν ἄλλων δαιμόνων ἔχει κράτος,
κείνης δὲ δοῦλός ἐςτι· ςυγγνώμη δ' ἐμοί.   950
ἔνθεν δ' ἔχοις ἂν εἰς ἔμ' εὐπρεπῆ λόγον·
ἐπεὶ θανὼν γῆς ἦλθ' Ἀλέξανδρος μυχούς,
χρῆν μ', ἡνίκ' οὐκ ἦν θεοπόνητά μου λέχη,
λιποῦςαν οἴκους ναῦς ἔπ' Ἀργείων μολεῖν.
ἔςπευδον αὐτὸ τοῦτο· μάρτυρες δέ μοι   955
πύργων πυλωροὶ κἀπὸ τειχέων ςκοποί,
οἳ πολλάκις μ' ἐφηῦρον ἐξ ἐπάλξεων
πλεκταῖςιν ἐς γῆν ςῶμα κλέπτουςαν τόδε.
[βίαι δ' ὁ καινός μ' οὗτος ἁρπάςας πόςις
Δηίφοβος ἄλοχον εἶχεν ἀκόντων Φρυγῶν.]   960
πῶς οὖν ἔτ' ἂν θνήιςκοιμ' ἂν ἐνδίκως, πόςι,
⟨   ⟩
πρὸς ςοῦ δικαίως, ἢν ὁ μὲν βίαι γαμεῖ,
τὰ δ' οἴκοθεν κεῖν' ἀντὶ νικητηρίων
πικρῶς ἐδούλως'; εἰ δὲ τῶν θεῶν κρατεῖν
βούληι, τὸ χρήιζειν ἀμαθές ἐςτί ςου τόδε.   965

Χο. βαςίλει', ἄμυνον ςοῖς τέκνοιςι καὶ πάτραι
πειθὼ διαφθείρουςα τῆςδ', ἐπεὶ λέγει
καλῶς κακοῦργος οὖςα· δεινὸν οὖν τόδε.

959-60 (quos citat Σ Lycoph. 168) del. Wilamowitz
961 πόςει P   post h.u. lac. indic. Murray
964 ἐδούλως' Dobree: -ευς' VP
965 ςου Dobree: ςοι V: om. P

will say that I have not yet discussed the point
in question, how I escaped secretly from your
house. He arrived with no insignificant goddess   940
on his side, did this man, Hecuba's evil genius,
either Alexander or Paris, however you may want
to call him. This is the person you left in your
house, you fool, while you took ship for Crete
from Sparta. Well then, I shall ask not you but
myself a question on this next point.
What was I thinking of to follow the stranger from
home and betray my house and my country?
Punish the goddess and become more powerful
than Zeus, who has the other gods under his power
but is himself the slave of this one. *I* should be   950
forgiven. At this you may raise a specious
argument against me. When Alexander was dead
and gone down to Hades, and the union arranged
by the gods was no more, I ought to have left
the house and gone to the Argive ships. I tried
to do that very thing. I have witnesses in the
warders of the towers and the watchmen on the
ramparts who often discovered me stealthily
letting my body down to the ground from the
battlements with a rope. [That new husband of
mine, Deiphobus, who took me by force, held
me as his wife against the Trojans' wishes.]   960
How then, my husband, would I die justly . . . .
(or) rightly at your hands, I whom Paris
married by force, and whose own situation
enslaved me instead of bringing me victory?
Wanting to get the better of the gods is an
ignorant desire on your part.

Chorus   My queen, defend your children and your
country and destroy the effect of her persuasion,
for she speaks well for all that she is guilty.
And this is a terrible thing.

127

Εκ. ταῖc θεαῖcι πρῶτα cύμμαχος γενήcομαι
    καὶ τήνδε δείξω μὴ λέγουcαν ἔνδικα.   970
    ἐγὼ γὰρ ῞Ηραν παρθένον τε Παλλάδα
    οὐκ ἐc τοcοῦτον ἀμαθίαc ἐλθεῖν δοκῶ,
    ὥcθ᾽ ἡ μὲν ῎Αργοc βαρβάροιc ἀπημπόλα,
    Παλλὰc δ᾽ ᾿Αθήναc Φρυξὶ δουλεύειν ποτέ.
    οὐ παιδιαῖcι καὶ χλιδῆι μορφῆc πέρι   975
    ἦλθον πρὸc ῎Ιδην· τοῦ γὰρ οὕνεκ᾽ ἂν θεὰ
    ῞Ηρα τοcοῦτον ἔcχ᾽ ἔρωτα καλλονῆc;
    πότερον ἀμείνον᾽ ὡc λάβηι Διὸc πόcιν;
    ἢ γάμον ᾿Αθάνα θεῶν τινοc θηρωμένη,
    ἢ παρθένειαν πατρὸc ἐξηιτήcατο   980
    φεύγουcα λέκτρα; μὴ ἀμαθεῖc ποίει θεὰc
    τὸ cὸν κακὸν κοcμοῦcα, μὴ ⟨οὐ⟩ πείcηιc cοφούc.
    Κύπριν δ᾽ ἔλεξαc (ταῦτα γὰρ γέλωc πολύc)
    ἐλθεῖν ἐμῶι ξὺν παιδὶ Μενέλεω δόμουc.
    οὐκ ἂν μένουc᾽ ἂν ἥcυχόc c᾽ ἐν οὐρανῶι   985
    αὐταῖc ᾿Αμύκλαιc ἤγαγεν πρὸc ῎Ιλιον;
    ἦν οὑμὸc υἱὸc κάλλοc ἐκπρεπέcτατοc,
    ὁ cὸc δ᾽ ἰδών νιν νοῦc ἐποιήθη Κύπριc·
    τὰ μῶρα γὰρ πάντ᾽ ἐcτὶν ᾿Αφροδίτη βροτοῖc,
    καὶ τοὔνομ᾽ ὀρθῶc ἀφροcύνηc ἄρχει θεᾶc.   990
    ὃν εἰcιδοῦcα βαρβάροιc ἐcθήμαcιν
    χρυcῶι τε λαμπρὸν ἐξεμαργώθηc φρέναc.
    ἐν μὲν γὰρ ῎Αργει cμίκρ᾽ ἔχουc᾽ ἀνεcτρέφου,
    Cπάρτηc δ᾽ ἀπαλλαχθεῖcα τὴν Φρυγῶν πόλιν
    χρυcῶι ῥέουcαν ἤλπιcαc κατακλύcειν   995
    δαπάναιcιν· οὐδ᾽ ἦν ἱκανά cοι τὰ Μενέλεω
    μέλαθρα ταῖc cαῖc ἐγκαθυβρίζειν τρυφαῖc.
    ειἕν· βίαι γὰρ παῖδα φήιc ⟨c᾽⟩ ἄγειν ἐμόν·

975 οὐ Hartung: αἲ VPΣ
978 λάβοι Hermann
979 πειρωμένη P
982 ⟨οὐ⟩ Seidler
985 c᾽ Hermann: γ᾽ VP
991 ὃν εἰcιδοῦcα P et gE: ὃν ἰδοῦcα V: ἰδοῦcα τοῦτον gB
993 cμίκρ᾽ Burges: μί- VP (μι- P)
998 ⟨c᾽⟩ Va: om. VP

Hecuba   First I shall align myself with the goddesses and
show that her words are unjust. I do not believe   970
that Hera and the virgin goddess Pallas reached
such a pitch of folly that the one was willing to
sell Argos to the barbarians, and the other,
Pallas, Athens to the Trojans to be enslaved.
They did not come to Ida for frivolous games and
the extravagance of a beauty contest. For
what reason would the goddess Hera conceive
such a desire to be beautiful? So that she could
possess a husband superior to Zeus? Would Athena
be looking for a wedding among the gods when
she specifically asked her father to let her remain
a virgin because she shunned marriage? Do not   980
make the goddesses out to be irrational, by
embellishing your own stupidity. You will not
convince the wise. You said that Cypris came to
Menelaus' house with my son (that is a ridiculous
suggestion). Could she not have transported
you, and all of Amyclae too, to Troy by just
remaining quietly in heaven? No, my son was
outstandingly handsome, and your mind, on
seeing him, transformed itself into Cypris. All
acts of human intemperance are Aphrodite,
and rightly does the name of the goddess begin   990
with the word for folly. Seeing my son, splendid
in his oriental clothes, and glittering with gold,
you went out of your mind. Having little at home
when you lived in Argos, you hoped that once
free of Sparta you could swamp the wealthy city
of Troy with your extravagance! Menelaus' palace
was not enough for your luxurious tastes to run
riot in!
Well now: you say my son dragged you away by

τίς Cπαρτιατῶν ἤιϲθετ'; ἢ ποίαν βοὴν
ἀνωλόλυξας, Κάϲτορος νεανίου   1000
τοῦ ϲυζύγου τ' ἔτ' ὄντος, οὐ κατ' ἄϲτρα πω;
ἐπεὶ δὲ Τροίαν ἦλθες Ἀργεῖοί τέ ϲου
κατ' ἴχνος, ἦν δὲ δοριπετὴϲ ἀγωνία,
εἰ μὲν τὰ τοῦδε κρείϲϲον' ἀγγέλλοιτό ϲοι,
Μενέλαον ἤινεις, παῖϲ ὅπως λυποῖτ' ἐμὸς   1005
ἔχων ἔρωτος ἀνταγωνιϲτὴν μέγαν·
εἰ δ' εὐτυχοῖεν Τρῶες, οὐδὲν ἦν ὅδε.
ἐς τὴν τύχην δ' ὁρῶϲα τοῦτ' ἤϲκεις, ὅπως
ἕποι' ἅμ' αὐτῆι, τἀρετῆι δ' οὐκ ἤθελες.
κἄπειτα πλεκταῖς ϲῶμα ϲὸν κλέπτειν λέγεις   1010
πύργων καθιεῖϲ', ὡς μένουϲ' ἀκουϲίως.
ποῦ δῆτ' ἐλήφθης ἢ βρόχοις ἀρτωμένη
ἢ φάϲγανον θήγουϲ', ἃ γενναία γυνὴ
δράϲειεν ἂν ποθοῦϲα τὸν πάρος πόϲιν;
καίτοι ϲ' ἐνουθέτουν γε πολλὰ πολλάκις·   1015
Ὦ θύγατερ, ἔξελθ'· οἱ δ' ἐμοὶ παῖδες γάμους
ἄλλους γαμοῦϲι, ϲὲ δ' ἐπὶ ναῦς Ἀχαιικὰς
πέμψω ϲυνεκκλέψαϲα· καὶ παῦϲον μάχης
Ἕλληνας ἡμᾶς τ'. ἀλλὰ ϲοὶ τόδ' ἦν πικρόν.
ἐν τοῖς Ἀλεξάνδρου γὰρ ὕβριζες δόμοις   1020
καὶ προϲκυνεῖϲθαι βαρβάρων ὕπ' ἤθελες·
μεγάλα γὰρ ἦν ϲοι. κἀπὶ τοῖϲδε ϲὸν δέμας
ἐξῆλθες ἀϲκήϲαϲα κἄβλεψας πόϲει
τὸν αὐτὸν αἰθέρ', ὦ κατάπτυϲτον κάρα·
ἣν χρῆν ταπεινὴν ἐν πέπλων ἐρειπίοις,   1025
φρίκηι τρέμουϲαν, κρᾶτ' ἀπεϲκυθιϲμένην
ἐλθεῖν, τὸ ϲῶφρον τῆϲ ἀναιδείας πλέον
ἔχουϲαν ἐπὶ τοῖς πρόϲθεν ἡμαρτημένοις.
Μενέλα', ἵν' εἰδῆις οἷ τελευτήϲω λόγον,
ϲτεφάνωϲον Ἑλλάδ' ἀξίωϲ τήνδε κτανὼν   1030
ϲαυτοῦ, νόμον δὲ τόνδε ταῖϲ ἄλλαιϲι θὲς
γυναιξί, θνήιϲκειν ἥτις ἂν προδῶι πόϲιν.

1012 βρόχοιϲ Burgesii amicus: -ουϲ VP   ἢ 'ν βρόχοιϲ Diggle
1015 ϲ' ... γε Burges: γ' ... ϲϲ VP

130

force. Which of the Spartans saw you? What
sort of cry did you utter? Yet Castor was still
there, a young man, and his twin brother, since   1000
they were not yet among the stars. And when
you had come to Troy and the Argives were on
your track and the murderous battle of spears
had begun, if you had news that Menelaus' side
was winning, you would commend him in order
to torment my son and to show him what a great
rival he had for your love. On the other hand
when the Trojan side was prospering, Menelaus
was nothing to you. In short, looking merely
to fortune, you worked it so that you could
follow that, and you had no wish to adhere to
integrity. Then you say that you secretly let
yourself down from the ramparts by rope – that   1010
it was against your will that you stayed there.
Well, where were you discovered hanging yourself by the noose or sharpening a sword? This
is what a woman of nobility would have done
missing her former husband. Yet I gave you
a great deal of advice on many occasions.
"Leave, my daughter; my children will make
other marriages. I shall conduct you secretly
to the Achaean ships. Put an end to the war
between the Greeks and ourselves." But this
was gall to you. You ran riot in Alexander's
palace and you wanted the barbarians to   1020
prostrate themselves before you. This was
important to you. And after all this you have
come out here all dressed up, presuming to
breathe the same air as your husband, you
despicable creature. More fitting had you come
humbly in rags, trembling with fear, your head
shaved bare. A sense of shame would be more
appropriate in you than brazenness, after the
wrongs you have committed in the past.
Menelaus, I end my speech thus. Crown Greece
with honour by killing this woman. This would   1030
be an act worthy of you. Establish this precedent
for all other women. Death for the woman who
betrays her husband.

Χο. Μενέλαε, προγόνων τ' ἀξίως δόμων τε cῶν
    τεῖcαι δάμαρτα κἀφελοῦ πρὸc Ἑλλάδοc
    ψόγον τὸ θῆλύ τ', εὐγενὴc ἐχθροῖc φανείc.   1035
Με. ἐμοὶ cὺ cυμπέπτωκαc ἐc ταὐτὸν λόγου,
    ἑκουcίωc τήνδ' ἐκ δόμων ἐλθεῖν ἐμῶν
    ξέναc ἐc εὐνάc· χἠ Κύπριc κόμπου χάριν
    λόγοιc ἔνειται. βαῖνε λευcτήρων πέλαc
    πόνουc τ' Ἀχαιῶν ἀπόδοc ἐν cμικρῶι μακροὺc   1040
    θανοῦc', ἵν' εἰδῆιc μὴ καταιcχύνειν ἐμέ.
Ελ. μή, πρόc cε γονάτων, τὴν νόcον τὴν τῶν θεῶν
    προcθεὶc ἐμοὶ κτάνηιc με, cυγγίγνωcκε δέ.
Εκ. μηδ' οὓc ἀπέκτειν' ἥδε cυμμάχουc προδῶιc·
    ἐγὼ πρὸ κείνων καὶ τέκνων cε λίccομαι.   1045
Με. παῦcαι, γεραιά· τῆcδε δ' οὐκ ἐφρόντιcα.
    λέγω δὲ προcπόλοιcι πρὸc πρύμναc νεῶν
    τήνδ' ἐκκομίζειν, ἔνθα ναυcτολήcεται.
Εκ. μή νυν νεὼc cοὶ ταὐτὸν ἐcβήτω cκάφοc.
Με. τί δ' ἔcτι; μεῖζον βρῖθοc ἢ πάροιθ' ἔχει;   1050
Εκ. οὐκ ἔcτ' ἐραcτὴc ὅcτιc οὐκ ἀεὶ φιλεῖ.
Με. ὅπωc ἂν ἐκβῆι τῶν ἐρωμένων ὁ νοῦc.
    ἔcται δ' ἃ βούληι· ναῦν γὰρ οὐκ ἐcβήcεται
    ἐc ἥνπερ ἡμεῖc· καὶ γὰρ οὐ κακῶc λέγειc.
    ἐλθοῦcα δ' Ἄργοc ὥcπερ ἀξία κακῶc   1055
    κακὴ θανεῖται καὶ γυναιξὶ cωφρονεῖν
    πάcαιcι θήcει. ῥάιδιον μὲν οὐ τόδε·
    ὅμωc δ' ὁ τῆcδ' ὄλεθροc ἐc φόβον βαλεῖ
    τὸ μῶρον αὐτῶν, κἂν ἔτ' ὦc' αἰcχίονεc.

1033 τ' ἀξίως Seidler: ἀξίως τε P: ἀξίως V
1035 ψόγον om. P   τὸ θῆλυ, κεὐγενὴc ... φανῆι Dobree
1040 cμικρῶι Diggle: μι- VP
1051 οὐκ ἔcτ'] οὐδεὶc Arist. rhet. 1394 B et (οὐθεὶc γὰρ) eth. Eud.
1235 B (∼gB)
1052 Με. Aldina : om. VP
1053 Με. praescr. VP
1059 αἰcχίονεc Hermann et fort. Σ¹ (ἀκόλαcτοι πάνυ): ἐχθίονεc VP

132

Chorus	Menelaus, act in a manner worthy of your house and your ancestors – take revenge on your wife and save yourself from a charge of cowardice on Greece's part, and appear noble even to your enemies.	
Menelaus	You and I have come to the same conclusion – that this woman, of her own free will, left my home to go to a stranger's bed. She introduced Cypris into her speech speciously. Go and find those who will stone you and make up for the long sufferings of the Greeks in one brief instant – die and learn not to dishonour me.	1040
Helen	No, by your knees, do not impute to me ills which belong to the gods. Do not put me to death. Have forgiveness for me.	
Hecuba	Do not betray the friends she has slaughtered. I implore you on their behalf and on behalf of their children.	
Menelaus	Be silent, Hecuba. I am not listening to her. I am giving the order to my servants to take her to the ships whence she will be conveyed on her way.	
Hecuba	Do not let her travel on the same ship as you.	
Menelaus	Why is that? Is she heavier than she was?	1050
Hecuba	Once a lover, always a lover.	
Menelaus	That depends on the state of mind of those in love. But it shall be as you wish. She will not board the same ship as I. What you say is not unreasonable. When she has come to Argos this miserable woman will die a miserable death as she deserves, and will inspire all women to be chaste. This is no easy thing. But her destruction will turn their folly to fear, even if they are worse than she is.	

Χο. οὕτω δὴ τὸν ἐν Ἰλίωι   [στρ. α
    ναὸν καὶ θυόεντα βω-   1061
      μὸν προύδωκας Ἀχαιοῖς,
    ὦ Ζεῦ, καὶ πελανῶν φλόγα
    cμύρνας αἰθερίας τε κα-
      πνὸν καὶ Πέργαμον ἱερὰν   1065
    Ἰδαῖά τ' Ἰδαῖα κιccοφόρα νάπη
    χιόνι κατάρυτα ποταμίαι
    τέρμονά τε πρωτόβολον ἕωι,
    τὰν καταλαμπομέναν ζαθέαν θεράπναν;   1070
    φροῦδαί coι θυcίαι χορῶν τ'   [ἀντ. α
    εὔφημοι κέλαδοι κατ' ὄρφ-
      ναν τε παννυχίδες θεῶν,
    χρυcέων τε ξοάνων τύποι
    Φρυγῶν τε ζάθεοι cελᾶ-   1075
    ναι cυνδώδεκα πλήθει.
    μέλει μέλει μοι τάδ' εἰ φρονεῖc, ἄναξ,
    οὐράνιον ἕδρανον ἐπιβεβὼc
    αἰθέρα τε πόλεος ὀλομένας,
    ἃν πυρὸς αἰθομένα κατέλυcεν ὁρμά.   1080

    ὦ φίλος, ὦ πόcι μοι,   [στρ. β
    cὺ μὲν φθίμενος ἀλαίνειc
    ἄθαπτος ἄνυδρος, ἐμὲ δὲ πόντιον cκάφος   1085
    ἀίccον πτεροῖcι πορεύcει
    ἱππόβοτον Ἄργος, ἵνα ⟨τε⟩ τείχη
    λάϊνα Κυκλώπι' οὐράνια νέμονται.

1064 cμύρνας Diggle: -ης VPΣ¹:
1065 ἱρὰν Heath
1067 κατάρυτα Seidler: κατάρρ- VP
1069 ἕωι Wilamowitz: ἁλίω VP
1070 ζάθεον Wilamowitz   interrogationis notam add. Denniston
1078 ἕδραν P   ἐπιβεβὼc Seidler: -βεβηκὼc VPΣ
1079 πόλεος Seidler: -εως VPΣ¹
1081 choro contin. Stephanus (et Neap. sec. Wecklein): Εκ. praescr.
VP
1086 ἀίccαν Hermann
1087 ⟨τε⟩ τείχη Seidler: τείχεα VP

Helen is led out. Menelaus follows

Chorus   Did you then, Zeus, betray in this way to the   1060
Achaeans, your temple in Troy and its altar
fragrant with incense, the flame of its sacrificial
offerings and the smoke of myrrh rising to the
heavens, hallowed Pergamum and the ivy-covered
glades of Mount Ida, their rivers running with
melting snow, and the far flung horizon lightened 1070
by the dawn's first shaft, that radiant and holy
place?
Gone are your sacrifices and the sweet-sounding
songs of choirs and the night-long festivals of
the gods held deep in the darkness; the moulded
gold images and the moon-shaped sacrificial cakes,
twelve in number. It concerns me, my lord, it
concerns me whether you care about these things
as you sit upon your airy heavenly throne while
my city has perished and the flaming onslaught
of fire broken it.   1080
My own dearest husband, you wander now in
death unburied and deprived of lustral water,
while I shall be taken in a swift-winged sea-
going ship to Argos, grazed by horses, where
men inhabit the sky-towering stone Cyclopean

τέκνων δὲ πλῆθος ἐν πύλαις
δάκρυσι †κατάορα στένει† βοᾶι· βοᾶι   1090
Μᾶτερ, ὤμοι, μόναν δή μ' Ἀχαιοὶ κομί-
    ζουσι σέθεν ἀπ' ὀμμάτων
κυανέαν ἐπὶ ναῦν
εἰναλίαισι πλάταις   1095
ἢ Σαλαμῖν' ἱερὰν
ἢ δίπορον κορυφὰν
Ἴσθμιον, ἔνθα πύλας
Πέλοπος ἔχουσιν ἕδραι.

εἴθ' ἀκάτου Μενέλα   [ἀντ. β
μέσον πέλαγος ἰούσας   1101
δίπαλτον ἱερὸν ἀνὰ μέσον πλατᾶν πέσοι
†αἰγαίου† κεραυνοφαὲς πῦρ,
Ἰλιόθεν ὅτε με πολυδάκρυτον   1105
Ἑλλάδι λάτρευμα γᾶθεν ἐξορίζει,
χρύσεα δ' ἔνοπτρα, παρθένων
χάριτας, ἔχουσα τυγχάνει Διὸς κόρα·
μηδὲ γαῖάν ποτ' ἔλθοι Λάκαιναν πατρῶι-   1110
    όν τε θάλαμον ἑστίας,
μηδὲ πόλιν Πιτάνας
χαλκόπυλόν τε θεάν,
δύσγαμον αἶσχος ἑλὼν
Ἑλλάδι τᾶι μεγάλαι   1115
καὶ Σιμοεντιάσιν
μέλεα πάθεα ῥοαῖσιν.

1090 κατάρροα Meridor (κατάρρυτα exspectes), -ν ἀμάτορα Jackson
1095 εἰναλίαισι Aldina: : ἐναλ- V: ἐν ἀλ- P
1100 εἴθ' Stephanus: ἔνθ' VPΣ
1102 πλατᾶν Burges: πλάταν VPΣ
1104 αἰθαλοῦν Diggle, δίπαλτον (et 1102 Αἰγαῖον pro δίπαλτον) Wilamowitz, Δῖον (cum διccον 1086) Schenkl
1105 πολυδάκρυτον Seidler: -δακρυν VP: -δάκρυον Wilamowitz
1113 θεάν Musgrave: θεᾶς θάλαμον VP: θεᾶς et θεᾶς μέλαθρον pro uariis
lectionibus agnoscit Σ
1116 Σιμοεντιάσιν Hermann: -τίσι(ν) VP
1117 ῥοαῖσιν post Musgrave (ῥοῆισιν) Blomfield: προῆσιν P: τρωῆισιν VΣⁱ

136

walls. A crowd of children at the gates cry
through their tears clinging and calling out again 1090
"Mother, the Achaeans are taking me away from
your sight, all on my own, to the dark-prowed
ship, either to Salamis with its holy temples or
to the peak of the Isthmus between two seas
where Pelops' palace has its gates."
While Menelaus' ship is on the high seas, may   1100
the Aegean's lightning fires, hurled by the hands
of Zeus, fall between the banks of oars, since he
is sending me weeping from Troy, away from my
country, to be a slave in Greece while she,
daughter of Zeus, actually has in her possession
the golden mirrors that young girls love so well.
May he never come home again to Sparta and his   1110
ancestral hearth, nor to the district of Pitane
with the bronze-gated temple of Athens, after
capturing her who brought shame to mighty
Greece by her disastrous marriage, and brought
suffering to the shores of Simois.

ἰὼ ἰώ,
καίν' ἐκ καινῶν μεταβάλλουcαι
χθονὶ cυντυχίαι. λεύccετε Τρώων
τόνδ' 'Αcτυάνακτ' ἄλοχοι μέλεαι   1120
νεκρόν, ὃν πύργων δίcκημα πικρὸν
Δαναοὶ κτείναντεc ἔχουcιν.

Τα. 'Εκάβη, νεὼc μὲν πίτυλοc εἷc λελειμμένοc
λάφυρα τἀπίλοιπ' 'Αχιλλείου τόκου
μέλλει πρὸc ἀκτὰc ναυcτολεῖν Φθιώτιδαc·   1125
αὐτὸc δ' ἀνῆκται Νεοπτόλεμοc, καινάc τιναc
Πηλέωc ἀκούcαc cυμφοράc, ὥc νιν χθονὸc
'Άκαcτοc ἐκβέβληκεν, ὁ Πελίου γόνοc.
οὗ θᾶccον οὕνεκ', οὐ χάριν μονῆc ἔχων,
φροῦδοc, μετ' αὐτοῦ δ' 'Ανδρομάχη, πολλῶν ἐμοὶ   1130
δακρύων ἀγωγόc, ἡνίκ' ἐξώρμα χθονόc,
πάτραν τ' ἀναcτένουcα καὶ τὸν 'Έκτοροc
τύμβον προcεννέπουcα. καί cφ' ἠιτήcατο
θάψαι νεκρὸν τόνδ', ὃc πεcὼν ἐκ τειχέων
ψυχὴν ἀφῆκεν 'Έκτοροc τοῦ coῦ γόνοc·   1135
φόβον τ' 'Αχαιῶν, χαλκόνωτον ἀcπίδα
τήνδ', ἣν πατὴρ τοῦδ' ἀμφὶ πλεύρ' ἐβάλλετο,
μή νιν πορεῦcαι Πηλέωc ἐφ' ἑcτίαν
μηδ' ἐc τὸν αὐτὸν θάλαμον οὗ νυμφεύcεται
[μήτηρ νεκροῦ τοῦδ' 'Ανδρομάχη, λύπαc ὁρᾶν],   1140
ἀλλ' ἀντὶ κέδρου περιβόλων τε λαΐνων
ἐν τῆιδε θάψαι παῖδα· cὰc δ' ἐc ὠλέναc
δοῦναι, πέπλοιcιν ὡc περιcτείληιc νεκρὸν
cτεφάνοιc θ', ὅcη coι δύναμιc, ὡc ἔχει τὰ cά·
ἐπεὶ βέβηκε καὶ τὸ δεcπότου τάχοc   1145
ἀφείλετ' αὐτὴν παῖδα μὴ δοῦναι τάφωι.

1118 καίν' ἐκ post Dobree (καιναὶ 'κ) Wilamowitz: καινὰ VPΣ¹
1123 Αγ. Elmsley: uide ad 709
1129 οὐ Seidler et Σ¹ ut uid.: ἢ VP
1130 δ' V: τ' P
1140 del. Herwerden, Paley (agnoscit Σ)

*Talthybius returns. His men bring on the
body of Astyanax laid on Hector's shield*

Chorus   Io, io,
            incessant relays of misfortunes keep coming upon
            our country in new ways. Unhappy women of
            Troy, look on the body of Astyanax here whom
            the Greeks have murdered and cruelly flung from   1120
            the walls as they might fling a quoit.

Talthybius   Hecuba, one ship is left, oars ready to carry
            the remainder of the spoils of Achilles' son back
            to the shores of Phthia. Neoptolemus himself
            has set sail because he has heard that Peleus
            has suffered some new misfortune: Pelias' son,
            Acastus, has cast him out of the country. There-
            fore not wishing to delay, he is already gone in   1130
            great haste, and Andromache with him. She drew
            from me many tears when she left as she mourned
            aloud her country and said a last farewell to
            Hector's tomb, and begged Neoptolemus to bury
            this, the body of your Hector's son, who lost his
            life when he was flung from the city walls. This
            bronze-backed shield which inspired terror among
            the Greeks, and which his father used to guard
            his body, she begged him not to take to Peleus'
            house nor into the very chamber where she would
            be taken to Neoptolemus' bed, [Andromache the   1140
            dead boy's mother,] but to bury the child on it
            instead of in a cedarwood coffin and a stone tomb.
            [a painful sight to see.] She begged him to give
            the child into your arms so that you could wrap
            its body in wreaths and winding sheets, in so
            far as you had strength and opportunity. This,
            since she is gone, and her master's haste
            prevented her from giving burial to the child

ἡμεῖς μὲν οὖν, ὅταν cὺ κοcμήcηιc νέκυν,
γῆν τῶιδ' ἐπαμπιcχόντεc ἀροῦμεν δόρυ·
cὺ δ' ὡc τάχιcτα πρᾶccε τἀπεcταλμένα.
ἑνὸc μὲν οὖν μόχθου c' ἀπαλλάξαc ἔχω·   1150
Cκαμανδρίουc γὰρ τάcδε διαπερῶν ῥοὰc
ἔλουcα νεκρὸν κἀπένιψα τραύματα.
ἀλλ' εἶμ' ὀρυκτὸν τῶιδ' ἀναρρήξων τάφον,
ὡc cύντομ' ἡμῖν τἀπ' ἐμοῦ τε κἀπὸ cοῦ
ἐc ἓν ξυνελθόντ' οἴκαδ' ὁρμήcηι πλάτην.   1155
Εκ. θέcθ' ἀμφίτορνον ἀcπίδ' Ἕκτοροc πέδωι,
λυπρὸν θέαμα κοὐ φίλον λεύccειν ἐμοί.
ὦ μεῖζον' ὄγκον δορὸc ἔχοντεc ἢ φρενῶν,
τί τόνδ', Ἀχαιοί, παῖδα δείcαντεc φόνον
καινὸν διειργάcαcθε; μὴ Τροίαν ποτὲ   1160
πεcοῦcαν ὀρθώcειεν; οὐδὲν ἦτ' ἄρα,
ὅθ' Ἕκτοροc μὲν εὐτυχοῦντοc ἐc δόρυ
διωλλύμεcθα μυρίαc τ' ἄλληc χερόc,
πόλεωc δ' ἁλούcηc καὶ Φρυγῶν ἐφθαρμένων
βρέφοc τοcόνδ' ἐδείcατ'· οὐκ αἰνῶ φόβον,   1165
ὅcτιc φοβεῖται μὴ διεξελθὼν λόγωι.
ὦ φίλταθ', ὥc cοι θάνατοc ἦλθε δυcτυχήc.
εἰ μὲν γὰρ ἔθανεc πρὸ πόλεωc ἥβηc τυχὼν
γάμων τε καὶ τῆc ἰcοθέου τυραννίδοc,
μακάριοc ἦcθ' ἄν, εἴ τι τῶνδε μακάριον·   1170
νῦν ⟨δ'⟩ αὖτ' ἰδὼν μὲν γνούc τε cῆι ψυχῆι, τέκνον,
οὐκ οἶcθ', ἐχρήcω δ' οὐδὲν ἐν δόμοιc ἔχων.
δύcτηνε, κρατὸc ὥc c' ἔκειρεν ἀθλίωc
τείχη πατρῶια, Λοξίου πυργώματα,
ὃν πόλλ' ἐκήπευc' ἡ τεκοῦcα βόcτρυχον   1175
φιλήμαcίν τ' ἔδωκεν, ἔνθεν ἐκγελᾶι
ὀcτέων ῥαγέντων φόνοc, ἵν' αἰcχρὰ μὴ cτέγω.
ὦ χεῖρεc, ὡc εἰκοὺc μὲν ἡδείαc πατρὸc
κέκτηcθ', ἐν ἄρθροιc δ' ἔκλυτοι πρόκειcθέ μοι.

1148 ἐπαμπιcχόντεc praemonente Elmsley Matthiae: ἐπαπίcχ- P
(-αμπ- p): ἀμπιcχόντεc V   ἀροῦμεν Burges: αἱρ- VP
1171–2 fort. corrupti
1171 ⟨δ'⟩ Reiske   αὖτ' Aldina: αὗτ' VP
1177 cτέγω Diggle: λέγω VPΣ et Athen. et Eust. in Il. p. 757. 47,
quo seruato δὴ pro μὴ Denniston

herself. As for us, when you have prepared
the body, we will bury it and then set sail. Do
what you have been enjoined to do as quickly   1150
as possible. One task I have spared you. As
I crossed the waters of the Scamander there, I
washed the body and cleaned the wounds.
Now I am going to break the ground to dig the
grave so that your tasks and mine, done together
with despatch, may set the ship on the path for
home.

Hecuba   Set down on the ground Hector's circular shield,
a painful sight and one I hate to see. Oh, you
Greeks, with more pretension in your weapons
than good sense, why have you perpetrated a
murder without precedent in fear of this child?   1160
Was it because you were afraid that he might
restore Troy one day once it had fallen? Your
strength meant nothing then. Even when Hector
flourished in the thick of battle and countless
other forces too, we were perishing, yet you,
now that the city is captured and the Trojans
destroyed, fear such a tiny child. I despise
the fear of a man who has not tested it by
reason. Oh my dearest child, how cruelly
death came to you! If you had died for the city
after reaching manhood and attaining marriage
and a kingdom equal in power to the gods, you
would have been happy – if indeed happiness
lies in such things. But, as it is, you are   1170
unaware of having seen and recognised these
things in your mind, and although they are
part of your heritage you had no experience
of them. How brutally, poor boy, your father's
walls, the towers built by Apollo, have shorn
those curls on your head which your mother
so often tended and kissed, and where the
blood now laughs out between the broken bones.
I will not hide the brutality of it. Your hands,
how sweetly like your father's they are, now
lying limp at the joints as I can see. Dear lips

ὦ πολλὰ κόμπους ἐκβαλών, φίλον στόμα,　　　　1180
ὄλωλας, ἐψεύσω μ', ὅτ' ἐσπίπτων πέπλους,
Ὦ μῆτερ, ηὔδας, ἦ πολύν σοι βοστρύχων
πλόκαμον κεροῦμαι πρὸς τάφον θ' ὁμηλίκων
κώμους ἐπάξω, φίλα διδοὺς προσφθέγματα.
σὺ δ' οὐκ ἔμ', ἀλλ' ἐγὼ σὲ τὸν νεώτερον,　　　1185
γραῦς ἄπολις ἄτεκνος, ἄθλιον θάπτω νεκρόν.
οἴμοι, τὰ πόλλ' ἀσπάσμαθ' αἵ τ' ἐμαὶ τροφαὶ
ὕπνοι τ' ἐκεῖνοι φροῦδά μοι. τί καί ποτε
γράψειεν ἄν σοι μουσοποιὸς ἐν τάφωι;
Τὸν παῖδα τόνδ' ἔκτειναν Ἀργεῖοί ποτε　　　1190
δείσαντες; αἰσχρὸν τοὐπίγραμμά γ' Ἑλλάδι.
ἀλλ' οὖν πατρώιων οὐ λαχὼν ἕξεις ὅμως
ἐν ἧι ταφήσηι χαλκόνωτον ἰτέαν.
ὦ καλλίπηχυν Ἕκτορος βραχίονα
σώιζους', ἄριστον φύλακ' ἀπώλεσας σέθεν.　　1195
ὡς ἡδὺς ἐν πόρπακι σῶι κεῖται τύπος
ἴτυός τ' ἐν εὐτόρνοισι περιδρόμοις ἱδρώς,
ὃν ἐκ μετώπου πολλάκις πόνους ἔχων
ἔσταζεν Ἕκτωρ προστιθεὶς γενειάδι.
φέρετε, κομίζετ' ἀθλίωι κόσμον νεκρῶι　　　1200
ἐκ τῶν παρόντων· οὐ γὰρ ἐς κάλλος τύχας
δαίμων δίδωσιν· ὧν δ' ἔχω, λήψηι τάδε.
θνητῶν δὲ μῶρος ὅστις εὖ πράσσειν δοκῶν
βέβαια χαίρει· τοῖς τρόποις γὰρ αἱ τύχαι,
ἔμπληκτος ὡς ἄνθρωπος, ἄλλοτ' ἄλλοσε　　　1205
πηδῶσι, †κοὐδεὶς αὐτὸς εὐτυχεῖ ποτε†.

1180 ἐκβαλὸν φίλιον V post ἐκβαλών dist. Burges
1181 πέπλους P: λέχος V
1184 ἐπάξω Nauck: ἀπ- VP
1189 σοι Burges: σε VPΣ: σῶι Dobree
1191 τοὐπίγραμμα γ' V (fort. -a γ' Vᵖᶜ, -a Vᵃᶜ): -γραμμ' P (-γραμμ' ἐν p)
1196 σῶι Barnes: σὸς VPΣ||
1199 ἔσταζεν P: -ξεν VΣ: -ζέ ς' Bothe
1203-4 πράσσων δοκεῖ ... χαίρειν Bothe
1206 εὐτυχεῖ Vp et gE: -χῆ P　　κοὔποθ' αὐτὸς εὐτυχὴς ἀεί Barthold
(αὐ- iam Scaliger)

that once uttered great promises that were   1180
doomed to failure when you clung to my dress
and said "Grandmother (when you die) I will
cut off a thick lock of my hair and bring
gatherings of my friends to your tomb and
utter affectionate words of farewell." But you
are not burying me, but I you, poor boy,
while you are still so young and I am an old
woman without a city or child left. Alas, those
many embraces and all my care of you and (all)
those nights have gone for nothing! What could
a poet write for you as an epitaph on your tomb?
"The Greeks once killed this child because they   1190
were afraid of him?" What a shaming inscription
for Greece that would be! You have not won
your father's heritage but you shall have his
bronze shield even if only as a coffin. O shield
that protected the fine arm of Hector, you lost
him even as he looked after you so well. How
sweet the imprint of his body that lies on your
sling, and the mark of sweat on your well-turned
rim, sweat which Hector in the thick of battle
let drip from his brow as he pressed you against
his chin. Come, bring adornment for the pitiful   1200
body, as much as our present condition allows.
Fate does not grant us the chance for much
display. But you shall get what I have. That
man who imagines he is secure in his prosperity
and rejoices is a fool. For our fortunes have a
habit of leaping about in different directions
like a capricious man, and no one is ever
happy of his own accord.

143

Χο. καὶ μὴν πρὸ χειρῶν αἵδε σοι ϲκυλευμάτων
    Φρυγίων φέρουϲι κόϲμον ἐξάπτειν νεκρῶι.
Εκ. ὦ τέκνον, οὐχ ἵπποιϲι νικήϲαντά ϲε
    οὐδ' ἥλικαϲ τόξοιϲιν, οὓϲ Φρύγεϲ νόμουϲ   1210
    τιμῶϲιν †οὐκ ἐϲ πληϲμονὰϲ θηρώμενοι†,
    μήτηρ πατρόϲ ϲοι προϲτίθηϲ' ἀγάλματα
    τῶν ϲῶν ποτ' ὄντων· νῦν δέ ϲ' ἡ θεοϲτυγὴϲ
    ἀφείλεθ' Ἑλένη, πρὸϲ δὲ καὶ ψυχὴν ϲέθεν
    ἔκτεινε καὶ πάντ' οἶκον ἐξαπώλεϲεν.   1215
Χο. ἒ ἔ, φρενῶν
    ἔθιγεϲ ἔθιγεϲ· ὦ μέγαϲ ἐμοί ποτ' ὢν
    ἀνάκτωρ πόλεωϲ.
Εκ. ἃ δ' ἐν γάμοιϲι χρῆν ϲε προϲθέϲθαι χροῒ
    Ἀϲιατίδων γήμαντα τὴν ὑπερτάτην,
    Φρύγια πέπλων ἀγάλματ' ἐξάπτω χροόϲ.   1220
    ϲύ τ', ὦ ποτ' οὖϲα καλλίνικε μυρίων
    μῆτερ τροπαίων, Ἕκτοροϲ φίλον ϲάκοϲ,
    ϲτεφανοῦ· θανῆι γὰρ οὐ θανοῦϲα ϲὺν νεκρῶι·
    ἐπεὶ ϲὲ πολλῶι μᾶλλον ἢ τὰ τοῦ ϲοφοῦ
    κακοῦ τ' Ὀδυϲϲέωϲ ἄξιον τιμᾶν ὅπλα.   1225
Χο. αἰαῖ αἰαῖ·
    πικρὸν ὄδυρμα γαῖά ϲ', ὦ
    τέκνον, δέξεται.
    ϲτέναζε, μᾶτερ   Εκ. αἰαῖ.
Χο. νεκρῶν ἴακχον.   Εκ. οἴμοι.   1230
Χο. οἴμοι δῆτα ϲῶν ἀλάϲτων κακῶν.
Εκ. τελαμῶϲιν ἕλκη τὰ μὲν ἐγώ ϲ' ἰάϲομαι,
    τλήμων ἰατρόϲ, ὄνομ' ἔχουϲα, τἄργα δ' οὔ·
    τὰ δ' ἐν νεκροῖϲι φροντιεῖ πατὴρ ϲέθεν.

1207 πρόχειρον Wecklein (noluit Dobree)
1211 post h.u. lac. indic. Scaliger
1212 προϲτίθημ' Herwerden
1218 γάμοιϲι χρῆν Prinz: -οιϲ ἐχρῆν VP
1220 om. V
1227 lectio una cum numeris incerta est: cf. Chr. Pat. 1518
1230 Χο. ... Εκ. Aldina: om. VP   νεκρῶν Aldina: -ὸν VPΣ
1234 φροντιεῖ Chr. Pat. 1383 sicut coni. Matthiae: -ίϲει VP

Chorus	Here on hand are your women who bring from the Trojan spoils adornment to place on the body.
Hecuba	My child, it is not for your victory over companions with horses or bow (practices respected, but not excessively so, by the Phrygians) that your grandmother lays upon you precious things from possessions once your own. As it is, Helen, so hated by God, has robbed you, and in addition destroyed your life and brought ruin to our whole house.
Chorus	Ah, you have touched my heart deeply, you who were once a great lord in my city.
Hecuba	I put upon you the glory of Phrygian robes, things you should have worn at your marriage to some preeminent Asian princess. O beloved shield of Hector, receive this crown, you who once glorified in victory and were mother of a thousand emblems of conquest. Dead with this body, you are yet deathless. Better by far to honour you than the weapons of the cunning and unprincipled Odysseus.
Chorus	Aiai, aiai. The earth will receive you my child, bitter object of our laments. Cry aloud, our mother . . .
Hecuba	Aiai.
Chorus	. . a dirge for the dead.
Hecuba	Alas!
Chorus	Alas indeed, for sufferings that are unforget-table!
Hecuba	I shall treat your wounds with bandages, a poor doctor I am, since I can say the name but not produce the effects. Your father will take care of you among the dead.

1210

1220

1230

Χο. ἄρασσ' ἄρασσε κράτα   1235
     πιτύλους διδοῦσα χειρός.
     ἰώ μοί μοι.
Εκ. ὦ φίλταται γυναῖκες.
Χο. †Ἑκάβη, cὰc† ἔνεπε· τίνα θροεῖς αὐδάν;
Εκ. †οὐκ ἦν ἄρ' ἐν θεοῖcι† πλὴν οὑμοὶ πόνοι   1240
     Τροία τε πόλεων ἔκκριτον μιcουμένη,
     μάτην δ' ἐβουθυτοῦμεν. εἰ δὲ μὴ θεὸς
     ἔcτρεψε τἄνω περιβαλὼν κάτω χθονός,
     ἀφανεῖc ἂν ὄντεc οὐκ ἂν ὑμνηθεῖμεν ἂν
     μούcαιc ἀοιδὰc δόντεc ὑcτέρων βροτῶν.   1245
     χωρεῖτε, θάπτετ' ἀθλίωι τύμβωι νεκρόν·
     ἔχει γὰρ οἷα δεῖ γε νερτέρων cτέφη.
     δοκῶ δὲ τοῖc θανοῦcι διαφέρειν βραχὺ
     εἰ πλουcίων τιc τεύξεται κτεριcμάτων·
     κενὸν δὲ γαύρωμ' ἐcτὶ τῶν ζώντων τόδε.   1250

Χο. ἰὼ ἰώ·
     μελέα μήτηρ, ἣ τὰc μεγάλαc
     ἐλπίδαc ἐν cοὶ κατέκναψε βίου·
     μέγα δ' ὀλβιcθεὶc ὡc ἐκ πατέρων
     ἀγαθῶν ἐγένου
     δεινῶι θανάτωι διόλωλαc.   1255
     ἔα ἔα·

1235 κράτα Bothe, Seidler: χειρὶ κράτα V(κρά-)P
1238-9 Εκ. ... Χο. om. V
1239 θαρcήcαc' Hermann   ἔνεπε Seidler: ἔνν- VP
1242 δὲ μὴ Stephanus: δ' ἡμᾶc VPΣ¹
1245 ὑcτέρων Wecklein: ὑcτέραν P: ἀοιδοῖc V: ὑcτέραιc Wilamowitz
1250 κενὸν VpΣ¹¹ (κενὸc δὲ κόμποc Chr. Pat. 1452): καινὸν P et gĖ
1251 μήτηρ Dindorf: μάτηρ V: μᾶτερ P: μῆτηρ Σ¹
1252 ἐν Porson: ἐπὶ VP et gE   κατέκναψε Porson: -γναψε VP:
-cκαψε gE
1253-4 ἐξ ἀγαθῶν (deletis πατέρων et ἐγένου) Hermann, ut fieret
responsio inter   1251-5 et 1256-9

146

Chorus	Strike your head again and again, beating with your hands like the rhythm of moving oar strokes. Alas, alas!
Hecuba	My dearest women . . .
Chorus	Hecuba, speak your thought. What cry do you wish to utter?
Hecuba	So the gods amounted to nothing after all! 1240 There was only my suffering and their discriminating hatred of Troy. My sacrifices were useless. And yet had not God turned the world upside down, we should have acquired no significance, and should have remained unsung, instead of giving themes of song for future generations. Go now, and bury the body in its poor tomb. For it has such garlands as befit the dead. I think it makes little difference to the dead if a person is richly bedecked. This is merely an empty pretension for the living. 1250

The body is carried off

Chorus	Io, io. Wretched mother, whose great hopes for life were torn apart in you. Though blessed with wealth and high born, you died a grim

147

τίνας Ἰλιάσιν τούσδ' ἐν κορυφαῖς
λεύσσω φλογέας δαλοῖσι χέρας
διερέσσοντας; μέλλει Τροίαι
καινόν τι κακὸν προσέσεσθαι.

Τα. αὐδῶ λοχαγοῖς, οἳ τέταχθ' ἐμπιμπράναι   1260
Πριάμου τόδ' ἄστυ, μηκέτ' ἀργοῦσαν φλόγα
ἐν χερσὶ σώιζειν ἀλλὰ πῦρ ἐνιέναι,
ὡς ἂν κατασκάψαντες Ἰλίου πόλιν
στελλώμεθ' οἴκαδ' ἄσμενοι Τροίας ἄπο.
ὑμεῖς δ', ἵν' αὑτὸς λόγος ἔχηι μορφὰς δύο,   1265
χωρεῖτε, Τρώων παῖδες, ὀρθίαν ὅταν
σάλπιγγος ἠχὼ δῶσιν ἀρχηγοὶ στρατοῦ,
πρὸς ναῦς Ἀχαιῶν, ὡς ἀποστέλλησθε γῆς.
σὺ δ', ὦ γεραιὰ δυστυχεστάτη γύναι,
ἕπου· μεθήκουσίν σ' Ὀδυσσέως πάρα   1270
οἶδ', ὧι σε δούλην κλῆρος ἐκπέμπει πάτρας.

Εκ. οἲ 'γὼ τάλαινα· τοῦτο δὴ τὸ λοίσθιον
καὶ τέρμα πάντων τῶν ἐμῶν ἤδη κακῶν·
ἔξειμι πατρίδος, πόλις ὑφάπτεται πυρί.
ἀλλ', ὦ γεραιὲ πούς, ἐπίσπευσον μόλις,   1275
ὡς ἀσπάσωμαι τὴν ταλαίπωρον πόλιν.
ὦ μεγάλα δή ποτ' ἀμπνέουσ' ἐν βαρβάροις
Τροία, τὸ κλεινὸν ὄνομ' ἀφαιρήσηι τάχα.
πιμπρᾶσί σ', ἡμᾶς δ' ἐξάγουσ' ἤδη χθονὸς
δούλας. ἰὼ θεοί· καὶ τί τοὺς θεοὺς καλῶ;   1280
καὶ πρὶν γὰρ οὐκ ἤκουσαν ἀνακαλούμενοι.
φέρ' ἐς πυρὰν δράμωμεν· ὡς κάλλιστά μοι
σὺν τῆιδε πατρίδι κατθανεῖν πυρουμένηι.

Τα. ἐνθουσιᾶις, δύστηνε, τοῖς σαυτῆς κακοῖς.
ἀλλ' ἄγετε, μὴ φείδεσθ'· Ὀδυσσέως δὲ χρὴ   1285
ἐς χεῖρα δοῦναι τήνδε καὶ πέμπειν γέρας.

1256 Χο. praescr. V: Εκ. P   τίνας semel Haun. (sec. Wecklein):
bis VP   τούσδ' Lenting: ταῖσδ' P: παῖσδ' V
1260 τέταχθ' ἐμπιμπράναι Dindorf: τέταχθεν πιμ- V: -χθε πιμ- PΣˡ
1262 χερσὶ V: χειρὶ P
1269 δ' Blaydes: τ' VP
1271 πάτρας P: χθονός V
1277 ἐμπνέουσ' q et Chr. Pat. 1704 sicut coni. Wakefield
1284 Τα. V: Χο. P

death. But look! Who are the men I see on
the heights of Ilium, waving fiery torches in
their hands? This must mean some new agony
for Troy.

Talthybius re-enters

Talthybius   I address you captains who have orders to   1260
set fire to this city of Priam – do not let the
flame rest idle in the hand, but launch the fire
upon it, so that once Ilium's citadel is razed we
may set out for home from Troy with gladness.
And you, daughters of the Trojans, so that my
one order has double effect, start moving towards
the Greek ships when the leaders of the army
sound the high echoing call of the trumpet,
that you may be dispatched from this land. You
go with them, unhappiest of old women. These
men, sent from Odysseus, have come in search   1270
of you. The ballot sends you from your own
home country to be his slave.

Hecuba   Ah, I am wretched indeed! This is now the
ultimate and final outcome of all my suffering.
I am leaving my country, and my city is lit
with flame. Come, aged feet, make what difficult
haste you can, that I may salute the city in its
wretchedness. O Troy, who once breathed forth
your greatness among barbarian peoples, you
will now be robbed of your glorious name. They
are burning you and they are already dragging
us from the land as slaves. O Gods! Yet why   1280
do I call upon the gods? They did not listen
when they were appealed to before. Come let
us rush into the pyre. Best for me to die with
this country of mine as it burns.

Talthybius   Your suffering has driven you out of your
mind, poor woman. Men, lead her off, no
delaying. You must deliver her into Odysseus'
hands, sending her as his prize.

149

Εκ. ὀτοτοτοτοῖ.　　　　　　　　　　　　　　　　　　[στρ. α
　　Κρόνιε, πρύτανι Φρύγιε, γενέτα
　　†πάτερ ἀνάξια τῆς Δαρδανίου†
　　γονᾶς, τάδ᾽ οἷα πάσχομεν δέδορκας;　　　　　　1290
Χο. δέδορκεν· ἁ δὲ μεγαλόπολις
　　ἄπολις ὄλωλεν οὐδ᾽ ἔτ᾽ ἔστι Τροία.

Ἐκ. ὀτοτοτοτοῖ.　　　　　　　　　　　　　　　　　　[ἀντ. α
　　†λέλαμπεν Ἴλιος, Περ-　　　　　　　　　　　　1295
　　　γάμων τε πυρὶ καταίθεται τέραμνα
　　καὶ πόλις ἄκρα τε τειχέων†.
Χο. πτέρυγι δὲ καπνὸς ὥς τις οὐ-
　　ρίαι πεσοῦσα δορὶ καταφθίνει γᾶ.
　　[μαλερὰ μέλαθρα πυρὶ κατάδρομα　　　　　　1300
　　δαΐωι τε λόγχαι.]

Εκ. ἰὼ γᾶ τρόφιμε τῶν ἐμῶν τέκνων.　　　　　　[στρ. β
Χο. ἒ ἔ.
Εκ. ὦ τέκνα, κλύετε, μάθετε ματρὸς αὐδάν.
Χο. ἰαλέμωι τοὺς θανόντας ἀπύεις.
Ἐκ. γεραιά γ᾽ ἐς πέδον τιθεῖσα μέλε᾽ ⟨ἐμὰ⟩　　　1305
　　καὶ χερσὶ γαῖαν κτυποῦσα διccαῖc.
Χο. διάδοχά coι γόνυ τίθημι γαίαι
　　τοὺς ἐμοὺς καλοῦσα νέρθεν
　　ἀθλίους ἀκοίταc.
Εκ. ἀγόμεθα φερόμεθ᾽　Χο. ἄλγος ἄλγος βοᾶιc.　　1310

1287 ὀτοτοτοτοῖ post Schroeder (ὀττ-) Diggle: ὀττοτοτοτοτοῖ VP:
item 1294
1289 ἀνάξια τῆς δαρδανίου P: ἄξια τᾶσδε δαρδάνου V
1296 καταίθεται fort. non agnoscit Σ
1298 οὐρίαι Wilamowitz: οὐρανία VPΣ
1300–1 non hic suam sedem habent: post 1297 trai. Hermann
1303 post ἒ ἔ habet V μέλαθρα τῶ πυρὶ καταδέδρακεν, quod est
scholium ad 1300 pertinens
1305 γ᾽ Seidler: τ᾽ VP　　μέλε᾽ ⟨ἐμὰ⟩ Hermann: μέλεα VP
1306 κτυποῦσα Σ sicut coni. Musgrave: κρύπτουσα V: -cι P
1307 διάδοχά tamquam e V Dindorf: -όν VPΣ¹

150

Hecuba	Otototoi. Son of Cronos, lord of Phrygia, our ancestor, have you seen what we suffer, the dishonour done to the race of Dardanus?	1290
Chorus	He has seen, but the great city that is no longer a city has perished and there is no Troy.	
Hecuba	Otototoi. Ilium is blazing – Pergamum's buildings are consumed with fire and the citadel and the summits of the walls.	
Chorus	Our land, fallen to the spear, dissipates into nothingness like smoke on a wing of wind. [With violence the houses are overrun with fire and the enemy spear.]	1300
Hecuba	Oh land that nurtured my children.	
Chorus	Alas!	
Hecuba	Oh children hear me, take note of your mother's cry.	
Chorus	It is the dead you cry to with your lament.	
Hecuba	I let my aged body sink to the ground and I beat the earth with both hands.	
Chorus	I in turn kneel to the earth and call upon my wretched husband in the world below.	
Hecuba	We are being led, taken away	1310
Chorus	Your cry is of pain.	

151

Εκ. δούλειον ὑπὸ μέλαθρον. Χο. ἐκ πάτρας γ' ἐμᾶς.
Εκ. ἰὼ ἰώ, Πρίαμε Πρίαμε,
     cὺ μὲν ὀλόμενος ἄταφος ἄφιλος
     ἄτας ἐμᾶς ἄιστος εἶ.
Χο. μέλας γὰρ ὄσσε κατεκάλυ-   1315
     ψε θάνατος ὅσιος ἀνοσίοις σφαγαῖσιν.

Εκ. ἰὼ θεῶν μέλαθρα καὶ πόλις φίλα,   [ἀντ. β
Χο. ἒ ἔ.
Εκ. τὰν φόνιον ἔχετε φλόγα δορός τε λόγχαν.
Χο. τάχ' ἐς φίλαν γᾶν πεσεῖσθ' ἀνώνυμοι.
Εκ. κόνις δ' ἴσα καπνῶι πτέρυγι πρὸς αἰθέρα   1320
     ἄιστον οἴκων ἐμῶν με θήσει.
Χο. ὄνομα δὲ γᾶς ἀφανὲς εἶσιν· ἄλλαι δ'
     ἄλλο φροῦδον, οὐδ' ἔτ' ἔστιν
     ἁ τάλαινα Τροία.
Εκ. ἐμάθετ', ἐκλύετε; Χο. περγάμων ⟨γε⟩ κτύπον.   1325
Εκ. ἔνοσις ἅπασαν ἔνοσις Χο. ἐπικλύζει πόλιν.
Εκ. ἰὼ ⟨ἰώ⟩, τρομερὰ τρομερὰ
     μέλεα, φέρετ' ἐμὸν ἴχνος· ἴτ' ἐπὶ
     δούλειον ἀμέραν βίου.   1330
Χο. ἰὼ τάλαινα πόλις. ὅμως
     δὲ πρόφερε πόδα σὸν ἐπὶ πλάτας Ἀχαιῶν.

1312 ἰώ bis V: semel P
1315 Χο. Seidler: om. VP   κατεκάλυψε Stephanus:
κατακαλύψει VP
1316 ἀνοσίοις L. Dindorf: -αις VP
1317 Εκ. Seidler: om. VP
1318 Χο. P: om. V   Εκ. Seidler: om. VP
1319 Χο. Seidler: om. VP
1320 Εκ. Seidler: om. VP   καπνοῦ Seidler
1322 Χο. Seidler: om. VP
1325 Χο. Seidler: om. VP   ⟨γε⟩ Seidler
1326 Εκ. Seidler: om. VP   Χο. Kirchhoff: om. VP
ἐπικλύζει Burges: -κλύσει VPΣⁱ
1327 Εκ. Kirchhoff: om. VP   ⟨ἰώ⟩ Kirchhoff
τρομερὰ bis P: semel V
1329–30 (ἴτ' κτλ.) Hec. continuat Seidler: Talth. trib. VP
ἐπὶ Burges: ἐπὶ τάλαιναν VP
1331 Χο. post Seidler Dindorf: om. VP

Hecuba	. . . to a house of slavery.
Chorus	. . . and away from my country too.
Hecuba	Oh Priam, Priam, graveless and friendless in death you are unaware of my destruction.
Chorus	Black death closed his eyes, holy amid unholy butchery.
Hecuba	O temples of the gods and my beloved city.
Chorus	Alas!
Hecuba	You are possessed by the murderous flame and the force of the spear.
Chorus	You will straightway fall to the beloved earth and become nameless.
Hecuba	The dust like smoke winging to the sky shall prevent me from seeing my home.
Chorus	The name of the land will be lost. Things everywhere are vanished and poor Troy no longer exists.
Hecuba	Did you grasp, did you hear?
Chorus	Yes, the sound of the towers falling.
Hecuba	An earthquake over the whole city . . .
Chorus	. . . engulfs it.
Hecuba	Io, io. Make your way, my shaking, trembling limbs. Forward into the day of slavery.
Chorus	Mourn the unhappiest city. But go none the less to the ships of the Achaeans.

1320

1330

Hecuba is led off. Talthybius and the Chorus go out

153

The *Trojan Women*: Structure

COMMENTARY

Hypothesis

This hypothesis summarises the background to Euripides' plot without being an accurate synopsis of the actual play. It is, and was, therefore of limited use to those interested in the shaping techniques employed by the dramatist, but possibly of interest to mythographers and to those whose curiosity is and was merely in the basic story. Its origin is probably a "Collection of Stories from Euripides" composed some time before the first half of the Second Century A.D. It is attached to the manuscripts but a version on papyrus dating from the early Second Century A.D. is to be found in *Oxyrhynchus Papyri*, XXVII, no. 2455 frag.13. For detailed discussion of this fragment and for tragic hypotheseis in Euripides see E.G. Turner, 'Euripidean Hypotheses in a new papyrus', *Proceedings of the Ninth International Congress of Papyrology* (Oslo 1958; published 1962), 1-17; Zuntz (1963) 129-146, esp. 143ff; J. Rusten, *GRBS* 23 (1982), 357-67.

"seen to the burial of the dead": "the dead" here is plural and does not relate well to the content of the play in which there is only one dead person buried by Hecuba, namely her grandson Astyanax. For this reason Diggle suggests the singular *ton anairethenta*.

Prologue 1-97

The scene is the sacked city of Troy and the audience would see makeshift tents belonging to the Greeks. The central door would represent the opening to one of these. Hecuba is lying stretched out on stage asleep (37) and the standing Poseidon and then Athena thus dominate her. The difference in their positions emphasises the gods' power and the human's abject state. The audience must imagine the smouldering city (8) in the background and its walls which, a symbol of Troy's former grandeur, are to come crashing down in the closing scene of the play (1324-5).

The formalised prologue where one character sketches the background to the action is commonplace in Euripides. Four other plays have a god as the speaker, namely *Alcestis* (Apollo), *Hippolytus* (Aphrodite), *Ion* (Hermes) and *Bacchae* (Dionysus). Although Euripides was often radically critical of gods, he was not above using them to further his plots and he never expressed complete disbelief in their existence. They are a part of the mythical furniture he inherited and continued to use. After Poseidon's speech Athena enters and a formal dialogue ensues. Balance shows in the sections of distichomythia (51-68), followed by stichomythia (69-76), followed by one short speech of comparable length by each (10 and 11 lines). The formality of structure is matched by the formality of style (see note on 48).

Poseidon's presence here is dramatically very important, not just for the past background but for the future action he and Athena will together shape. For the Greeks, all unaware, will be shipwrecked on their way home, and it is important that the audience knows this tragedy awaits them since this knowledge sheds an ironic light on the Greeks' actions throughout the play. All they seem to achieve will come to nothing – a point Cassandra also makes later in the play when she prophesies her own and Agamemnon's death as well as Odysseus' troubles on the high seas (430 ff.). The Trojans may be victims of defeat, but the victorious Greeks too will meet with disaster. These consequences for the Greeks strictly reach beyond the play's action – the speeches of Poseidon, Athena and Cassandra are all we have to remind us of it – but this is after all primarily a play about Troy and the Trojans, and too much stress on the Greeks' future fate would upset this focus. I do not agree with Lee that the Greeks are equally tragic figures whose hubris is a major theme. This would detract from the play's heart which is Troy and the Trojans. And indeed Poseidon's prophecy about the Greeks puts the suffering of the Trojans into a wider and new perspective.

1-2 "I come ... Poseidon": The words at the beginning and end of the sentence, *Hēkō ... Poseidōn*, emphasizing the name at the end, enclose the qualifying clause "having left the salt depths of the Aegean Sea". To get a comparable emphasis I have translated "I am Poseidon. I come, etc."

5 Phoebus: Apollo. He and Poseidon built Troy during their years of service to Laomedon, when they had tried to deprive him of his rule. Zeus put them in servitude to him as a punishment. (This part of the earlier Trojan legend is referred to in the ode at 799 ff.) Such participation in Troy's founding by the gods earns it the epithet "holy". See 123, 1065.

5 "encompassing stone towers": *purgous* is the first reference to the towers or walls which are to feature so strongly in the play, and it is no accident that they are given pointed description here by the word *lainous* "stone" and the phrase *orthoisin ... kanosin* "with straight rule". They are part of the stage-set and symbolize Troy's greatness, they are the scene of Astyanax' death, and they collapse at the end of the play. They are described in detail, e.g. by the chorus at 814 where *kanōn* "rule" is again used, by Hecuba at 1174, in passing references at 12, 46, 725, 1011, 1121, 1174, and they also inspire the metaphor *purgoō* "build tower-high" at 612 and 843. (See introductory note on Hecuba's monody, 98-152).

6 *kanōn*: a rule or ruddled line used by masons and carpenters, e.g. *H.F.* 945.

6-7 In this play Poseidon is an ally of the Trojans. In Homer he is their enemy. See *Iliad* 14. 357 ff., 21. 435 ff.

9 *Parnasios*: Parnassus is a mountain in Phocis.
Detailed narratives about the Wooden Horse are later than Homer, as in the Cyclic epics (*Little Iliad* and *Iliupersis*) and in the *Iliupersis* of the lyric poet Stesichorus. Virgil narrates the story in detail in the second book of the *Aeneid*. (See Austin's Introduction and K.W. Gransden, 'The Fall of Troy', *G & R* 32 (1985), 60-72).

12 Diggle has adopted the reading of the MSS PQ *baros*

"weight, burden" rather than that of V *bretas* which would mean "image" or "idol", and which since it is always used only of a god, is not strictly appropriate here. It could, however, be argued that the Trojans regarded the horse as a divine portent, and that *bretas* is therefore a more striking word than the more neutral *baros*, and probably right. Biehl draws attention to 525 *xoanon* "image".

13-14 These lines look very much like an explanatory note by an earlier interpreter of the play. They are not strictly necessary to Poseidon's speech. On the oddness of the language, particularly *keklēsetai*, "it will be called", see J.R. Wilson *AJP* 89 (1968), 66 ff. and Lee's suggestion of an actor's interpolation.

15 "The sacred groves are desolate ...": *erēmos*, "desolate" and *erēmia*, "desolation" are recurring words in the play. *Erēmia* is used at 26 and the emphatic *erēmiai* at 97 is picked up again at an equally emphatic passage at 564 within a very bold metaphor; cf. also 603. Note Poole 264.

17 "Zeus the Protector" (of the Hearth): particularly ironic since Priam was cut down at the altar of the very god whose power was supposed to be to protect suppliants. A brilliant and detailed description of this incident is given in Virgil's *Aeneid* 2. 526 ff.

20 "a following wind": *prumnēthen ouron* is literally "a fair wind from the stern."
"after ten long years": *dekasporōi chronōi* is literally "after ten sowing times".

23-4 After the Judgement of Paris when Paris awarded the prize to Aphrodite, Hera and Athena turned against the Trojans. Hera was particularly associated with Argos.

25 Just as the gods deserted mortals in death (see Artemis at the end of the *Hippolytus*) so gods tended to desert sacked cities (see Aesch. *Septem* 217-18, "The Gods, they say, / of a captured town desert her", and Virgil, *Aen*. 2. 351-2.

29 The river Scamander whose other name was Xanthus ran across the Trojan plain; the modern name is Menderes su. *klēroumenōn*: present tense, since the process of allocation is still going on, and forms a large part of the action of the early part of this play. I have translated "waiting to be allocated" to allow for this continuity.

159

31   "sons of Theseus": *Thēseidae* is just a way of saying "Athenians". Although the particular sons of Theseus were Acamas and Demophon, it is unlikely only they are meant here.

34-5 Helen is put with the other captives but Hecuba implies at 1022-3 that she has somehow managed to dress better than they. This rankles with Hecuba.

36-7 It is by way of a stage direction to the audience and producer indicating Hecuba's position.

40   This reference to Polyxena foreshadows the news which is given to Hecuba by Talthybius at 264 in somewhat oblique fashion, and is later confirmed by Andromache at 622-3. *lathrai* "secretly", i.e. "unknown to her" is the superior reading of V, which Diggle adopts. *oiktra* "pitiably", the reading of PQΣ and adopted by Lee, merely reduplicates *tlēmonōs*.

41 ff. Similarly Poseidon foreshadows the fate of Cassandra referred to at 249 and prepares the way for her extended scene 308-461. When Cassandra rejected Apollo's advances, he punished her by ensuring that the gift of prophecy which he had bestowed on her would never be taken seriously.

47   "Pallas Athena, Zeus' daughter" prepares the way for Athena's entrance in the following line.

48-50 "Is it possible to speak to?": *exesti ... prosennepein;* These words neatly enclose the description of Poseidon. It is hard to reproduce the original word order in a literal translation but in freer ones, such as Vellacott's and Lattimore's, note how they rearrange the English phrases to give emphasis to the final word "speak".

53   "I thank you": *epēines'* is literally "I approve of". The aorist expresses instantaneous judgement.

59-60 *nin* is governed by *es oikton ēlthes* (the periphrasis standing as a transitive verb). See Diggle, *Studies* 58.

60   "burnt to ashes": *katēithalōmenēn* (direct object in agreement with *nin*) is an emendation of Elmsley adopted by Diggle. This avoids the clumsy change of construction necessary were the genitive *katēithalōmenēs* of the MSS kept.

67   literally "why do you leap from one attitude to another at different times in this way ...?"

"just as chance dictates": *hon an tuchēis*. The *hon* has been attracted to the case of the missing antecedent, and the sense is *hon an tucheis* ⟨*philōn*⟩, literally 'whoever you chance ⟨to love⟩'. Not much reflection perhaps on the moral constancy of gods but entirely in keeping with the Homeric concepts of gods acting for favourites on whim. But Athena does give some reason for her change of attitude.

69 The change to single stichomythia here indicates a greater urgency.

70 Ajax' rape of Cassandra is told in the Cyclic epic – the *Iliupersis*. Cassandra was dragged by him from Athena's shrine. This was not however the Great Ajax, son of Telamon, but the Lesser Ajax, son of Oileus.

71 "He neither suffered anything at the Achaeans' hands nor was reproached": *akouō*, in a passive sense "to hear oneself called" often with e.g. *kakōs*, "be ill spoken of", is a common usage. Here *dein'* goes with it as well as with *epathen*.

75 "their return home an unhappy one": *dusnoston* ... *noston* is an oxymoron, literally "a journey that is no pleasant journey". That oxymoron was a familiar feature of Euripides' style, Aristophanes recognized in his parody in the *Frogs* at 1334, 1331. See Kannicht on *Helen* 363.

78 "enormous": *aspeton* is literally "unspeakably great".

83 "huge waves": *trikumiais* is literally "with third waves" since these were thought to be the highest. See Plato, *Rep.* 472a cited by Lee.

84 Probably, as Lee says, one of the smaller gulfs of Euboea implied by the word *muchon* "innermost part", "small area", rather than the whole stretch of the South East coastline.

90 The Capherean Cliffs in being associated with Nauplios *may* recall the *Palamedes* (see Scodel 66ff. who argues against the view taken by Koniaris 92ff.)

94 "Lets out its sails": *exiei kalōs* refers to letting out the reef ropes (i.e. of the sails), not the anchor ropes, for Athena wants to strike at the Greeks when they are already at sea.

95-7 These words carry one of the main themes of the play, developed also by Cassandra, that the victors may after all turn out to be just as vanquished as those they have conquered.

On the punctuation and the addition of ⟨*sph'*⟩ see Diggle, *Studies* 58-59.

Hecuba's monody 98-152

Hecuba, the aged Queen of Troy and the protagonist of this play, is lying down on stage near the tents of the Greeks (139). She has been asleep throughout the dialogue with the two gods and now raises her head to sing a lonely monody or solo aria in which she expresses her grief at her present predicament. The monody is a particularly apt vehicle for the expression of strong emotions (see Barlow 43ff.) and this play contains two - the other being Cassandra's at 308ff. Nothing could be further from the cool spoken exchanges between the two gods than this passionately sung lament with its cryptic images, protesting questions and bitter acknowledgement of discomfort and loss.

It falls into three parts - the first 98-121 expressing Hecuba's own grief, the second 122-137 addressing the cause of it, the Greek expedition to Troy and its visible symbol, their ships, and the last 138-152 reverting to her own state and linking it with that of the chorus, thus motivating their subsequent entry and comment at 153. Its metre is anapaestic of both the regular kind found in recitative (98-121), and the more irregular kind found in straight lyric (122-152). For more detailed analysis see Lee 80 and 84-5, and Dale (1968) 57ff.

The monody is shot through with nautical imagery, both metaphorical (at 102-4, 108, 118) and literal (122ff.) and this indicates a preoccupation. Hecuba reveals also elsewhere (see 686ff.) her fear of ships. The metaphorical language indicates a subconscious preoccupation, and the literal an overt acknowledgement of the fact that the Greek ships are lurking just offshore to take her and the other women away. They too are anxious about the ships as the ensuing dialogue shows (159-160, 162, 180-181); note also the last line of the play. Such a play between literal and metaphorical imagery is apparent elsewhere also in the link between the metaphor *purgoō* (612, 843) and the constant reference in the action to the actual towers of Troy, looming in the background (e.g. 5, 12, 46, 725, 1011, 1121, 1174) until they tumble at the very end of the play, a symbol of Troy's greatness reduced finally to mere dust.

98   "poor one": *dusdaimōn* contains the notion of an unhappy lot or divine destiny, and this sense of a divine destiny (*daimōn*) which controls the lot of individuals is maintained throughout this stanza by its repeated use alone or in compounds i.e. 98 (*dusdaimōn*), 101 (*daimonos*), 102 (*daimona*), and 112 (*barudaimonos*).

99-100   "This is no longer Troy nor we the Queen of Troy":
By this paradox Hecuba expresses her recognition that
the destruction of Troy is complete and she herself has
lost her identity.
102   "sail according to the strait's current": *plei kata
porthmon* is literally "sail down the strait in direct line
with the current" i.e. "sail in accordance with inevitable
events." Note the nautical metaphor sustained in the next
few lines and the forceful repetition of *plei kata* "sail in
accordance with".
108   "reduced": *sustellomenos* is again a nautical metaphor;
literally "shortening sail".
110   "Why should I be silent? Or why not be silent?": (*ti me
chrē sīgān; ti de mē sīgān.*) Note the repetition here of
"why" and "be silent" enhanced by both the repetitive
sound and rhythm (each element contained within its own
anapaestic metron) of the Greek words, which echo the
rocking movement of Hecuba's body.
112-114   'It was not altogether without cause that Aristophanes
ridiculed our poet for his overdrawn portraits of squalid
royalty'. (Paley). Yet Hecuba's reference to her physical
discomfort seems to me to be legitimately realistic rather
than absurd. On the general use of such contrasts
between the elevated and mundane within lyric passages
see Barlow 50-53.
115ff.   Hecuba is envisaged here as rocking her body from
side to side as if, she implies, she were a ship in motion
on the waves. The metaphor is contained in the word
toichous meaning "ships' benches" or "sides" (*Helen* 1573)
and is almost impossible to render in English adequately.
Literally the meaning is "to both ships' sides of my
limbs". As Lee says 'Her back (*nōton akanthan t'*) is the
keel, while her sides (*amphoterous toichous*) are the sides
of the vessel'. The submerged metaphor here is
psychologically revealing again of the old woman's
preoccupation with ships. A rocking motion in mourning is
a practice still common in Mediterranean countries today
but may sound bizarre to the restrained English!
119   *epious':* literally "proceeding to", is an emendation of
Musgrave, a small change from the MSS *epi tous,* and one
which eases the sense, for there is no parallel for *epi* to
mean "in accompaniment to".
121   "joyless troubles": *achoreutous* is literally "without
dancing" and hence "without joy".

163

122   Hecuba now turns to the real ships of the Greek expedition, not the ships of her imagination, and the transition seems natural and psychologically plausible. The lyric anapaests begin here.

125   "fair harbours": Paley takes this to refer to the harbours along the East coast of Greece and the Aegean islands visited by the approaching Greek expedition.

126   *paiani*: the paean was sometimes used of a war-cry in victory (see Aesch. *Pers.* 393, Lys. 2.38.) and is hence called "hateful" here for its connotations to Hecuba and the people of Troy. The *aulos* is properly "a pipe" but I have translated "flute" to provide variety with *suriggōn*.

127   "tuneful": pipes may still be "tuneful" even though their sound is in this case hateful to the Trojans.

128-9 "to hang upon": *exērtēsasth'* is literally "you hung (from your sterns) the woven product of Egypt". This is an incredibly pompous way of referring to anchoring cables made of Egyptian byblus i.e. papyrus fibre. The allusion is explained by the scholiast. Diggle daggers because of the tortuousness of the expression and the unexampled use of *paideian* meaning 'product'.

132   Castor and Pollux were Helen's brothers. In *Iliad* 3.242 the brothers are said to be "dreading the words of shame and all the reproach that is on me" (sc. Helen).

133   The *Eurotas*, one of the longest rivers in the Peloponnese, is used as a metonymy for Sparta.

136   Diggle's text is daggered here because of the metrical irregularity (see Lee ad loc.).

137   "has run me aground": *exokellō* is a nautical word (see Herod. VII, 182); note the reversion here to ship imagery

142   "drastically, pitifully shorn": *ekporthētheis* literally meaning "ravaged", "devastated" refers here to Hecuba's shorn head. Note how the compound with *ek* implies "thoroughly" cropped. It was customary for women in mourning to crop their hair and this may be seen on many vase paintings depicting lament for the dead. A particularly clear example is on the white lekythos in the Met. Mus. of Art N.Y., A.R.V. 561: Robertson, *Greek Painting* 147.

143   *chalkenchēs*: "bronze-speared", only occurs here. With its heroic, epic flavour it is like *kallipeploi* "beautifully dressed" at 338, i.e. ironically used to contrast the once

glorious with the now wretched state of the Trojans.

144   daggered because of metrical anomaly, and because *dusnumphai* is also anomalous in form.

146-7   There are awkwardnesses here apart from the metrical ones e.g. the repetition of *hōsei* and *hopōs* "like", only one of which is strictly necessary, but the MSS at *Hec.* 398 may afford a parallel and the meaning is clear, i.e. that Hecuba like a mother raising a cry for her nestlings will raise a cry for the women of Troy, but it will not be the same as the one she once sang in happier days. Dindorf's nominative *ornis* 'as the mother bird' would make the sense clearer.

150   The MSS have *diereidomena* "leaning on", referring to Hecuba's dependence on Priam's sceptre or power, whether literal or metaphorical, but Herwerden's *diereidomenou*, which Diggle accepts, makes the sense more general, i.e. the *dance* being led while Priam looks on, leaning on his sceptre (genitive absolute). See his defence of this reading in *Proc. African Class. Assoc.*, XIV (1978) 31.

The Parodos

The Parodos is divided into two Sections, (a) the kommatic section at 153-196, a dialogue between the Chorus and Hecuba, and (b) the lyric ode by the Chorus 197-229.

(a) The chorus is divided into two groups, one entering and addressing Hecuba at 153, the other entering and addressing her at 176ff. The first group appeals to the second to come outside at 166. Lines 166 and 176 suggest that the chorus come out by the central door, not the parodoi. On the problems see Hourmouziades 24-25.

The tone of fear and despair so apparent in Hecuba's monody is mirrored here by the women's anxious questions about the preparations of the enemy fleet and their own likely futures as slaves to Greeks in Greece.

The metre here is lyric anapaests rather than the marching anapaests more common in parodoi. (See West (1982) 121, 122 n.108.) Such a use suggests a closer emotional involvement with the preceding aria of Hecuba than the more distant marching anapaests would have allowed.

153-4   The Chorus may well wonder at the drift of Hecuba's words which are preoccupied with riddling nautical metaphors and with a description of the Greek ships. What they do not yet know is that these ships are now ready to sail.

154,157   "From indoors", "inside": *dia gar melathrōn* and *tōnd' oikōn* in 157 refer to the tents. *Melathron* and *oikos* can be used not only of house and palace, but also of other dwelling places e.g. a cave Soph. *Phil.* 147 Eur. *Cyc.* 491 Homer *Od.* 9. 478, and, as here, a tent *Il.* 24 471, 572. Soph. *Ajax* 65. Eur. *Hec.* 59, 1019.

156   "fear stabs the hearts": *dia de sternōn phobos aissei.* *Aissō* describes the swift motion of the sword as it is stabbed e.g. Homer *Il.* 11. 484, 5. 81, 17. 460, or of pain as it stabs through the head Eur. *Hipp.* 1351, cf. 165.

171   "to be degraded by the Argives": *aischunan Argeioisin.* This is how the scholiast explains the phrase and it seems the most likely. Parmentier's interpretation 'to shame *me before* the Greeks' is difficult linguistically, and the only other possible interpretation "to bring shame to the Greeks" would be dramatically inappropriate for Hecuba to say.

173   "Ah Troy, unhappy Troy": the address to Troy here as a person, with its emphatic repetition, characterises the

166

women's close identification with their city. It is as if Troy is also one of the suffering Trojan women. Cf. 780 *talaina Troia*, 1277-8 *ō megala dē pot' ampneous' ... Troia*, and the last but one line of the play 1331 *iō talaina polis*; cf. *Hec.* 905, 913.

"you are gone": *erreis*. Hecuba mourns Troy's annihilation also at 99, 582, 1292.

175   *dmathentes* are "the dead", literally those "overcome" by death cf. *I.T.* 199, 230, *Alc.* 127.

180   "at the sterns": *kata prumnas.* Dr Alan Lloyd of Swansea suggests the point of this phrase, emphatically placed as it is, is that when the ships have been beached in the normal way, stern first, the people at the stern are the last to be able to use their oars as the ship gets clear. Hence once these get busy, the ship is well and truly afloat and on its way.

182   Diggle has adopted two suggestions of the Aldine editor here which greatly ease the sense. 1. *orthreusousan psuchan* for the MSS *orthreuou san psuchan* and 2. 183 to be attributed to Hecuba not the Chorus as in the MSS.

1. *orthreuō* means "to lie awake before dawn" (see LSJ). If therefore the small correction is right (since the middle imperative gives no sense), the reference is to Hecuba's wakeful vigil since dawn and the words go closely with *ekplēchtheis'*, "my spirit awake since dawn, struck by panic" (literally "I have come, struck in my wakeful spirit by panic". *psuchan* is a retained accusative with the passive *ekplēchtheisa*).

2. The advantage of giving these lines to Hecuba is that they provide the required balance to her voice part also at 159-160.

190-193   "where on earth ...": the repeated interrogatives *pou pai* indicate anxiety. cf. Soph. *Ajax* 913, Eur. *I.T.* 1435. This antistrophe has been full of questions.

"drone-like": *hōs kēphēn.* Like Hecuba will be, drones are dependent, and like she will be too, they are supported in their slave-like status by others, as Tyrrell points out. Lee cites Dodds on *Ba.* 1365.

193   "a feeble adornment of the dead": *amenēnos* is used in Homer of the dead. *Od.*10. 521 *nekuōn amenēna karēna*, 11. 29, 49. Its usual meaning is "weak" or "feeble". Here however an unHomeric oxymoron is produced by the linking with *agalma*. Hecuba is being ironical in seeing herself as a poor sort of adornment even to the dead.

167

(b) This ode expressing the Chorus' imaginings of where they might end up in Greece is the only one in the play that does not concentrate upon Troy. Although it is dramatically plausible that the women should be anxious about their future destination at this point (indeed they have already expressed such anxieties in 187-190 and this ode underlines these), it is less convincing, as well as anachronistic, that they should praise Athens in this way and go into details about other places little known in Mycenaean times, such as Sicily and Thurii. Perhaps Euripides was flattering his audience here, pandering to their pride in their city and to their current interest in Sicily which culminated in the great expedition about to be undertaken in 415 B.C., but if so, he has sacrificed dramatic verisimilitude to topical allusions, which in this case are scarcely appropriately contained by their context. Nonetheless there is some unity of theme in that the places are described in terms of their fountains and rivers – Peirene for Corinth, Eurotas for Sparta, Peneus for Thessaly and Crathis for Thurii.

The ode is similar in its general content to the first stasimon of the *Hecuba* where the reference to Athens (particularly where, at 466-473, the Chorus imagine themselves taking part in the Panathenaeic festival) is even more at odds with its dramatic context.

The metre: lyric anapaests with heavily spondaic rhythm – e.g. at 197, 198, 200, 202, 203, 204, 210, 211, 213 and at corresponding places in the antistrophe.

200   "No longer shall I move the whirling shuttle back and forth"...: *exallassō* which normally means "change", here appears to mean "turn from one direction to another" i.e. "move back and forward" of the movement of the shuttle. This simple sentiment "I shall no longer be doing the familiar things" seems more natural than to take *exallassō* with *luman* as Diggle suggests in his full apparatus comparing *Hel.* 380, i.e. "I shall change my outrage by not plying the Trojan shuttle" i.e. since there will be no Trojan loom to work I shall change one outrage for another".

201   "the home of my parents": *tokeōn dōmata* is Parmentier's emendation which Diggle adopts for MSS *tekeōn sōmata*, 'the bodies of my children', on the grounds that the Chorus cannot see any such thing. There are no children on the stage, but what the Chorus can see in the background are their family homes. The change involves

168

the alteration of two letters only, each resembling the original very closely.

203   "the beds of Greeks": *lektrois - Hellanōn;* the plural is used here in a generalising way for the singular. Note how the singular *hexō* in 202 changes to plural at 208 *elthoimen.*

205ff.   For a detailed analysis of the geographical descriptions in this main part of the ode see H.D. Westlake, *Mnemosyne* 6 (1953) 181ff. His view is that the descriptions are not merely ornamental but that the poet is directing the attention of his audience to contemporary events – those of 415 as seen through Athenian eyes – but without attempting to influence public opinion.

205   Peirene was a fountain in Corinth. Pindar calls Corinth 'city of Peirene' *Ol.* 13. 61.

209, 219   "land of Theseus": this is Athens since he was King there. See 31n.

210   "the swirling of the Eurotas": the Eurotas, a river in Sparta, becomes almost a poetic shorthand for indicating this region. See *Hec.* 650, *Hel.* 124, 162, 210, 350, 493, 1492, *I.A.* 179, *And.* 437, *I.T.* 400.

214   The river Peneus flows through Thessaly, passing through the Vale of Tempe between Mount Olympus and Mount Ossa on its way to the Thermaic Gulf.

218   For the demonstrative *ta* see Diggle, *Studies* 6.

220   The volcanic eruptions of Mount Etna in Sicily were thought to be due to Hephaestus' work in the forge underneath the mountain. Pi. *Pyth.* 1.25ff.

221   "the land opposite Phoenicia": Phoenicia is here used for Carthage which was a Phoenician Settlement.

223   "for its garlands of valour": *stephanois aretas.* This seems to be a reference to Pindar's Victory Odes which celebrated the success of Hiero and other Sicilians in the games.

225   "near the Ionian Sea": no sense can be made of *nautai* here; near a *sailor* in the Ionian Sea? It does not fit in either grammatically or metrically with the surrounding phrases. Hence the daggers. See L. Parker, *CQ* 8 (1958), 86.

227   The river Crathis had dyeing properties (see Pliny *N.H.* XXXI. 2, Strabo VI. 263, Ovid *Met.* 15. 315-16). It flows into the Tarentine Gulf South of Thurii.

1st Episode 230-510

In the first part of this episode we see the entrance of the Greek herald Talthybius who comes to tell Hecuba the allocation of women captives. Cassandra has been picked out as Agamemnon's concubine, Polyxena has been sacrificed at Achilles' tomb, Andromache is to be given to Achilles' son and Hecuba to Odysseus. Hecuba does not grasp the full significance yet, but the audience would know that it will mean death for Cassandra, has meant death for Polyxena and will ultimately mean death for Hecuba.

The major part of the episode is given to Cassandra who is seen as both unhinged in mind by her own fate, yet at the same time uncannily perceptive of how things really stand and of what will happen when the Greeks have left Troy.

As in the Agamemnon we hear her first in a wild frenzy which she expresses in an aria of unheeding, mad and uninhibited joy, then in a calm rational state where she argues the paradoxical case that the defeated Trojans are really better off than the victorious Greeks. Lee laments the shortness of the mad spectacle (108) and claims that "soon we are confronted with a more prosaic, unexciting Cassandra who argues with inappropriate calmness". But this is to approach the presentation too naturalistically, as Lee appears to recognise later (125). What the poet shows us is two facets of Cassandra's mental state, separated out for dramatic purposes – unhinged frenzy and clear prophetic perception. The two are not inconsistent – merely contained and condensed into different modes so that we may appreciate the tone of each more clearly.

In the same way we see two facets of Alcestis in her play – her lyric delirium when she is dying (244-272), and her calm iambic speech when she makes arrangements for her family after her death (280-325). Such creative contrasts are very much part of a Greek dramatist's way of proceeding. Each mode evokes a different response.

235-307   Hecuba's anxiety in this short scene between herself and the herald is stressed by the fact that she is given lyric lines while Talthybius speaks in iambic trimeters. The contrasting use of metre to express differing emotional levels is frequently seen in Euripides. Again look at the death scene in the *Alcestis* 244-279 where Alcestis utters lyric lines, while Admetus, slow and uncomprehending, speaks in trimeters. Only when Alcestis has fainted does Admetus go into lyric himself (273-279).

170

Euripides has skilfully shown Hecuba's maternal character here by making her ask after her children and daughter-in-law first before coming to herself.

235 "because": the *gar* expresses the reason for using Hecuba's name - "I can call you Hecuba, because you know me of old".

249 "picked out, chosen": *exaireton* describes things given as a special honour, not assigned by lot. Cassandra was regarded as a coveted prize since prophetesses were highly regarded in antiquity as people with special gifts endowed by Apollo (not always however willingly received or benevolently given by the god, since Apollo, in her case, made her a prophetess after she had refused his advances, and ensured that her prophecies would never be believed).

252 "as concubine": *skotia* "dark" or "secret" is used of a clandestine union - hence "concubine" as opposed to "wedded wife". Cf. 44 and *Ion* 860.

256 Cassandra's rôle as concubine is now inconsistent with her former special position as virgin priestess - hence her sacred emblems must be discarded. See 451ff.
kladas is a rare form of *klados* meaning "branch", "twig" or "bough", an emendation, which Diggle accepts, of PQ's *kleidas* "keys", in the context of garlands which are made up of twigs and leaves.

259 Talthybius does not understand why anyone should want a half-crazed priestess, nor can he understand why it is not an honour to be ordered to serve a king. His ordinary perception of things is nicely contrasted with Hecuba's protective attitude and special concern for her daughter's plight.

262 Polyxena's fate has already been alluded to by Poseidon in lines 39-40. Hecuba does not however grasp the significance of Talthybius' euphemistic words and imagines that this is some sort of guardianship of the tomb. She has no idea it means Polyxena's death, and she therefore goes on to ask about her daughter-in-law Andromache. The irony is nicely presented.

269 "What did I hear you say?": literally "what's this you uttered?" The verb *laskō*, often used of loud cries or screams (inappropriate here), seems also to be used more neutrally of oracular language in the sense of "utter". See A.M. Dale's note at *Alc.* 343-7.

270   "Does she still live?": *aelion leussei* is literally "see the light" (i.e. of day, of the sun). The direct question is not directly answered, and Hecuba, perhaps in wishful thinking, lets it go. But it registers at a subconscious level since she later acknowledges it at 624-5. 'This was what Talthybius meant, that speech cryptic, yet now so clear' (Lattimore).

275   "the help of a stick to walk with...": *tritobamonos* literally means "walking on three legs", "forming a third foot" and describes the staff which does just this. Cf. *Rhesus* 215 *dibamos eimi*.

280   "double": *diptuchos* refers merely to the fact that there are two cheeks, but at 287 "double talk" has a sinister qualitative meaning.

282   The graphic and villainous portrait of Odysseus here is appropriate not only because it adds to the general image of barbarous Greeks the poet is conveying. But Odysseus was particularly unscrupulous in his false accusation of Palamedes in the previous play of the trilogy which the audience would doubtless recall. Further, it is he, specifically, who thinks up the death of Astyanax and persuades the assembly to execute it (Talthybius refers to this at 721) so that this passage prepares the ground for that incident later in the play.

    Such an extended and abstract character sketch as this, by one character describing another person, is rare in Greek tragedy.

284   "lawless monster": *dakos* is properly "a bite", hence is used of any animal whose bite is dangerous.

288   "turning love into hate": literally "making what was formerly friendly unfriendly again.

289-290   These lines are daggered for metrical reasons.

293   "But which Achaean or Greek...?": Both *Achaiōn* and *Hellenōn* are words for "Greeks", perhaps used here to distinguish between those of the Peloponnese and those of Northern Greece. Parmentier draws attention to Eur. *El.* 1285 where *Achaiis gē* is used of the Peloponnese.

    The Chorus' question is never answered, for dramatic reasons. Talthybius has already given the vital information about the main characters – the Chorus are never named individually and to itemise them here would detract from the plight of the central characters. The Chorus' collective question however is in keeping with their own anxiety which echoes that of Hecuba and all the Trojan women.

298   Cassandra's wild brandishing of torches inside the tents (the stage building) leads the herald to wonder whether the women have resorted to violence. Cassandra's turbulent and sudden eruption onto the stage with flaming torches provides an exciting moment visually and contrasts well with Hecuba's preceding more static monody. Her entry is thus marked by spectacle just as Andromache's is by the arrival of the chariot loaded up with Trojan loot. Both moments lend impact to the action. Two women thus enter, in a very similar plight, but the way the dramatist depicts them could not be more different.

308-340   <u>Cassandra's monody</u>

Cassandra sings a lyric monody in a mixture of dochmiac metre, resolved imabics and glyconics. Dochmiacs are associated with high excitement and emotion, here particularly 308, 310-2, 325, 327-9: see Dale (1968) 110. Compare for instance the climax of Creousa's monody *Ion* 894-6, 906-9, or the dochmiacs interspersed with iambics at *Bacchae* 1169ff. Brandishing torches and in a highly excited state she sings a wedding hymn, imagining she is celebrating her marriage to Agamemnon in Apollo's temple. It is of course a mockery of the real situation and the ironies are many. One of them is that the song has some of the natural exuberance a girl might feel at her wedding. It has elements of normality in it which are specially ironic here because they are totally inappropriate to this one person for whom the married state was never contemplated. This is in addition to the obvious further irony that her true position is nothing like a marriage anyway, since it is an enforced slavery which will only bring misery and cause her to be indirectly the cause of Agamemnon's death.

There is a stroke of genius here in portraying madness as normality gone wrong, or rather inappropriately applied. In the right circumstance this would be a perfectly natural song for a Trojan princess to sing on her wedding day. For Cassandra however it is tragic. I do not agree with Lee who says that here 'she sees her fate as it really is'. In my view her madness at this point protects her from seeing her fate as it really is. This perception is left for the calmer iambic portions which follow. Nor do I agree with Lee that it is 'vindictive'. It is meant to have the unclouded simplicity and happiness of one who in madness is oblivious to the real circumstances.

The language of the song is narrow in range, repeatedly stressing marriage within the context of religious observance. Cassandra's words include *hieron* (sacred temple) 310, *sebō* (I revere) 308, *hosios* (holy) 328, *thuēpolō* (I sacrifice) 330. Marriage is persistently emphasised in the five times repeated refrain, *ō Humenai' anax* (Lord Hymenaeus), *gametas* (bridegroom) 311, *gamoumena* (bride-to-be) 313, *gamois* and *gamon* 319, 339 (weddings), *numphan* (bride) 337 and *posin* (husband) 340 given prominence by its position at the end of the aria. *Makarios* (blessed), another word with religious connotations (see note on 311), is repeated at 311, 312, 327 and 336, stressed through being three times at the beginning of lines and once, a superlative, at the end. *Choros* (dance) occurs at 325 and 328, and *choreue*, *choreuma* at 332.

Such repetitive vocabulary underlines Cassandra's obsessive fervour and single-minded delusion of a sacral occasion misconceived and wrongly applied, but expressed in terms consistent with her function as a priestess.

308 Since the torch was used at Bacchanals as well as at weddings, and Cassandra is in a raving state and called *mainas* at 349 by Hecuba (a word especially used of frenzied Bacchic revellers) and uses the Bacchic cries *Euhan Euhoi* at 326, no doubt the colouring of both kinds of ceremonial ritual is intended to be conveyed here. Cassandra has taken upon herself the rôle of carrying the torch. This normally belongs to the bride's mother. See Σ to A.R. 4.808, Eur. *Med* 1027, *Pho.* 344, *I.A.* 732.

310 "O Lord Hymenaeus": Hymen or Hymenaeus is the god of marriage and always invoked in wedding ceremonies as presiding over them. See Ar. *Peace* 1334-5, *Birds* 1736-7.

311 "blessed": *makarios*, is a word with ritual connotations both for the marriage song and the Bacchanal, just as the word "blessed" has ritual associations of prayer for us. For marriage see Ar. *Birds* 1722-5 Eur. *Hel.* 1434ff., *I.A.* 1076-9, 1404ff. For Bacchic ritual see *Ba.* 72ff.

323 Hecate is, I think, primarily invoked here as associated with fire and torch-bearing. See Diggle's note on

174

Phaethon 268 and Roscher's examples *Myth. Lex.* I. 900 *Hekate in der Kunst.* But she has more sinister associations with the chthonic powers of sorcery and black magic and the scholiast is probably right to observe that she is also relevant because she has connotations of death. Medea invokes her for sinister purposes at *Med.* 397 and the Chorus at *Ion* 1048.

326 *"Euhan Euhoi"*: These are cries used in Bacchanalian revels, cf. Ar. *Lys.* 1294, Soph. *Trach.* 219, *Ba.* 141. Hesychius says *Euhan* came from an Indian word for ivy, a plant sacred to Dionysus.

329 *"Apollo"*: Since Apollo is intimately associated with Cassandra (note her cries to him in Aesch. *Ag.* 1073, 1077, 1080-81, 1085-86), it is fitting that her imagination should envisage the whole ceremony as taking place in his temple even though the very idea of marriage is alien to his purpose for her. She is still under his influence. See note on 451. On the use of *en daphnais* meaning "crowned with bay leaves" rather than referring to Apollo's temple "among the bay trees" see Diggle, *Studies* 60.

332 *choreum' anage, poda son*: Diggle's reading here is very close to that of P(Q) *choreu' anage poda son*; it simply adds one letter, giving *anage* an object and leaving *poda* to go with *helisse*. V's *anagelason* "laugh out loud", much bolder, though perhaps more in keeping with madness, is unworkable metrically.

338 "beautifully dressed": *kallipeploi*. A particularly ironic epithet more reminiscent of the grandeur and glory of days gone by than the miserable rags the women now wear. But the image fits Cassandra's distorted vision. The epithet occurs in P. *Pyth.* 3.25. See note on 143.

342 "blithely": The use of *kouphon* here suggests "lightly" almost in the sense of "heedlessly". Hence my translation "blithely".

343 "O Hephaestus": Hephaestus was the fire-god, and so appropriate to torch bearers at weddings.

348 "You are not carrying the torch straight": *ou gar ortha purphoreis*. *Orthos* can mean either "straight" in a physical sense or "correct". Hecuba is ever practical and the simplest explanation seems to me the best dramatically, that Hecuba seizes one of the torches which Cassandra is brandishing wildly, presenting a danger to all around her. It is a direct qualification of the previous

phrase "Give the torch to me". The other explanation, which Lee favours, is that Hecuba takes the torch because Cassandra is not performing the ritual correctly. But surely we are past that stage. Cassandra is mad. Would Hecuba plausibly worry about ritual correctness at such a moment? I doubt it. Talthybius has also foreshadowed the danger of the torch by his comments at 298.

351   "torches": the plural here, *peukas*, would seem to indicate that Cassandra is carrying a torch in each hand. Hecate is depicted in art as frequently carrying more than one torch.

353ff.   Here begins Cassandra's iambic speech. The ultra-delirious mood of the mad wedding song has gone, as the words at 355-6 and 366-7 make plain. Instead there is a cold, clear-eyed, prophetic view of her rôle, one in which legitimate pride and triumph surface that she alone will be the victorious agent by which the mighty Greek leader Agamemnon will be brought down. *Nikēphoron* "triumphant", "conquering", "victorious" at 353 is therefore an appropriate compound, carefully chosen, and carefully emphasised through its position at the end of the phrase and line. It has a tradition of heroic contexts going back to Aeschylus and Pindar (cf. Pind. *Ol*. 1.116; 13.14 Aesch. *Cho*. 148, *Eum*. 477). This word is later to be echoed by the same word in the same place at 460 (see note). Both reinforce the sense throughout Cassandra's two long speeches (353ff, 424ff) not only that the Trojans are really better off than the Greeks, but that she herself, a mere woman and an apparent victim, will alone be able to do what no other Trojan, even Hector, has achieved, namely to defeat Agamemnon and avenge Troy.

356   Apollo was called Loxias from the word *loxos* "oblique". This referred to his giving of ambiguous oracles. See Jebb's note on Soph. *O.T*. 853.

Cassandra persists in calling her union with Agamemnon "a marriage" as Helen describes her disastrous liaison with Paris as a "marriage" (932). Although *gameō* and *gamos* are more usually used of legitimate wedlock, *gameō* occurs in the context of non-marital union at Homer *Od*.1. 36; cf. 44 and 398 of this play. It may be that there was no other word. Contrast this word-use however with that of *damar* at 660 and see note.

176

359   "I shall kill him": *ktenō gan auton*. Cassandra does not of course directly kill Agamemnon, but that she is to be indirectly the cause of his death is seen to weigh so heavily on her mind that she puts it in this way.

       Cassandra's prophecies of the disasters awaiting the Greeks, particularly Agamemnon and Odysseus, complement the more general prophecies of the Greeks' future fate made by Poseidon in the prologue. Her prophecy however is particularly tragic since it will involve her own death too.

365ff.   Cassandra now goes on to demonstrate logically that it is really the Trojans who are the victors. They have won glorious and everlasting reputations in defending justly their native country, families and friends whereas the Greeks have suffered absence of family and fatherland and deprivation of decent burial. Her point, added to the knowledge that the surviving Greeks will also suffer on the way home, is a powerful one.

370   "this clever general"; *sophos* is ironical as is *kleinos* "famous" describing Agamemnon above (358).

371   "killed what he loved": refers to the sacrifice of Iphigeneia by Agamemnon at Aulis.

374   "banks of the Scamander": see 29n.

383-5   These lines, particularly 383, have been suspected on stylistic grounds (see the *apparatus*.) It is also open to question whether their content is appropriate here. Cassandra has just finished the points she wishes to make about disadvantages to the Greeks. It would be natural for her then to proceed to advantages for the Trojans, rather than to introduce a new point about the Greeks' brutal treatment of the Trojans (one interpretation of *aischra*, "shameful events"), or even to harp back after so long an interval on Agamemnon's troubles at Mycenae (another interpretation of *aischra*). Neither is in point here.

384   *mousa*: is "inspiration" as most commonly expressed in music, song or poetry.

387   "they died": *ethnēiskon* parallels the *ethnēiskon* above at 375. The Trojans, like the Greeks, met their deaths, but unlike them they had a just cause and found decent burial at the hands of their families. The *imperfect* suggests a continuing process.

397 "his valour would never have been revealed": literally "he being brave would have escaped notice". Posthumous fame is a strong source of consolation to the defeated Trojans. See Hecuba's words at 1242-45 and note on 1244.

400 These words supplement those of Poseidon in the prologue at 95ff. For such anti-war sentiments elsewhere see *Hel.* 1151ff.

407 "you sing things which your song perhaps leaves obscure": literally "you sing things which perhaps you will prove were obscure when you sang them".

411-12 Although the herald understands it in a somewhat narrow context, this theme of people not being what they seem, more widely interpreted, is central to the whole trilogy. Alexandros was not what he appeared to be, although he, unlike Agamemnon, appeared humble and was really elevated. Palamedes appeared a traitor and was really innocent. Agamemnon appears wise and eminent but is really a fool who ultimately counts for nothing.

415-16 Talthybius has no doubts about madness. He is as wary of it as the majority of people usually are. But his "ordinariness" provides nice relief. See W.H. Friedrich, *Euripides und Diphilos* (München, 1953) 73.

416 "would never have wanted her *bed*": *lechos ge*. The particle *ge* stresses the thought that he would never have been so foolish as to seek her bed, though he might have employed her as a slave.

420 "a good match", *kalon numpheuma*, is ironical. Talthybius writes off both Cassandra and Agamemnon as lacking any kind of common sense such as he would recognise as important.

422-3 "The woman ... a good person": Odysseus' wife Penelope.

424 "clever pretensions": *deinos* is here used pejoratively in the sense of "too clever" as at Pl. *Euth.* 3c and *Tht.* 176d1; cf. *Ba.* 971 where I suspect there is a play on the different meanings of *deinos* including this one, and echoing perhaps 655.

425 This contempt for heralds is expressed elsewhere in Euripides at *Hcld.* 120ff. *Supp.* 426ff., *Or.* 888ff.

Although unable to comprehend Cassandra, Talthybius shows himself to be compassionate towards Andromache and Hecuba, and even goes beyond his duties later to take upon himself the preparation of Astyanax' body for burial. One of the interesting things in the play is the way this Greek's sympathy for the Trojans grows as their suffering accumulates, and this dramatic touch robs the play of any crude division of characters into simple black and white. On his rôle generally see Gilmartin (1970) 213ff.

430   The story of Hecuba's end is told at the end of the *Hecuba* when Polymestor prophesies at 1261ff. 'You shall drown at sea. You shall climb to the masthead and fall ... changed to a dog, a bitch with blazing eyes ... And when you die, your tomb shall be called ... Cynossema, the bitch's grave, a landmark to sailors' (transl. W. Arrowsmith).

431   The change of subject is very abrupt here.

434   We must suppose, as Paley says, that some words such as 'having wandered over places where' have dropped out. But this whole passage, 435-43, is extremely condensed, being little more than a skeletal catalogue, and it seems to me that Tyrrell, and Pearson *CR* 4 (1890), 425, are right in thinking it an interpolation. Its shorthand style is quite unlike the rest of Cassandra's utterances and its language is either weak e.g. *hōs de suntemō* 441, *kaka muria* 443, or odd - *petras* is without construction as it stands, *morphōtria* "changer" only occurs here, and appears to be a feminine form from a non-existent word *morphōtēr*, and 440 as it stands in the MSS. is untranslatable and even with Bothe's emendation, which I have translated, sounds odd.

436   The stages in Odysseus' journey here referred to are described in the *Odyssey* 12. 101ff, 235ff, (Charybdis); 9. (Cyclops): 10. 233ff, (Circe); 5. 313ff, (Shipwreck): 9. 83ff, (Lotus eaters); 12. 262ff, 394ff, (Cattle of the Sun); 11 (Journey to the Underworld).

441   refers to the ill-omened sound of cooking flesh. It is "ill-omened", *pikran*, because after this feast Odysseus lost all his men.

444ff.   Cassandra now goes into trochaic tetrameters. The change of metre brings emphasis to her closing lines which spell out more clearly than previously the horror of her own death and that of Agamemnon. Compare the way Lyssa in the *H.F.* goes into trochaic tetrameters first in a brief exchange with Iris at 855-857, then in a speech of 16 lines where she prophesies the extreme violence with which she will drive Heracles mad. Both passages are highly charged.

444 "hurl": *exakontizo* is a metaphor from javelin-throwing. See Collard on *Supp.* 456.

446 "dishonourable ... dishonourably": *kakos* ... *kakōs*. Note the emphatic repetition of sound and meaning in the Greek.

447 repeats the sentiment expressed by Talthybius at 411-12. Agamemnon's power is illusory since he is enslaved by his passion for Cassandra and this brings him death.

448ff. Cassandra creates a graphic visual image of her death just as she does in Aesch. *Ag.* 1260ff.

451 Cassandra bids farewell to the marks of her office as priestess, the woollen headbands sacred to Apollo, by tearing them off and flinging them to the winds. So does Cassandra in the *Agamemnon* 1264ff relinquish her holy office. In retrospect and compared with what she now faces, the god seems to her *philtatos* ("the god I loved so dearly", 451) and the gift of prophecy which he bestowed on her valuable, although at the time she resented it. It is interesting that in the *Ion*, a more extreme case of resentment against Apollo, Creousa nonetheless when in great danger still falls back on the god's protection (1285) after blaspheming against him earlier. The influence of Apollo once felt was not lightly discarded.

453 literally "go from my flesh by tearing".

457 "It is one of the Furies you will be taking ...": As Diggle argues, *Studies* 62, "Cassandra is saying that three Furies will take vengeance on Agamemnon when he arrives home, and these three will be herself, Clytemnestra and Aegisthus".

460 See 353, cf. *El.* 872. It is significant that with the masculine, heroic concept implied in *nikēphoros*, Cassandra now ranks herself (459) with the men of the family, Priam, Hector and her other brothers, now in the Underworld.

462 Hecuba faints. Her attendants go to her assistance, but she chooses to remain where she is, on the ground.

466-510 Apart from her opening monody, this is the one place in the play where Hecuba can expand upon her own position. Otherwise her rôle is very much one of response and concern for others - to and for the Chorus, to and

180

for Cassandra, to and for Andromache, to and for her grandson's burial and responses to Talthybius and Helen.

Her statement, summed up in the words "all that I suffer, and have suffered and shall suffer" follows this order in that it goes from her present weakness and despair to an account of her past life and the horrors she witnessed, as Priam was cut down at the altar and Troy taken, to a vision of a life of slavery in the future. She then returns to her present physical weariness.

A mere 45 lines, the speech yet vividly and succinctly conveys events and feelings which belong particularly to Hecuba.

468 "I suffer and have suffered and shall go on suffering": *paschō te kai pepontha kati peisomai* is a beautifully apt and neat line embracing present, past and future of the same verb. Lee finds them 'not suitable in Hecuba's mouth in her sorrowful state'. Does he then expect a heroine of Greek tragedy to be inarticulate?

470 "there's something to be said": for *echei ti schema* cf. *I.A.* 983.
Hecuba's ambivalence towards the gods is seen throughout the play. At 612 she rails against them for bringing the great down. At 884 she is uncertain to what force she should address her prayers. At 1240 she regrets the sacrifices she made to no avail.

472 "One last time": since the compound *exaisai* implies "to sing one's last song". See Pl. *Phd.* 85a where it is used of the swan.

474ff. Polyxena rehearses her past happiness in a similar way, *Hec.* 349ff.

481 "Priam, their father ...": *ho phutourgos* is actually a rarer word than just "father". But "sire" or "begetter" now sound so unnatural in English that I have translated "father" for the sake of naturalness.

482-3 The murder of Priam by Neoptolemus at the household altar of Zeus Herkeios is told in detail by Virgil, *Aeneid* 2. 506ff.

485 "to marry carefully selected bridegrooms": *es ... exaireton* is literally "with a view to the chosen worth of bridegrooms".

489 "to crown my misery": *thrigkos* is a metaphor from the coping stone at the top of a cornice. The verb *thrigkoō* occurs at *H.F.* 1280 in the sense of "crowning" a house with misery. See Bond ad loc.

181

491ff. cf. *Hec.* 361ff.

495 "poor, decrepit back": *rusoisi nōtois* is literally "shrivelled" or "wrinkled back".

496 "my tattered flesh dressed in tattered rags": *truchēra peri truchēron chroa peplōn lakismat'*; note the repetition of this rare word *truchēros* first literally, then metaphorically.

500-510 These lines in returning to Cassandra, in reminding the audience of Polyxena and in contrasting Hecuba's own present state with her past, recapitulate and summarise, as they conclude, the first episode and even earlier. (Note especially *sumbakche* 500 echoing *bakcheuousan* 341, *exebakcheusen* 408, 502 recalling 260-261, and 505ff recalling the opening and close of Hecuba's monody 98-9, 150-2.)

501 "your chaste life": *hagneuma* implies both "chastity" and "social status" and Cassandra has lost both. In English however there is no word which carries both connotations. I have chosen to translate the former since *elusas* perhaps is reminiscent of the Homeric phrase *luse ... partheniēn zōnēn Od.* 9. 245; cf. Eur. *Alc.* 177.

506 "daintily": by using the phrase *habron ... poda* Hecuba thinks of happier times when she no doubt wore pretty shoes and her feet seemed light and dainty in contrast to now. She refers to the times she used to dance at 151-2.

507 "straw pallet": *stibas* refers to the place where Hecuba was lying at the beginning of the play.

508 "head-rest": *krēdemnon* is a woman's head-dress and refers here to a place for the head i.e. the stony ground which must be her pillow. But the word also has, from Homer, metaphorical connotations of the rocky battlements which crown Troy (see *Il.* 16. 100, *Od.* 13. 388). And the adjective *petrina* invites that association, so that we have here a double image of stony ground as headrest for Hecuba and also rocky battlements destructive to anyone who is flung from them.

509-10 A familiar Greek sentiment. See Hdt. I. 32, Aesch. *Ag.* 928, Soph. *O.T.* 1528-30, *Trach.* 1-3, Eur. *And.* 100 ff., *Supp.* 161ff., *El.* 95ff., *I.A.* 161ff.

First Stasimon 511-567

The first stasimon, as the others in this play, concerns Troy and its people. The style is not philosophical or moral in tone but descriptive, and its imagery brings alive in sensuously evocative language the city's life on the night Troy was betrayed by the invasion through its gates of the Wooden Horse. Scenes of false jubilation are contrasted with the subsequent desolation when the Greeks rampaged through the private apartments of the palace. Every Trojan woman has lived through this experience and the telling of it is therefore at the heart of the play.

Its reality is built up by the dramatist in a series of images suggesting sight, sound and texture. Sight for instance in the magnificently gold-decked horse, encapsulated in the single and unique compound *chruseophalaron*; in the dark and sinister ship's hull used to compare the shape and colour of the horse; in the bright torch flares glowing in the dark, expressed in the oxymoron *melainan aiglan*, and in the shaking hands of children, *cheiras eptoēmenas*, clutching at their mothers' dress. Sound is evoked in the description of pipes (544), thudding feet (546) and song (547), as well as in the bold image at 555-6 "a bloody shout possessed the city". Texture is stressed in a number of epithets suggesting the material composition of things - "the mountain pinewood" (533), the "polished ambush" (534), "the circling ropes of spun flax" (538) and the stone temple floor (540). But it is not enough to separate out the effects on the senses, for they interpenetrate one another. Thus the sound of thudding feet and singing cuts through the darkness with its intermittent gleams of torchlight, so that sound and dark and light become indistinguishable. Thus a shout is described with a word which also has connotations of the redness of blood, *phoinia* (555), and an abstract word "ambush" (534) is given a tangible, textural adjective to suggest the surface of wood within which it is hidden.

And as if purely descriptive language falls short - at the end the poet goes into metaphor. The Greeks' brutal decapitation of the Trojan men is evoked in two words *karatomos erēmia*, "headless desolation", while the Trojan women, taken as so much human loot to breed sons to Greek men, are called *neanidōn stephanon ... Helladi kourotrophon*, a phrase so condensed that it is almost untranslatable in English except by using more words "a crowning prize of young women to breed sons for Greece".

183

The metre of the ode is mainly lyric iambic with a dactylic opening which may be to evoke Epic echoes (see my note on 511-13). Unlike the second and third stasima, the form here is strophe and antistrophe followed by an epode rather than strophe, antistrophe, strophe, antistrophe. The epode draws attention to the Chorus' personal involvement – its first words are "I for my part ..." whereas the descriptions in strophe and antistrophe are general.

511ff. *Amphi moi Ilion, ō /Mousa, kainōn humnōn /aison* ... *ōidan epikēdeion:* literally "of Ilium, Muse, sing a funeral lament in new strain ...". The appeal to the Muse here recalls the epic beginnings of the *Iliad* and *Odyssey*, and the whole phrase *amphi moi ō Mousa*, or variations of it, is the classic beginning of several Homeric hymns e.g. those to Pan, Poseidon, the Dioscuri, Helios, Selene. Why should the poet wish to echo those features here? Not only because the theme of the Trojan war is an epic one, as Lee says, but because an epic beginning signals something important, grand and impressive, and the chorus wish to register some familiar credentials for this. But they then go on to imply in their subsequent words, *kainōn humnōn*, that the old forms and themes are to be told in a new way and the Muse pressed into service for a new kind of song. This is the lyric lament for Troy's destruction seen uniquely not through the eyes of warriors, but through those of a group of women. Their account is not the traditionally heroic one of glorifying war, yet it deserves, the poet implies, to be as important as epic in what new things it has to observe. There is of course some irony too in this implied measuring of old attitudes against new ones.

Other epic elements in the ode are the tmesis at 522, the genitive ending *linoio* in 537 and the unaugmented verb, if Diggle's conjecture is right, *aeiron* at 546. Epithets such as *xestos*, "polished", (533), *kelainos*, "dark", (539) and *melas*, "black", (549) particularly in the feminine form *melaina*, as here, are common in Homer. But the interesting difference is that whereas Homer applies such adjectives to *material* objects, Euripides is here applying them to abstract words in metaphor or oxymoron i.e. 534 *xeston lochon* "polished ambush" and 549 *melainan aiglan* "black gleam".

513 *humnos,* usually a song in praise of gods and heroes, is here put into service as a song sung in sympathy for the

184

victims of war.

"funereal": *epikēdeios* appears to be a Euripidean coinage and is also used in the *Alexandros* with *ponoi*, "sufferings". (fr. 16. 12 Snell).

516 "the four-wheeled wooden horse": *tetrabamonos* ... *apēnas* is literally "the conveyance going on four" i.e. either "feet" or more probably here "wheels". I have translated *apēnas* by "wooden horse" here, combining it with *hippon* in 519, since "conveyance" sounds so stiff. Virgil, *Aeneid* 2. 235 appears to echo this passage.

520 *chruseophalaron* (only here) literally means "with golden cheek pieces of the horse's head harness". I have added the word "magnificently" in my translation to bring out the emphasis of the unique compound. *Chruseo* - compounds are common in Euripides and may derive from the lyric tradition. Analogous compounds with *chruso-* are common in Pindar for instance, while the adjective *chruseos* occurs about fifty times. In the lyric poet however such compounds are ornamental and complimentary, whereas here the implication is of something malignant and sinister. A new context therefore for an old style epithet with heroic associations. On the false allure of gold objects in this play see 820, 1107 and Introduction to the Second Stasimon, 799-859.

526 "the Trojan goddess, Zeus' daughter" is Athena who had a temple on the Trojan Acropolis. The Wooden Horse was taken in as a propitiatory gift to her.

530 "took to their hearts" is literally "embraced" – or "held" – "destruction in disguise".

534 *xeston*: this adjective "polished" logically goes with *peukan*, "pine", but has been transferred to "ambush", the body of men inside the horse. The contrast is between the smooth gleaming outer surface, so attractive to look at, and the treachery inside.

535 *theâi*: "to the goddess", whereas the old Oxford text accented *théai* which would mean to bring "into view". *theâi* is a natural reference to Athena who receives the gift of the Wooden Horse.

537 "virgin goddess of the immortal steeds": *azugos* refers to Athena's unmarried state, *ambrotopōlou* "of the immortal steeds" (only here) probably refers to her love of horses and chariots as a goddess of war (see Lee's note).

540 "source of death to our country": *phonea patridi* is Diggle's neat emendation for the MSS *phonia*. The latter

which would refer to the stone temple floors "running with blood", "blood-red", is tempting for the added sense of colour and texture it gives to an already sensuous picture. But unfortunately it is almost impossible to make sense of it with *"patridi"*; "blood-stained to our country's disadvantage" sounds very strained. See Diggle in *Studies* 63–64.

546 *aeiron hama* is Diggle's emendation for the MSS *aerion ana* and means "they raised their tapping feet", thus raising their feet and making a tapping sound at the same time. See his note in *Studies* 64–66. The unaugmented epic form is in keeping with the epic beginning to the song. The MSS reading is senseless unless *t'* is deleted in 547. It would then mean "amidst the beating of feet raised in the air, they sang etc. ..."

550 *edōken hupnōi,* as it stands, lacks two short syllables which it needs to correspond with the strophe and some corruption is evident. But no satisfactory remedies have yet been found although many have been suggested. The "brightness of the torches gave a dark gleam" is all right, but "amid" – or "to" – "sleep" does not make good sense.

551 "the mountain dwelling daughter of Zeus" is Artemis, as is suggested by the gloss on *koran* in the MSS. Homer represents her as favouring Troy during the war (see *Iliad* 5. 447).

562ff. I take this to mean the Trojan men were decapitated at the altars, and the Trojan women, mourning their murdered husbands, were raped in the bedrooms to produce sons for Greece. *kourotrophos*, an epithet used by Homer of the benign and nurturing qualities of Ithaca, *Od.* 9. 27 "my land is rugged but knows how to breed brave sons", is here incorporated in a bitter and deliberately anti-heroic metaphor.

2nd Episode 568-798

This episode consists of three scenes, a lyric duet between Andromache and Hecuba or *kommos* 577-607, an iambic dialogue between Andromache and Hecuba 608-708, and an iambic dialogue between Andromache and Talthybius 709-798.

After the *kommos*, Andromache in iambic speech recounts the death of Polyxena which Hecuba had half suspected but blotted from her mind when Talthybius hinted at it earlier. Now she has to face it fully. Andromache follows this dialogue with a long speech in which she recalls her dead husband Hector and expresses her horror of the future. To her, death seems preferable. Hecuba expresses some hope in the thought of Astyanax growing up to bring new life to Troy, only to have this hope dashed when Talthybius enters to announce the fate in store for her grandson. Even he is appalled by this decision of the Greeks instigated by Odysseus and says so. Andromache laments for her son before handing him over to Talthybius to take away.

In this episode the themes of Polyxena's fate and Astyanax' fate look back and forward, to the prologue and to the epilogue respectively. This, together with the continual presence of Hecuba, helps to cement the play's fabric.

568-577   Andromache enters on a cart, her small son Astyanax in her arms. On the cart also are Hector's weapons (573-4) taken by the Greeks as loot to convey to Greece with the captives, and emphasising therefore that Andromache too is simply regarded by the enemy as so much loot to be disposed of as they think fit (614). The entrance of mother and son as captives on this cart in this setting contrasts strongly with the grand entrance of Agamemnon to his palace on a royal chariot also piled high with Trojan loot in Aeschylus' *Agamemnon*.

570   "close to her heaving breast": *para eiresiai maston. eiresia* is a metaphor from rowing alluding to the beat of oars. It appears here to mean the rise and fall of the breast in agitation. There is no parallel elsewhere in classical works for such a use.

576   It was the ancient practice to hang spoils from war in the temples. See Aesch. *Septem* 277 ff. and Eur. *El.* 6-7.

577-607   The metre of this duet is, first, syncopated iambic, 577-581, 582-586, 587-590, 591-594, then dactylic 595-607. The dialogue is composed of half-lines where each speaker partly responds to what her interlocutor has said, and

187

partly pursues her own line of thought. These utterances, so falteringly articulated by the poet, dramatically indicate a degree of despair on the part of the women where words are made to seem in danger of breaking down altogether, so great is their grief. Such broken dialogue is characteristic of the later rather than the earlier plays of Euripides. See particularly the divided trimeters at *Pho.* 980 ff, 1273ff. *Or.* 1235-1239, 1598-1617 and the split trochaic tetrameters at *Or.* 774ff. *Ion* 530ff. *Pho.* 603ff. *I.A.* 1341ff.

578   literally "why are you lamenting a paean that is mine?" *paian* is here a metonymy for *thrēnos* meaning 'song of grief'.

584   "Yes, and,": *dēt'* is an affirmative answer echoing the previous utterance. See G.P. 276.

591   "You destroyer of the Greeks": *luma* here is the same as *lumē* meaning 'ruin' as at Aesch. *P.V.* 692.

592-3   Diggle's text which, rightly in my opinion, makes these words refer to Hector, involves accepting two emendations – *dē poth'* (Seidler) and *Priamōi* (Musgrave). Most of the MSS have *despoth'* and *Priame*. This would make the words refer to Priam. But '*presbugenes*' means 'first born' and must surely describe Hector, quite apart from the other point that Hector is more likely to be the "*lum'* *Achaiōn*" than Priam.

597   "your son": Paris. He escaped death when Hecuba, his mother, in spite of her foreknowledge that he would be the ruin of Troy, refused to kill him, but exposed him on a hillside where he was brought up by shepherds. This is the subject from which the plot of *Alexandros* derives.

599   "At the feet of Pallas Athene": *para Palladi*. The bodies are found near the statue of the goddess in the precincts of the temple itself.

600   The dative *Troiai* is the now commonly accepted reading, and the subject of *ēnuse* (lit. "obtained", "achieved") is Paris, as the scholiast saw. The nominative of VP *Troia*, which could only mean "Troy has come to slavery" "has reached slavery", is much less appropriate since it is Paris who is being talked about as Troy's destroyer in these four lines.

603   *erēmopolis*: does the *erēmos* part of the compound apply to Hecuba or the city? i.e. "bereft of a city" or "having a desolate city"? The word *erēmia* elsewhere in the play

(26, 97) alludes to the desolation of the city itself, and therefore should be interpreted "of the desolate city" i.e. "characterised by having a desolate city". Note also its use at 564.

611 "Do you see this?": it is probable that at this point Andromache gestures at herself and Astyanax in the chariot.

612 The metaphor *purgous'* "they build tower-high" has resonances for the mighty towers of Troy which were physically built up by the gods and must come tumbling down. The word is used metaphorically here and literally at 843 and there is connection between the two uses, as also with the figurative and literal play with the theme of ships. Troy's real towers are the concrete symbol of the gods' metaphorical building of men's hopes (see Introduction p.32).

613 "that which merely *appears* powerful": *ta dokount'.* Hecuba's words are prophetic. The Greeks at present appear powerful, but they too are to be destroyed by the gods as Cassandra and Poseidon have earlier forecast.

The rôle of the gods in this play is ambivalent. In spite of the prologue, they are frequently seen by the Trojans as hostile to Troy and as having abandoned the city to its fate. See particularly the ode of the chorus addressed to Zeus, the betrayer of Troy, at 1060-1080, and the implications of their words at 821-857. Hecuba too expresses her despair and scepticism about them at 1240-1242. It is one of the elements in the tragedy that the women cannot even rely on a belief in the efficacy of the gods or feel that their sacrifices have accomplished anything. It is true Hecuba has a rather strange prayer at 884 which expresses some sort of belief in justice, but that is before she has seen the injustice of Helen's victory in the debate scene, where Menelaus spares Helen's life in spite of Hecuba's powerful pleas to him to take it.

618 Ajax had dragged Cassandra from her temple earlier (70). Now Agamemnon appears to threaten her.

619 "You are unfortunate in another way too": Andromache means that the death of Polyxena as well as the fate of Cassandra is an additional disaster for Hecuba to bear.

625 Note the repetition in the Greek *ou saphōs ... saphes.*

626 "from this cart" seems to imply that Andromache has not yet got down from her cart as she did when she wrapped

189

Polyxena for burial, and it may be that she remains in it for the whole scene before being carried away in it after Astyanax has been removed at 782. There is no explicit reference to her getting down from it.

629 *prosphagmatōn* (628) means "sacrifice". The plural of *prosphagma* in this sense is used at *Hec.* 265, where the single figure Helen is being canvassed as the sacrificial victim at Achilles' tomb.

630 "Her death is a fact now": *olōlen hōs olōlen* is literally "she died as she died", implying that the event is over now and must be accepted and the least said about it the better. There are many phrases of this nature in Euripides, on which see Denniston's note on *El.* 1141.

634-683 I believe that this speech of Andromache has been underestimated. Conacher writes of it (142) 'Andromache's speech is disappointing: a set rhetorical exercise on two unrelated themes ... Only the peroration addressed to Hector's shade saves it from banality'. Lattimore in his introduction to his translation describes it as 'padding'. Scodel (11) who finds many of the speeches in the *Trojan Women* 'inappropriate to both characters and situations' says of this one, which she takes as an example of inappropriateness, 'Andromache about to be dragged off to the bed of an enemy, discusses propriety of behaviour in women, and the respective merits of life and death'. Yet to take these themes as irrelevant is to miss the point completely. Both are integral to Andromache's situation. For it is *because* she has been seen as a model wife and an example among women, that she has been selected by Neoptolemus. Her fame has reached even the Greek camp. And it is *because* she has been by nature and character a good wife to Hector that she finds herself in a dilemma now. For the very qualities she recognises as having made her a good wife to one man, Hector, – her quietness and submissiveness, virtues she sees as most befitting a woman – would presumably potentially make her a good wife to others too. Except that fidelity to that one man is also part of her character and fame as a wife, and that precludes her from acquiescing in the situation in which she now finds herself.

What is interesting however is that the poet in giving Andromache the mental processes in this speech to come to terms with her predicament, represents her facing it squarely and tackling head-on the alternatives implied in it (661-6) before finally reaffirming her loyalty to her husband 667ff in a great crescendo of love and despair. She knows the cost of these feelings (that she will earn the hatred of her new master and be unable to "open her heart to him" as she puts it) and this is why Hecuba, her husband's own mother, no less devoted to his memory than Andromache, nonetheless advises her differently (699-700) - that she should be a good wife also to Neoptolemus. Hecuba has to try to give her hope by recommending the easiest way for her to survive. She is also thinking of Astyanax whom she does not yet know will be torn from his mother.

The desperation of Andromache here is like the desperation of Cassandra's madness. Both women are torn apart by the abnormal circumstances in which they find themselves: some violation of their natural responses occurs, and they are forced to extremes of bitterness which in normal times would appear to run against the natural grain of their dispositions.

634-5 "Mother, mother, listen to an argument well reasoned enough to comfort your mind": *O tekousa*, "You who gave birth to me", is odd since Hecuba did not give birth to Andromache who is her daughter-in-law. Moreover *kalliston logon* and *terpsin* both seem inappropriate, since Andromache's words are far from bringing pleasure to Hecuba. Diggle therefore rightly brackets the lines following the original suggestion of Dindorf. The next line immediately picks up Hecuba's point.

638 Diggle daggers this line as being incomplete in sense, and suggests that something has dropped out, such as 'he who has not yet seen the light suffers no pain, not having experienced life's troubles'. This would give better sense. But as the line stands one must supply *ho katthanōn* from the previous infinitive, i.e. the dead man feels no pain after having experienced (life's) troubles. The points being made here and in the next lines are therefore 1. being dead is better than having experienced the miseries of life but 2. in life it is better never to have known prosperity if one subsequently loses it, for then one always regrets it.

640 "is mentally bewildered because of his former prosperity": Bluck supports his interpretation of this genitive *eupraxias* as one of cause, and the meaning of

191

alatai as "distressed in mind" or perhaps "distraught in mind" in an article in *CQ* II (1961), 125-6.

649 Respectable Greek women were supposed to remain indoors. This is what Medea protests about so much in her speech to the women of Corinth, drawing a contrast with the freedom of men (*Med.* 244-5). See also *H.F.* 44ff., *Pho.* 1276, *I.A.* 1029ff.

653 "from my own resources": for *oikothen* in this sense see LSJ 3.

660 Andromache describes herself as *damar* "wife" although she is never legally married to Neoptolemus. The word is usually applied to a legitimate spouse and often stresses the status and dignity of that rôle (see Stevens on *And.* 4). The use of it here by Andromache therefore, "the perfect wife" trapped in an uncharacteristic situation, may be deliberate in order to create irony, pathos, and a convincing trait of character. See also 356n. Euripides may also be deliberately recalling the *Andromache*.

661ff. The dilemma of ambivalence here expressed is much more developed than it is in the *Andromache* where it is glossed over and never treated dramatically as part of the character's plight. One can imagine a modern dramatist making much more of it. *Hektoros ... kara*: literally "head of Hector". *kara* is frequently used in tragedy in periphrasis for the person e.g. Soph. *O.T.* 40, 1207, *Ant.* 1, *El.* 1164, *O.C.* 1631.

662 "If I open my heart to my present husband": *anaptuxō phrēna* is a phrase suggesting a spontaneous warmth and generosity, which would come naturally to Andromache, but which she must none the less resist in these exceptional circumstances.

665 *euphronē*: literally "the kindly time", which is a euphemism for the night.

667 "loathe": *apeptus'*, which contains the sense of spitting, is a strong word. For the aorist in the present sense cf. 53.

669 "A horse separated from its mate": literally "a filly separated from another filly with whom it has been reared". This comparison by way of illustrative example shows how strongly rhetorical Andromache's speech is. It is however very much to the point, as I have explained earlier.

673-4 These lines are reminiscent of Homer, *Il.* 6. 429ff.

Both passages use four nouns in succession to describe
Hector's qualities, but the nouns here in 674
"understanding, rank, wealth and courage" are abstract
and therefore colder and more distant than Homer's simple
persons.

'Hektor, thus you are father to me, and my honoured mother,
You are my brother and you it is who are my young husband'
(transl. Lattimore)

The extreme verbal neatness of 674 is somehow at the
expense of a strong emotional effect achieved in the
Homer and just missed here.

679   Thus Andromache reverts to the point from which she
       started at 630-1 and regards it as now proved.

683   "However pleasant such delusions": *hēdu d'esti kai
       dokein* is literally "but it is pleasant just to imagine".

686   Hecuba's preoccupation with ships is continued in this
       passage (see the note on 102ff). She has never been on a
       ship before, but Euripides depicts her imagination
       working powerfully as she describes her own plight in
       terms of the thing she fears most – ships. These await
       her and she must face them at the end of the play. See
       the last words of the Chorus at 1332.

687   Hippolytus in the matter of sex similarly relies on
       knowledge by hearsay and from painting rather than
       having direct experience (*Hipp.* 1004ff.).

695   literally "I let (my troubles) be and hold my tongue".
       See Diggle, *Studies* 66.

696   "terrible wave": *kludōn* is of course metaphorical here,
       but neatly fits in with the preceding image so that we see
       the play between literal and metaphorical.

697-8 "Stop mourning now for Hector": *tas men Hektoros
       tuchas/eason* is literally "let go now the fortunes of
       Hector".

700   "Honour your new master and give your husband
       incentive to love you for your conduct": *delear* is literally
       "bait" or "incitement". *tropōn* explains *tima*. Lee's
       'allurement consisting in your charming ways' misses the
       point. Andromache was no Helen – she was famed for her
       prudent behaviour. Hecuba's view is a much more
       pragmatic and practical one throughout than that of her
       daughter or her daughter-in-law. She stops Cassandra
       from burning the place down, advises Andromache to
       adapt to her new situation as best she can, and she
       performs the funeral rites for Astyanax. She is committed

to survival except for one moment at 1282-3 when she suddenly tries to rush into the flames of burning Troy. That moment is all the more dramatic for being the only one where her resolve to survive weakens.

704 "your children": *ek sou genomenoi paides* appears to mean here Andromache's future children by Neoptolemus. It would however be more fitting to have a reference to descendants who were Astyanax' children rather than Andromache's, so that the pure Trojan line would continue. It is for this reason that Lee accepts P's *ex hou* for *ek sou* and *einai* for *hin'ei* of the MSS in the previous line, to go closely with *ōphelem'*. The meaning would then be "to bring up my grandson to be one day the greatest assistance to Troy, whose children etc. ..."

709-798 In this scene Talthybius haltingly brings himself to announce the Greek decision to kill Andromache's son by throwing him from the walls of Troy. With this announcement goes the one last hope to which the Trojan women have been clinging - that the boy would grow up to avenge his father's death and Troy's defeat. (See 704n.) Talthybius' shame at the edict shows in his bitter words at 731-2 "we are powerful enough to fight one woman", and in his advice to Andromache not to provoke the Greeks into doing anything more brutal still. The climax of the scene is Andromache's response in her speech at 740-779 (see note). Andromache finally leaves the stage without her son and it is left to Hecuba to utter the last words to him before his death.

711 "the grandsons of Pelops" are Agamemnon and Menelaus.

712 "the hint of hateful news to come": *hōs ... kakōn* is literally "how you start on a prologue of misfortunes".

716 Euripides gives Andromache unconscious irony here since Astyanax will indeed be left as the last remaining trace of the Trojans (*leipsanon*), but as a corpse not a living being.

717 The words *kaka* and *kakon* are used five times successively at the end of lines 717-722 (as well as at 712 and 727 (*kakois*)). This may be careless writing, but I have varied the translation in three out of the five times in the interests of a suitable dramatic impact in English.

720 "what you tell me": literally "as I hear it".

721 It is not surprising that the villain of the *Palamedes* should also be the deviser of this barbaric act. His rôle

194

here has been prepared for by Hecuba's words in the previous scene at 281ff.

723   "to allow to live": *trephein* is literally "to rear".

726   Talthybius goes beyond his mere rôle as Herald here, and from his sympathy with Andromache presumes to give her advice. When up against naked power it is better not to struggle in case something even worse happens. He is thinking that the decency of the child's burial might be denied. The absurdity of a whole army ranged against these powerless women is brought out. Indeed the play is throughout concerned with amoral naked force versus common decency – the old *phusis-nomos* controversy which Thycydides raised as a problem in the Melian dialogue. Like the Melians, the Trojans are powerless against naked oppression and it was of the Melians Euripides' audience were no doubt thinking when this play was presented (see Introduction). Talthybius, though a Greek, has standards of decency and is appalled at the excesses of his countrymen.

732   "give up struggling": *ou machēs eran* is literally "not long for a battle".

733   "provocative": *epiphthonon* as it is likely to bring enmity or retaliation from the Greeks. Andromache might attempt to conceal the boy (as she does in Seneca's version) or to commit suicide.

740-779   Andromache's speech is very powerful when declaimed aloud, giving great scope to the actor with its seven apostrophes (740, 745, 749, 757, 758, 764, 766), its rhetorical questions, and the gathering crescendo engendered by the piled up personifications (768-770), the forceful one-word curse at the beginning of 772, and the asyndetic string of imperatives at 774.

742   *apoktenei* "will kill" is the reading of P. V. has *apōlesen* "has destroyed" but the imminent death of Astyanax is what is being referred to here.

743   743, if genuine, is identical with a line in the *Alexandros* (fr. 44 Snell = fr. 58 Nauck²), where Paris laments he is being killed because of the very thing which is usually a source of preservation to others, "excellence of mind". Here it is nobility which should be the source of preservation, but which is here an agent of destruction. Scodel (74), straining credibility in my view, makes a parallel between Paris and Astyanax – 'the murder attempt

195

on the cowherd and the slaying of Astyanax are both motivated by irrational fear', and argues that this passage 'must be one of the strongest self-echoes anywhere in Euripides; the repetition of an entire line can hardly be carelessness or accident'. But there seems to me not only to be no similarity between the circumstances of Paris and Astyanax – but that one would be dramatically undesirable – and it is much more likely that this line crept in by mistake under influence from the earlier play and that 742–3, as Nauck thought, are spurious, duplicating as they do the thought of 744.

744 "to your advantage": literally "has not come opportunely".

751 A common simile in Euripides. See Megara's words at *H.F.* 71ff, Andromache's at *And.* 441 and the child's at *And.* 504–5.

755–6 "You will break your neck in a deathly fall": *es trachēlon ... pesōn* is literally "falling on your head", i.e. "breaking your neck". LSJ cites this passage and translates thus. *Pēdēm'* is an internal accusative and depends on *pesōn*. *pēdēma* is literally a "leap" but is best translated here as "fall".

757 "beloved one": *hupagkalisma* is literally "that which is clasped in the arms".

758 "scent of your skin": *pneuma* from meaning "breath" can mean "that which is breathed forth" hence "odour", "fragrance": see *Hipp.* 1391.
The stress on the physical here to convey emotion is typical of Euripides in so many places – in the speech of Hecuba over Astyanax' body in this play, for example, particularly 1178ff and 1196ff, or in Medea's farewell to her own children at *Medea* 1075. I have tried to show in my book *"The Imagery of Euripides"* (passim) that sharp awareness of the power of the world of the senses underpins Euripides' style in many centrally dramatic passages.

760 "I ... became worn out ...": *kataxainō* is literally to "card wool" and so comes to be used metaphorically of "wearing to shreds".

762 "embrace her who gave you birth": for this sense of *prospitnō* see *And.* 537.

763 "my neck": *nōtoisi* is strictly "back" but almost all translators translate "neck".

196

764   "O Greeks who have devised barbarian atrocities": *ō barbar' exeurontes Hellēnes kaka*: these lines might be said to contain the heart of the play. It is supposedly civilised Greeks who are really the barbarians, and the barbarians who are the civilised ones – a slur on the values on which Greeks had prided themselves for so long. It is somewhat inappropriate however that Andromache should think in terms of Greeks and barbarians at all, since she herself was a Trojan, and therefore in Greek terms by definition a barbarian. But clearly Euripides is here expressing himself as a Greek and forgetting consistency of character.

768   "Of the avenging Curse": *Alastoros*. *Alastōr* is, according to Hesychius, a surname of Zeus describing him as the avenger of evil deeds. But tragic poets, as here, use it to designate any deity or demon who avenges wrongs done by men, cf. Aesch. *Ag.* 1501 (Fraenkel's n. has a full bibliography on *alastōr*), 1508, *Pers.* 354 Soph. *Trach.* 1092, Eur. *Pho.* 1556. Note its use later in this play, 941n.

771   Again an inappropriate reference to barbarians from Andromache. Here the word simply means "non-Greek" without the loading of 764.

772   Helen's eyes were legendary. In Aeschylus' *Agamemnon* Menelaus is found gazing mournfully into the empty eye sockets of Helen's statue, regretting the absence of reality, *Ag.* 418-419. See also *Ag.* 742 and Eur. *Hec.* 442ff.

774   Note the three imperatives in asyndeton. The verb *riptō* "fling" is repeated in the Greek.

779   Andromache leaves the stage at this point, after Talthybius has taken the child Astyanax from her arms.

784   The Trojan walls or towers are described as a crown at *Hec.* 910.

786   "Take him": addressed to the attendants who came on with Talthybius.

The Second Stasimon 799-859

The destruction of Troy by Greeks and its betrayal by gods is the theme of this ode. The chorus describe an earlier sacking of the city by Heracles and Telamon, who destroyed with fire its mighty walls. Heracles had rescued Hesione, Laomedon's daughter (Laomedon was King of Troy and had four children, Hesione, Priam, Ganymede and Tithonus) but had been cheated of his reward and therefore mounted an expedition against Troy. The city had once been favoured by the gods through the elevation of two of these children, Ganymede and Tithonus, to positions of honour on Olympus, but now even they, and the gods with them, seem indifferent to their city's present fate. The ode ends with the wry comment "But the gods' love is lost to Troy".

This ode has won praise from commentators. Paley calls it 'elegant', Tyrrell 'exquisite', Lee 'beautiful', but none of them explain how or why it deserves such epithets. Like the other stasima it depends strongly upon a series of visual images for its effect: comment is at a minimum though strong when it occurs. The chorus evoke the island of Salamis, sea-washed, bee-haunted, leaning in the direction of the Acropolis, shining Athens with her grey olive trees, Heracles fastening his ship's cables by the river Simois, Trojan walls falling under red blasts of fire, Ganymede tripping lightly amid gold wine cups, crowded beaches filled with cries for the dead and lost, dew-drenched bathing places and running tracks, the face of Ganymede serene in its youthful charm, white-winged Dawn looking down on Troy's destruction, and a starry gold chariot snatching Tithonus into the sky. These images are woven together to form a coherent focus upon Troy's plight – her destruction once before, her destruction now all over again, and her desertion by the Gods. The unobtrusive skill by which such a joining is made, is what gives the ode its power. Part of that power lies in continued contrasts – part of it in the personal tone which the addresses at the beginning of both strophes and the second antistrophe give – most of it in skilful deployment of other stylistic devices.

In the first strophe and antistrophe two Greek heroes, Telamon and Ajax, are predominant. They are characterised in terms of two ornamental vignettes: a serene picture of Athens and Salamis which are the haunts of Telamon, and a picture of Heracles anchoring his ships on the river Simois. Both contrast with the picture of Troy's burning walls which concludes the antistrophe.

198

In the second strophe and antistrophe several gods are portrayed in terms of highly ornamental scenes on Olympus. A callously serene Ganymede amid his gold wine cups, white-winged Aurora, and Tithonus in gold chariot. Again, these decorative pictures form a contrast, this time with Trojan beaches below thronged with crying women and children.

Choice of words and style maximise these contrasts of destructive beauty with unadorned suffering. Decorative epithets, particularly compound ones, and other words with heroic connotations (e.g. the unique compound verb *sunaristeuōn* "performing in concert superlative deeds of valour", and the high-flown *Hellados ... anthos*, "flower of Greece") offset with their elaborate ornamentation the plainness of the language describing Troy's scenes. Note too how the prolonged sentence structures carrying such high-flown language are brought up short by two curt, austere, six-word sentences at the end of the second strophe and antistrophe, (837-8) "The Greek spear has destroyed Priam's land", (857-9) "The god's love is lost to Troy". Such plain brevity, summarising the two sources of threat to Troy, effectively concludes the preceding extended ornamentation.

To dismiss the decorative elements as merely a kind of black irony incorporating false values is not adequate however, for it was a Greek audience who listened to the familiar opening picture of "shining" Athens with its "sacred hill", "grey olive", and neighbouring Salamis, "bee-haunted" and "washed by waves". Such an image in conjunction with the picture of their great hero Heracles would have brought pleasure and pride to the audience, but as the ode unfolded it would also have brought a new perspective and the juxtaposition with Trojan scenes would have ensured that the heroic and the glorious could not remain the bright, untarnished image it might have had, say, had this been a Pindaric Ode. Pindaric echoes cultivated through the metre, language and praise of Heracles are thus embedded in a new context.

The contrasts are not either simply "Greek" versus "Trojan", for Ganymede and Tithonus are *Trojan* princes who have betrayed their own city. Their beauty is the more sinister for being treacherous and the gold objects surrounding them remind one of the treacherous connotations of gold elsewhere: the Wooden Horse for instance with its gold trappings (520), or Helen gazing into her gold mirrors (1107) – both occurring in other choral odes.

Because of the skill of its style and construction this ode is a good example of how inadequate translation may be in rendering the full effect of the Greek. 1. The song makes use of impressive compound epithets, *melissotrophou* (799), *perikumonos* (800), *toxophorói* (804), *pontoporon* (811), *kalligalana* (837), *leukopterou* (847), *teknopoion* (852) – ("bee-cherishing, wave-washed, bow-bearing, sea-going, beautifully unruffled, white-winged, child-begetting"). Some of these, *melissotrophou, perikumonos, kalligalana,* appear to be inventions of Euripides, others have resonances from Homer and the lyric poets, e.g. *toxophorói* and *pontoporon,* while *leukopteros* only occurs in one other instance in Aeschylus. It is impossible for a translator (a) to render these plausibly by one concentrated word, as in the Greek, since we do not naturally use compound epithets in English; (b) to convey in translation the rareness of the single word in the Greek. "Where the bees thrive" for *melissotrophou,* for instance, sounds commonplace and is not strictly accurate, whereas "bee-cherishing", which is what the word actually means, sounds both bizarre and artificial; (c) to convey the Homeric and lyric resonances. The special colour such echoes would add to this context are entirely lost in translation. The metre for instance, is dactylo-epitrite, reminiscent of some of the great Pindaric odes, over twenty of which are in this metre. The ornamental style with its compound epithets and visual effects of colour, light and texture (in words such as *glaukas, liparaisi, phoiniki, chruseiais, drosoenta, kalligalana, leukopterou, chruseos* – "grey-green", "shining", "red", "gold", "dewy", "beautifully unruffled", "white-winged", "gold") is also strongly reminiscent of Pindar. He uses *liparos* for instance thirteen times – ten times of cities and three times of Athens itself. *Chruseos* is a favourite epithet, used 35 times. Compounds of colour (e.g. *glaukochrōs,* "grey-coloured", of the olive, at *Ol.*3. 13, *glaukōpis* and *glaukōps,* "grey-eyed", or variations with *leukos,* "white", – *leukippos, leukopōlos,* "with white horses", *leukōlenos,* "white-armed") occur regularly as do compound adjectives in general. 2. The tight-knit word order of the Greek which makes certain calculated emphases is impossible to reproduce exactly in English. For instance, at the end of three verse units 801, 802, 803 we have *elaias* olive, *Athana* Athena and

Athenais for Athens underlining Athena's closeness with Athens and her importance in giving it the olive. Further, the adjective *glaukas* is next to *Athana* and although it agrees grammatically with *elaias* in the line above, by its proximity to *Athana* it reminds the audience also of the goddess' epithet "grey-eyed". Thus by grammatical allegiance and by position, this adjective does two jobs at once. 3. Some words are impossible to render accurately in English because of the multiple connotations they have in Greek. In this ode *pitulos* (817) is such a word. Commentators suggest that one translate it "onslaught", which is one of its meanings. "Twice in two onslaughts the bloody spear destroyed etc. ..." But this word also has associations of repeated movement which "onslaught", simply meaning "a vigorous attack", does not convey. It is used, for instance, of the sweeping movement of oarblades striking the water, the rhythmical thuds of raining blows, the regular splash of falling tears or wine into a cup. (On the range of the word see Barrett on *Hipp*. 1464.) Should it not then be translated in this context as "battering"? The O.E.D. defines "battering" as "to strike with repeated blows of an instrument or weapon or with frequent missiles; to beat continuously and violently, so as to bruise or shatter". This is just the meaning one wants here. This effect is possibly reinforced by the treble alliteration in *dis de duoin* and in *pituloin - puri* (if the latter is correct. See note on 817) -another effect hard to reproduce in translation. 4. The Greek is often very condensed where only an expansion will do in English. Such a phrase is *kanonōn ... tukismata ...* literally "chisellings after the plumbline". What these words convey is "walls of stone worked and squared by the chisel and measured by plumb-line". (*tukos* is a chisel for working stone and *kanōn* is the line by which stones were marked for squaring). The two economic Greek words conjure up a sense of shape and texture but they can only do this in English if they are considerably expanded. (Alliteration is also at work in that sentence.) 5. A sustained sound effect in the middle of the second strophe enhances the contrast between Ganymede's frivolity in heaven and the scene of desolation below. The wailing and laments are onomatopoeically conveyed in the concentration of diphthongs or long vowels in *geinamena, daietai, ēïones - haliai iakchon oiōnos hoion - boōs' ... hai - eunas, hai ... paidas, hai ... geraias.* (There are eight "ai" sounds in those words - reminiscent of the cry *aiai*?).

These are just a few of the effects in Greek which are almost impossible to render in a translation, particularly a prose one.

799 Telamon, brother of Peleus and father of Ajax and Teucer, was King of Salamis. He helped Heracles destroy Troy (804-6) when Laomedon, its king, cheated Heracles of his reward (809-10) for rescuing Hesione (Laomedon's daughter) from a sea monster (Apollodorus II. v.9,III.xii 7).

801 *tas epikeklimenas ochthois hierois*: literally "lying over against the sacred hill" i.e. the Acropolis of Athens from which the island of Salamis can be seen.

801-2 Athena traditionally gave Athens the olive (see *Ion* 1433ff.).

803 The epithet *liparos* "shining" is first bestowed on Athens by Pindar, *Isth.* 2.20 and fr. 64. After that it became almost a cliché, see Aristophanes' parody at *Ach.* 640 "to be a heavenly crown" i.e. the olive was for Athens a crowning glory which had the approval of the gods.

804 "bow-bearing": *toxophorōi* a heroic word sometimes used of gods in Homer and lyric (cf. Homer *Il.* 21. 483, Simon. 107.4, Pind. *Pae.* fr. 19. 30, *Pyth.* 5.41).

804-5 "performing in concert deeds of valour": the word *sunaristeuō* occurs only here although *aristeuō* is common in Homer e.g. *Il.* 6.208 where it defines the heroic ideal *par excellence*, 11.409, cf. Pind. *Nem.* 11.14.

805 Alcmena's son is Heracles. He is a favourite subject in Pindaric Odes. (See entry under *Heracles* in Slater, *Lexicon to Pindar* (1969)).

807-8 The original text is irrecoverable here. See Diggle's note in *Studies* 67. What is probable is that *hot' ebas aph'Hellados* is a gloss. It adds nothing to the sense and the occurrence also of *Hellados* in the next line of the antistrophe makes it unlikely to be genuine here. What the gloss originally displaced however is not known.

809 "the flower of Greece": cf. Aesch. *Ag.* 197, *Pers.* 59, 252, 925.

810 "the reward of the mares": the reward Laomedon offered was a special breed of horses given to him by Zeus.
The river Simois rose on Mount Ida and flowed past Troy.

811 "sea-going": *pontoporos* is common in Homer and cf. Soph. *Phil.* 721, *Aj.* 250 (both lyric passages).

813   "took from his ships his well-aimed bow": *cheros eustochian exeile naōn* is literally "he took the good aim of his hand from his ships", a somewhat strange poetic periphrasis for his "bow".

814   *Phoibou*: the walls of Troy were built by Apollo and Poseidon for Laomedon, who had cheated them of their reward. Hence Poseidon sent a sea monster to ravage the land and it was from this that Heracles rescued Hesione and was in turn cheated of *his* reward by Laomedon. (Apollod. II. v.9). See Introduction to the stasimon.

817-18   "the bloody spear destroyed the Dardanians around their walls": this with Diggle's emendation of *Dardanidas* for *Dardanias* sounds to me rather weak. The stress in the lines 814-818 is on the destruction of the *walls by fire* - walls are a strong motif in the play as dramatic imagery (see note on 5) and they have been particularly emphasised at 814. It seems preferable to keep *Dardanias* and accept for the unintelligible *peri* the emendation suggested by Seidler - *puri*. The meaning would then be "twice, in two batterings, the murderous army destroyed the walls of the Trojan land by fire". This neatly reiterates the emphasis of walls and fire in 814-815.

821   Ganymede, Laomedon's son, was chosen by Zeus to be his cup-bearer on Olympus. Note how the ornamental description of him, suggesting frivolity, flanks on either side the serious central picture of the Trojan beaches with its refugees.
   "In vain then": for all the favouritism Zeus showed Ganymede in appointing him to this office, it did nothing in the end to help Troy. The chorus imply that this was negligence on the part of both Zeus (846 and see especially the more explicit condemnation in the next ode (1060ff.)) and Ganymede who can only go on smiling while his country suffers.

841   *Erōs*: Love was responsible for firing Zeus with desire for Ganymede and Aurora for Tithonus. Yet both Zeus and Aurora in spite of their love for these Trojans, neglected the city of Troy.

845   "with that": *to men* appears to refer to the content of the previous stanza i.e. to the relation of Zeus and Ganymede and the fact that Zeus showed no concern for Troy in spite of this relationship.

847   "white-winged": for *leukopteros* cf. Aesch. *P.V.* 993, Eur. *Hipp.* 752.

849-56   <u>Hemera</u> is Eos, Dawn. She arranged for Tithonus to be transported to Olympus where Zeus at her request gave him immortality: Apollod. III. xii. 4-5.

852   Eos and Tithonus had two sons Memnon and Emathion: Hes. *Th*. 984ff., Apollod. III. xii. 4-5.

     "child-begetting": *teknopoion*, here describes the husband, but is more commonly used of the wife, "child-bearing", cf. Hdt. I. 59, V. 40.

858   "But the gods' love is lost to Troy": the word *phroudos* expressing something "vanished" and "lost" is a recurring one in the play (see also at 41, 1071, 1123, 1130) and is often emphasised either by position as at 41, 1130, or by the surrounding words. Here for instance there is alliteration in *philtra phrouda* and at 1323 there is the strong repetition of *allai ... allo* preceding it.

204

Third Episode 860-1059

Menelaus enters announcing he has come to fetch Helen. He will take her back to Greece and put her to death there. Hecuba warns him not to set eyes on Helen or "desire will win". She urges Menelaus to kill her. Helen however enters and asks for the opportunity to plead her cause. Menelaus is doubtful but Hecuba agrees to respond to her in formal debate and thus the great *agōn* between the two women begins.

Helen pleads her case within terms of divine responsibility, claiming that she was merely the victim of all-powerful Aphrodite; Hecuba argues on a secular level, claiming human responsibility to the effect that Helen was actor not victim. Helen makes the Judgement of Paris crucially important, Hecuba dismisses it as nonsense.

It is usually assumed that Hecuba's is the more rational argument of the two and that she wins on these grounds (see Lee xxiii). But the division is not so clear cut. Helen's argument is logically flawless if one accepts its terms, and Hecuba's is by no means rational throughout. If Hecuba wins, it is on other grounds than pure logic – moral feeling for instance, human sympathy and common sense.

Helen's first point is that Hecuba, as mother of Paris, is really responsible for the Trojan war and, even more, Priam, for not putting the infant to death after clear signs that he would bring ruin to his country. I am assuming that *ho presbus* in line 921 is a reference to Priam (see note on 921). Priam exposed the child when he could have killed it. It survived and tragedy was set in train from an act of compassion. No doubt the first play of the trilogy did stress Hecuba's and Priam's responsibility for future disasters – Cassandra is there for that very purpose – to measure the gravity of future consequences – and Hecuba and Priam are as guilty as Oedipus' parents were for the curse on the House of Laius. But the drama also dealt with the human factors involved, and this it is in Helen's interest to ignore. Technically she has a point – if one accepts the terms of her argument – and Hecuba does not answer her at all in this respect, not I think as Grube says, because raising this question will not appeal to Menelaus, but because there *is* no effective answer to it unless one changes the premise and says that such hunting for causes is futile.

Helen's second point is that if Paris had chosen Hera or Athena at the Judgement it would have been worse for Greece because Greece would then have been enslaved by Trojans. Hecuba's response to this is not direct. It is to deny that the Judgement ever took place at all.

I agree with Diggle in reading Hartung's *ou* for *hai* at 975 (see note on 975). The goddesses would never have been so frivolous as to set the Judgement up. Now, however reasonable this may sound, the audience is bound to accept from the *Alexandros* (Snell fr. 10) when it is prophesied that the Judgement took place, and from the prologue of this play, where one assumes Poseidon is attributing the destruction of Troy by Hera and Athena (23-24) to the Judgement, that events were as Helen has described them rather than as Hecuba would have them. Moreover we know from the previous choral ode that the gods *are* frivolous as the passage on Ganymede and Aurora suggests (821-858). Once again Helen is technically right, although one may sympathise with Hecuba's outrage at the gods' frivolity.

Helen's main point is that Aphrodite, as a result of the Judgement, was behind her abduction from Sparta. She was a mere victim. If even Zeus is a slave of Aphrodite, what chance had she? Helen is here using a common and ancient argument about the gods' power. Priam for instance in *Iliad* 3. 164 asserts that the gods are to blame for Helen's action, not she herself. Underlying Helen's words here is the more contemporary argument about the natural power of the strong to prevail over the weak. This is familiar from the Sophists and from the Melian dialogue and is prominent in Gorgias' *Encomium on Helen* (6), a work which Euripides was probably familiar with, although the precise dating of it has not been established.

In its own terms Helen's argument is irrefutable. What Hecuba does in reply is to change the ground and say that Aphrodite does not exist, except in men's minds, and is a mere excuse for human lust. Helen was seduced by Paris' appearance and wealth, and blamed the gods for what were her own appetites. Such an atheistic view was characteristic of certain aspects of contemporary thinking to which Euripides alludes elsewhere e.g. fr. 1018.

In my view neither Helen's divine, nor Hecuba's secular, arguments are intended to be viewed as "right". The truth surely lay somewhere in between. In the *Iliad* Helen blames herself for coming to Troy although no one will doubt that the figure of Aphrodite as she appears in Book 3 is a sinister and compelling figure who will brook no disobedience. Also in the *Iliad* Agamemnon blames Zeus for his quarrel with Achilles (19, 86-7, 137-8) yet still feels personally responsible enough to take action to make amends (9. 115ff., 19. 137-8). In Aeschylus' *Agamemnon* the words used at 218ff. of the sacrifice of Iphigeneia show that Agamemnon was held to be both driven by gods and also himself morally responsible. In Euripides' *Hippolytus*, the power of Aphrodite is visibly present, but this does not lead Phaedra to exempt herself from blame for, or indeed from, the need to resist her love for Hippolytus. She rejects the Nurse's pursuit of the line of defence that one cannot fight against the gods 486-7. These passages suggest that both divine *and* human responsibility are commonly taken into account.

Helen's last point – that she tried to escape without success is rebutted by Hecuba who declares it to be a lie. The audience have no means of knowing the truth in this case.

Hecuba ends her speech with a gratuitous, understandable and irrational (in that it is not part of the argument) outburst about Helen's appearance. She should have dressed in rags like the others. She should be trembling with fear. The anger of Hecuba at the last moment blots out logic.

Hecuba's speech is not as logically perfect as Helen's, neither is it as facile or as cold. It is full of human feeling – protest – outrage – scepticism – anger, and it convinces both the Chorus and Menelaus. It is a paradox of Helen's speech that while arguing all the time that she is a mere victim, she appears well in control of the situation, calmly manipulating Menelaus, putting Hecuba in the wrong, and gracefully extricating herself. It is a smooth performance, but has no depth of feeling and fails to persuade as Hecuba's passion does.

The irony is that Hecuba's triumph of persuasion fails to achieve what she wants. Menelaus, while paying lip service to her cogent words, refuses to accept her plea for Helen's instant death. He will take her back to Greece first and then kill her. Hecuba realizes that she has lost the battle. "He who once loves, loves for ever". Another irony – Menelaus is succumbing to Helen's beauty as Helen once had to Paris'. The power of *opsis*, appearance, which Gorgias so stresses in his *Encomium on Helen* (16-19), operates here too, and the gap between a reasoned mental conviction and the ability to act on it, yawns so widely that it casts the whole scene into irony.

The outcome has rendered the debate futile for Hecuba. By showing that persuasive words can persuade, but fail to lead to consistent action, Euripides may have in mind Gorgias' gross overestimation of them in his *Encomium* (10-14) and be demonstrating a different view. It is a view consistent with dramatic points he makes elsewhere. Medea is mentally convinced that what she is doing is wrong, but she does not act on her reasoned conviction (*Medea* 1078-1079). Phaedra is aware of the same dilemma (*Hipp.* 380-381). This is the stuff of which tragedy is made.

Kitto (1961) 212 argues that this scene would have been more effective 'had Menelaus given Hecuba another insult by acquitting Helen there and then'. But I do not think this is so. By making Menelaus show a weak prevarication which the audience know to be weak because they know from the *Odyssey* that Helen survived to a ripe old age in Sparta and was never in any danger, the poet achieves the maximum amount of irony. No such irony would exist were Helen acquitted on the spot.

This formal debate brings an intellectual tension into the play which relieves the atmosphere of lyric suffering which pervades the rest of it. None the less it contributes to the suffering in that Hecuba meets with yet another defeat.

I do not agree with Lee that Hecuba's character suffers in the *agōn*. 'She argues too coherently' he writes 'for a grief-stricken old woman and we are scarcely able to recognise the Hecuba of a hundred lines before'. The same point I made about Cassandra applies here (see 353n). Yet even within these terms Hecuba is skilfully drawn. Her outburst of pent-up anger at the end of her long speech showing her raw hatred of Helen comes as a fitting climax to the accumulation of griefs she has suffered up to this point. And if it is not as noble or as elevated in tone as we have seen before, it is certainly both natural and plausible and, as such, a tribute to the poet's realistic grasp of his subject. Hecuba is seen to give way to impulse here as she does at one moment when she tries to commit suicide at 1282 by rushing into the flames, and her portrait is the greater for being as subject to this as human beings usually are under extreme pressure.

860 "How bright the splendour of the sun is": Menelaus' naively cheerful and somewhat jarring beginning immediately strikes a new note. The blatant insensitivity of mood well characterises his disposition, and bodes ill

for Hecuba. He is happy because he will see Helen again, whatever he may indicate to the contrary. That is what these initial words signal to us the audience.

862-3 On the probable spuriousness of these lines, possibly an interpolation by an actor, see D.L. Page, *Actors' Interpolations in Greek Tragedy* (Oxford, 1934) 74. The lines are also discussed in detail by M.L. West, *BICS* 27 (1980), 16.

869 "the Spartan" is what the Trojans call Helen.

884 This prayer to Zeus, traditional in form (see Aesch. *Ag.* 160, Eur. *H.F.* 1263 and *Hel.* 711-712 for the formulae expressed in 885,) is none the less modern in its allusive definitions, for it refers to certain philosophical systems current in the time of Euripides. Menelaus acknowledges its modernity by his words at 889. The god which supports the earth, here identified with Zeus, is Ether: see K. Matthiessen, *Hermes* 96 (1968) esp. 699ff, who compares frags. 919, 941 and 944. The "inflexible law of nature" may be a reference to Heraclitus' balance of opposites in nature, and "Mind" is a reference to Anaxagoras who saw *Nous* as the animating principle of the Universe. (For a fuller discussion of this passage see Scodel 93-95.) This prayer is just the sort of thing Aristophanes satirizes Euripides for (see e.g. *Frogs* 891-2, *Clouds* 264-5).

887-8 The expression by Hecuba of a belief in divine justice is somewhat inconsistent with the scepticism she expresses elsewhere, e.g. at 469 and later at 1240, but it is appropriate enough in this particular context and ironic in view of the outcome.

891 The Greek word *helēi* is a pun on the name *Helenē*. A similar pun on Helen's name with this verb *haireō* occurs in Aesch. *Ag.* 689-90 *helenas, helandros, heleptolis*, literally "taker of ships, taker of men, taker of cities". Fagles renders 'Hell at the prows, hell at the gates, hell to the men of war'.

895 Note how confidently Helen begins by addressing Menelaus instantly and directly, making his name the first word in the sentence. She even complains about being mishandled by the attendants.

901 "No precise decision, but ...": Menelaus is immediately on the defensive as he is also at 911-912. "It is for your sake, not for hers, that I grant this".

209

903-4 "May I then ...", "Is it possible for me to ...":
Exestin oun is very formal and polite. Technically flawless, like the rest of Helen's speech. Compare the similarly polite and formal request of Athena at 48ff. where the chilly correctness is at odds with the momentous issues being discussed. In fact Helen's whole utterance is marked by formal pointers which mark out the external shape of her speech: 923, 931, 938, 945, 951, 961. Formality characterises Hecuba's reply also but the markers are more directed to points of substance in response to Helen than to the technically external shape of her speech: 970, 981-2, 998, 1010.

906 Since Menelaus shows no signs of taking Hecuba's advice to him at 891 to get out of Helen's sight, she now expresses the hope that Helen may convict herself in his eyes by arguing out the case with her.

912-3 Menelaus, with some self-deception, excuses his concession to Helen by saying he is making it for Hecuba's sake.

914 At this point the *agōn* between the two women begins. In such debates in Euripides the winner usually speaks second (except in the *Medea*) and there is often a third party present as in *Hec.* 1109 – end, *Hcld.* 120-287, *And.* 547-765, *Pho.* 442-637. On the character of such debates in the drama of this dramatist (formality, emotional colouring, devices of special pleading, narrative elements etc.) see C. Collard, 'Formal Debates in Euripides' Drama', *G & R* 22 (1975), 58-71.

918 is considered by most editors to be spurious. It is not necessary to the sense: indeed it misleadingly implies that Helen addresses Hecuba directly at some point whereas she never does. If this view is correct, *antitheis'* must stand without an object. "I shall reply, putting opposing arguments". Lee compares *Hcld.* 153.

921 "the old King": I incline to the view argued by Stinton 67 n.3 that *ho presbus*, "the old man", here refers to Priam. Priam is described as such at *Hec.* 160.
Helen's point that both Priam and Hecuba were to some extent culpable for allowing Paris to live, refers back to the *Alexandros*. In that play of course Cassandra was the only one to foresee the troubles to result from this act of compassion. Technically Helen is right – that was the beginning of all the trouble. In human terms however it is a poor kind of point to make.

922   "fatal semblance of the firebrand": *dalou pikron mimēma*.
This is the firebrand Hecuba dreamt she was giving birth
to, when pregnant with Paris. Cassandra refers to it in
the *Alexandros* (fr. 10 Snell).
"then called Alexander": is Stinton right that 'Helen is
deliberately needling Hecuba by using the name Paris,
and then correcting herself in mock apology'? 941-2, which
appear to be said without irony, seem to suggest that the
reference here is also "straight".
924   On the ancient sources for the Judgement of Paris story
see Stinton's first chapter.
933-4   Had Paris chosen either Pallas or Hera who promised
him military power, and imperial sway over Greece,
respectively, the Greeks would by now have been overrun
by Trojans.
938   "the point in question": literally "the things at the feet".
941   "this woman's evil genius": *ho tēsd' alastōr*. An *alastōr* is
originally an avenging spirit (see 768n.), then comes to
mean scourge or cause of evil as at Soph. *Trach*. 1092.
944   "you took ship ...": on the elliptical nature of the
phrase *apēras* with *nei* see Lee's note.
946   "What was I thinking of ...?": the *g'* emphasises
phronousa - i.e. "when I was *after all* in my right mind."
948   "the goddess": Aphrodite.
"become more powerful than Zeus": cf. *Supp*. 504.
948-9   This argument that even Zeus is a slave of Aphrodite
is a common one. It is made by implication by the Nurse
at *Hipp*. 447ff. for instance. The inestimable nature of
Aphrodite's power was recognised by Homer e.g. *Il*. 14.
198-9. See also Gorgias, *Hel*. 6 and 19.
952   "Alexander was dead": Paris was fatally wounded by one
of Philoctetes' poisoned arrows.
959-60   Bracketed by Diggle following Wilamowitz. In the
Alexandros Deiphobus, defeated by Paris at the games,
felt humiliated at being defeated by a slave and plotted to
kill Paris. It would have been revenge on his rival to
claim marriage with Helen himself on Paris' death.
     The line of argument is that Helen has been trying
to rejoin the Greeks, but was prevented by the Trojans.
Now she faces death from the husband she was trying to
rejoin. Mention of Deiphobus here interrupts this line of
thought. Moreover if the lines were to be retained, the
reference to two quite different sorts of *bia*, "force",

211

(959 and 962), one inspired by Aphrodite, the other the brute force of Deiphobus himself, would be confusing. Helen is making the point that Aphrodite is the only *bia* and she sums this up at 964-5.

963   "whose own situation ...": *oikothen* is here like *oikeios* "one's own". Cf. 653 and Pindar *Ol*. 3.44, *Isth*. 4. 12.

966-8   The chorus recognise Helen's skill at speaking but are not taken in.

973   "was willing to sell": the indicative *apēmpola* is used as if Helen's arguments about Pallas and Hera at 925ff. had been true. Hera would never be so foolish as to sell Argos to the barbarians nor Athena let Athens ever be the slave of Troy.

975   Diggle adopts Hartung's important emendation *ou*, "not", for *hai*, "who". Hecuba has been casting doubt by a *reductio ad absurdum* of the whole circumstances of the Judgement. Gods would just not have behaved like that. Now (reading *ou*) she is doubting that the Judgement ever took place, or at least that the goddesses came to Ida with such frivolous motives and for such childish games. They had no need and no motive for such antics. This is the kind of rationalist argument that Euripides makes his characters use elsewhere, e.g. Heracles at *H.F.* 1341ff. The reading *hai*, "who", would mean that they did come to Ida for just such frivolous purposes – which makes nonsense of the next few lines which are a flat contradiction of this.

982   It makes better sense to put a stop after *kosmousa* and then translate "I fear you will not persuade the wise".

986   "and all of Amyclae too ...": Amyclae, a famous city in the Peloponnese just south of Sparta, where Aphrodite was especially honoured (see Paus. III. 18.8., 19.6.)

988   "Your mind was turned into a Kupris": cf. fr. 1018 *ho nous gar hēmōn estin en hekastōi theos*, "Mind is the god in each one of us".

989   "acts of human intemperance": on this connotation of *mōros* see Denniston on *El*. 1035, and Barrett on *Hipp*. 642-4.

990   The beginnings of the words *Aphrodite* and *aphrosyne* "folly" are the same. On Euripides' love of such etymologies see Collard on *Supp*. 496.

991ff.   This passage contains three very strong verbs.

ekmargoomai, 992, "to go raving mad", and *enkathubrizō*, 997, "to riot" or "to revel in" are used only here. There is also *katakluzō*, 995, "to deluge, swamp", a very strong metaphor. All express the full force of Hecuba's scorn.

998 Hecuba misinterprets Helen here. Helen meant that Aphrodite was the force, not Paris, and her point was therefore a more profound one than Hecuba gives her credit for.

1000 Castor and Pollux, the 'heavenly twins', were Helen's brothers. They could have come to her rescue, Hecuba argues, since they were not yet deified.

1021 Prostration, a custom of the Orient (Hdt. I. 119), would have been a novelty to a Greek.

1020ff. In the last part of Hecuba's speech anger and moral indignation take over. It is the appearance of Helen all dressed up, which rankles with her, particularly since the Trojans are in rags.

1023 "all dressed up ...": *askeō* sometimes has a pejorative connotation, cf. Eur. *El.* 1073.

1024 "you despicable creature": *o kataptuston kara*. *kara* is literally "head" but is used frequently of people, either in affection e.g. Soph. *Ant.* 1, or more rarely in scorn, e.g. *Hipp.* 651. See 661n.

1025 "rags": *ereipia* are "fragments" of garments, or literally "wreckage".

1027 "a sense of shame": *to sōphron*, like *sōphrosunē*, while it can mean "sanity" or "discretion" comes to be used especially of the control of sexual desires (see LSJ).

1034 "Save yourself from a charge of cowardice on Greece's part": on the problems of 1034–5 see Diggle, *Studies* 68–70, who asks whether the context and sense does not demand here, not that Menelaus should have the charge of cowardice, but that he should remove the blame from *women* which Greece has heaped upon them because of Helen's conduct. He favours Dobree's conjecture to *thēlu, keugenēs* for *to thēlu t', eugenēs*.

1039 In the production of the play by La Mama Theatre Company of New York, Helen was actually stoned. In this text the notion of Menelaus that she should go and seek her own stoning is somewhat bizarre and exemplifies his own lack of resolve!

1047 This lack of resolve is further illustrated by the inconsistency of the order to her to go to the ships with

213

the mention of stoning above.

1050 This feeble joke by Menelaus is almost too heavy-footed even to be appropriate to him! It is a very rare instance of a joke in tragedy. On the problems, and for a view that it highlights Menelaus' insensitivity and sharpens the surrounding tragedy, see B. Seidensticker (1982) 89–91.

1052 Menelaus instantly caps Hecuba's generalisation in the previous line.

Third Stasimon 1060–1117

As in the other choral odes of this play the primary subject is the city of Troy and its lost happiness. Nostalgia again is the keynote. But this time the chorus express their loss in an outburst of bitterness against Zeus whom they see as having betrayed Troy quite callously and deliberately. "It concerns me my lord, whether you care, as you sit upon your heavenly throne, for my city as it perishes" (1077–9). Their anger at the irresponsibility of gods echoes their last ode where they drew a picture of the frivolous Ganymede among the uncaring Olympians in contrast to the human suffering of the women and children on the beaches below (821–838).

Note the extreme sensuousness (colour, light, shape, texture, movement, smell, sound, heat and cold) in the description of these first two stanzas, e.g. warm fire, fragrant incense, smoke, cold glacial rivers, green glades, snowy mountains hit by the morning sun. These qualities of description enhance the beauty of the Troy that has been destroyed, and make the trenchant point that the gods have destroyed even their own sacrifices and their own creation.

The ode is remarkable for its passionate personal note as each member of the chorus first addresses her husband whose shade she imagines wandering unquiet and unburied, and then goes on to give the words of her small child, fearful at being separated from her on the journey to Greece. Not only is such fervent subjective involvement unusual for a Euripidean chorus (an exception is *Hec.* 475ff.), but so also is the direct speech of the child. This is more commonly the province of messengers (see e.g. *H.F.* 988ff., *Ba.* 1118ff.) Such a strong personal tone is however fitting for the closing movements of the play where after the successive disappearance of Cassandra, Andromache and Helen, the stage is left to Hecuba and the ordinary women of Troy to sing a *kommos* (lyric dialogue) in farewell to their husbands and to Troy.

The reference in the last stanza to Helen and Menelaus and their return to Greece recalls their appearance in the previous scene, and is in harmony with the hatred for Helen expressed by Hecuba there.

The metre is aeolo-choriambic – a rhythm much used by Euripides (see A.M. Dale, *Metrical Analyses* (1981) Fasc. 2. *Aeolo-Choriambic* and esp. 100–101.)

215

1060 "Did you then betray in this way?": *houtō dē* indicates a
very strong, angry question. However a statement and
deletion of the question mark might be even more
effective, i.e. "*So*, then, Zeus you betrayed etc." This is
how Paley and Schiassi take it, getting the emphasis of
the first two words in an embittered statement, and I
think they are right.

1063 "the flame of its sacrificial offerings": *pelanōn phloga*.
Pelanos is properly a mixture of meal, honey and oil in
the form of a batter which could be poured, or sometimes
a cake.

1065 "hallowed": *hieran* emphasises the "blasphemy" the gods
have committed against their own special city. Troy was a
holy city (*zathean* at 1070 also underlines this point) for
two reasons. 1. It had divine connections stressed in the
second stasimon and it was built by gods as is pointed
out in the prologue, 5. 2. Its citizens were devout. See
the prologue 1 and 25ff., 1242 and most of all, this ode.

1066 Note the emotional repetition of *Idaia*.

1069 *heōi* is an emendation by Wilamowitz for metrical reasons
(see Lee ad loc.).

1071 "Gone": on *phroudos* see *phroudai* 858n.

1074 "moulded gold images": *tupoi* implies the shapes or
rounded outlines of the gold statues (it is used of
moulded figures).

1075 I have left *Phrugōn*, "of the Trojans", out of my
translation as it seems otiose. *All* these things
characterise the Trojans.
"sacrificial moon-cakes": *zatheoi selanai* is again a
reference to shape. *Selēnē* as well as meaning "moon" is a
full moon shaped cake used for sacrificial offerings. The
Souda lexicon defines it thus in relation to a reference in
the *Erechtheus* (fr. 350 Nauck) '*Selēnai* are flat circular
cakes' and says that the word is used as a synonym for
pelanoi (see 1063).

1077 Note the anxious and forceful repetition of *melei*, "it
concerns me, my lord, it concerns me".

1077-8 literally "mounting your heavenly throne and
(occupying) the sky".

1080 See lines 815ff. of the second stasimon. The destructive
power of fire is a prominent image in the play.

1081 Collective singular. Each member of the chorus is thinking
of her dead husband.

"wander about": *alainō* is an alternative of *alaomai*: see *El.*
204, 589. The souls of those who were unburied did not
find permanent rest in Hades but wandered round unquiet
outside.

1083 "unburied, and deprived of lustral water": *athaptos,
anudros*. Note the rhythm of these Greek words both
beginning with *a* and ending in *os* and both having the
same number of syllables; cf. *Ba.* 995, *Hel.* 689–90 and
Kannicht's note.

1085ff. The recurring nightmare of the women – that they
will be transported to places in Greece of which they
have only heard report. See 205–228.

1086 "grazed by horses": *hippoboton* is an Homeric epithet e.g.
Il. 2.287, *Od.* 4. 606.

1087–8 The great stone walls at Mycenae and Argos were built
by the Cyclopes who were famed as craftsmen. See Eur.
H.F. 15, 944, *El.* 1158, *I.A.* 152.
"where": *hina* <*te*>; epic generalising *te*. Cf. Homer *Il.*
22. 325, Eur. *Pho.* 645, *I.A.* 1495.

1089 The women's children are a recurring concern, see
557–559; these general references echo the particular
depiction of Astyanax, and his mother and grandmother
throughout the play.

1090 "calling out again and again": note the repetition of *boai*.
Something has gone wrong with the text here and Diggle
daggers *kataora stenei*. *Stenei* is most unlikely to be
right when we already have the forceful repeated verb
boai.

1097–9 "the peak of the Isthmus between two seas": refers to
Acrocorinth between the Saronic and Corinthian gulfs.
The Isthmus of Corinth forms the entrance to the
Peloponnese.

1104 Unlike the new O.C.T. most editors print *Aigaiou* with a
capital "*A*" which I have translated "Aegean's",
understanding a word for sea e.g. *pelagous* to be implicit
with it. The sense is clear and lightning is common in the
Aegean. Diggle daggers and emends in his apparatus to
aithaloun which means "burning", "blazing" and he
compares *Pho.* 183, Aesch. *P.V.* 992, Hes. *Th.* 72. A
full exposition of the difficulties of *Aigaiou* is set out by
him in *Studies* 71–72.

1107-9 "gold mirrors": *chrusea enoptra*. Here the gold objects Helen amuses herself with are indicative of what is frivolous and sinister. See the similar description of Ganymede and his gold cups at 821, of Paris and his golden robes at 992, and the gold trappings of the wooden horse at 520.

"actually has in her possession": *echousa tunchanei* is perhaps sarcastic. The fact that Helen is daughter of Zeus is also damning to her, since Zeus has been criticised in the first strophe of this ode already.

1112 Pitana was a district of Sparta.

1113 "bronze-gated temple of Athena": *chalkopulon te thean;* *thean* is shorthand for *naon theas*, "the temple of the goddess", the goddess being Athena. *theai ... Palladi,* the goddess and the proper name with it, are also used for the *temple* of Pallas at 599. Pausanias III.17.2 describes a temple of Athena on the Acropolis of Sparta surrounded by bronze plates.

1114 *helōn*: a pun on the name Helen. See 891n.

Exodos. 1118 to end

a) 1118–1215
b) 1216 to end.

a) 1118–1215 The chorus announce Astyanax' death. Talthybius reports Andromache's departure and her last request for her dead son, and Hecuba laments over the body of Astyanax. These episodes are remarkable for a Greek tragedy in that they are all made exceptionally personal. Usually it is an uninvolved messenger who reports a violent death at length. Here the death of Astyanax is announced in a few lyric lines only. Talthybius the enemy herald, and therefore supposedly the uninvolved character, has taken the unprecedented step of preparing the child's body for burial himself – he has washed it in the river before going to dig the grave – a voluntary act, unexpected and unasked for, since it was Hecuba whom Andromache named to prepare the body for burial. This act of generosity on Talthybius' part ensures that we cannot see this play merely in terms of wicked Greeks and innocent Trojans, as some of its interpreters have done (see note on 1150).

Hecuba's spoken lament, supplementing as it does the short speech of Talthybius, adds a yet more personal climax to the action.

1118 literally, "new misfortunes coming in exchange for other unprecedented misfortunes in an unexpected way". *kainos* can mean "new, strange, untoward, unprecedented", and *kain'* here is adverbial.

1121 It is hard to get all the words into the translation: literally "a cruel missile from the walls". *diskēma* is a quoit or thrown object.

1123 literally "one oar's sweep of a ship", implying that the oars are ready in the one ship left to sail.

1127-8 According to this version, Acastus, the son of Pelias, King of Iolcos, drove Peleus, Neoptolemus' grandfather, out of Iolcos. Peleus subsequently went to meet Neoptolemus on his way back from Troy but was shipwrecked and died on Cos.

1129 Diggle here accepts Seidler's emendation *ou* "not having pleasure in delay" for the MSS *ē* which is awkward grammatically. Paley gives a periphrasis which makes sense, but appears to be unparalleled, i.e. *thasson ē*

219

hōste meinai dunasthai, kaiper epithumōn, which he renders as "too quick to indulge in delay".

1135 "lost his life": *psuchēn aphēken* is an Epic phrase, perhaps to give the sense of a death worthy of a great warrior like his father.

1136ff. The infinitives *poreusai* and *thapsai* in this long sentence depend on the *eitēsato* "begged" in line 1133.

1140 is bracketed by Diggle who presumably regards the line as superfluous to the sense which is clear without it. "Andromache the mother of this corpse" is surely unnecessary. *Lupas horan* would be in apposition to the rest, meaning "a painful sight to see", i.e. the shield.

1143 *dounai* still dependent on *eitēsato*.

1148 There is debate whether *doru* means "spear" or "ship" here. Either is common. Since it is most unlikely that the hostile Greeks would raise a spear over Astyanax' tomb, the latter meaning is preferable here.

1150ff. Talthybius has taken the task which would normally belong to relatives entirely upon himself – a sign that his initial detachment has been changed by observing the suffering of these women. An interesting dramatic presentation and one which Sartre in his version plays down to its detriment, by giving Talthybius signs of impatience, 'I'll help you dig– it needn't be very deep. As I say, our ship's waiting. After ten years I can hardly believe it'. (Transl. R. Duncan, p. 70). On Talthybius' humanity see Gilmartin (1970) 213–222.

1155 Talthybius leaves at this point so that Hecuba may deliver a lament over the shield holding the child's body.

1156ff. Hecuba, standing over the great bronze shield of Hector which bears the body of her grandson, his son, delivers a formal speech which is to accompany the decking of the corpse. It is not a lyric lament and it is not a straight report of his death – it is rather a reflection, in speech, of the significance of his death for Greeks and Trojans, of the relation of his short life to hers, and to Hector's. The three generations of this Trojan family are brilliantly interwoven, and the poet achieves this partly by focussing throughout the speech on minute observable physical realities which link them, on the small face and head of the child, now marred by the stones of Troy's walls, on the tiny wrists, replicas of Hector's, broken in the fall, on the mouth which once

spoke to Hecuba, and on the shield of Hector which, as
the child's coffin, still carries the mark of his father's
body on its sling and the stain of his sweat on its rim.
Such description however is not overdone so that it
becomes maudlin. (On Euripides' economy and restraint in
such contexts see Barlow 71-72.) In this speech it is
interspersed with general reflections on the present and a
vivid evocation of the child's words to his grandmother
whom he once confidently thought to outlive. Such
particular details are finally put into general perspective
by a philosophical reflection at the end.

1156 "well-rounded": the word *amphitornon*, referring to the
rim, only occurs here.

1158 "pretension": *ogkos* originally means "bulk" or "body" or
"mass", then comes to mean metaphorically "pride" or
"dignity" or "pretension", "self-importance" in a
pejorative sense. The latter is the best meaning here.

1171-2 All editors draw attention to the obscurity of these
lines. I have followed Lee's interpretation of taking *oisth'*
with *idōn* and *gnous*, 'you are aware of having seen',
etc., but I am not certain that it is correct. Another
interpretation would be "But as it is, having seen and
recognized these things in your heart (i.e. with your
feelings), you still do not know them and have not
experienced the heritage in your house". At any rate it
is agreed that a distinction is here being made between
an early *theoretical* recognition of one's inheritance,
either by the mind or feelings, and entering into it *in
practice* (something which Astyanax' early death
prevented).

1173 Here one notes the great difference of Hecuba's version of
this damage to Astyanax' body, from the way in which a
messenger would have described it, had Euripides chosen
to be more conventional. The apostrophe (never a mode
used by the messenger) is tender and personal.

1175 "tended": *ekēpeus'* is a metaphor from the careful
tending of plants in a garden (see LSJ).

1176 "laughs out": *ekgelai* is an extremely bold, not to say
grotesque, metaphor. The reference is to the wound in
the head gaping between pieces of bone, and is a visual
rather than an aural one. Paley compares *Julius Caesar*
III.1, 'Over thy wounds now do I prophesy, / Which like
dumb mouths do ope their ruby lips'. None the less this

221

and the following lines are positively restrained compared with the physical horrors elaborated by Seneca in his *Troades* 1110ff.: 'His bones are fragmented and crushed by the violent fall, his weight cast down to the earth below has blurred the features of his noble body, his face and those lineaments of his glorious father; his neck is broken by the impact of the flint, his head split open and the brain squeezed out from inside – the body lies there a shapeless horror'. (Transl. E. Fantham). It is probable that Seneca had the Euripides in mind. See E. Fantham's note in her edition of Seneca's play, on 1110b – 1117.

1177 "not to hide what is ugly": *aischros* is "shameful" and therefore "morally ugly". *Stegō* is the brilliant emendation of Diggle for the less comprehensible *legō*. Euripides is not playing down the bold metaphor as he would be if he had used *legō*, but explaining its necessity required by the extreme violence.

1179 "now lying limp at the joints as I can see": *arthra* can mean "neck" or "ankle-joints" or perhaps refers here to the wrists broken in the fall.
Note *moi* which again personalizes.

1181 "doomed to failure" is literally "you deceived me", i.e. by your promises never to be fulfilled.

1182 Astyanax implied, "when you die, I will do all these things as a loving relative naturally should".

1186 "I am an old woman without a city or child left": Note the alliteration of *apolis, ateknos, (athlion)*. A poetic cliché from some points of view (cf. 1083n., *Hec.* 669, *I.T.* 220 where similar words in alliteration occur), but like most clichés it describes accurately a central human crisis.

1188 "all those nights ... gone for nothing": *hupnoi t'ekeinoi* is literally "those sleeps", i.e. probably of Astyanax watched over by Hecuba, rather than Hecuba's *sleepless* nights since there is no word implying interrupted sleep.

1194-5 cf. *H.F.* 1099-1100.

1196-7 The sharp physical details are characteristic of Euripides' style in messenger speeches, although here they are given much more pesonal significance by the fact that Hecuba says them.

1199 "as he pressed you against his chin": *prostitheis geneiadi* is literally "putting (i.e. the shield) to his beard". The sweat ran from Hector's chin onto the rim of his shield:

he would hold it just below his eyes so that his beard touched it.

1200 "Come, bring ..." are addressed to extras on the stage (*haide* 1207) who would come on with adornments for the body, and carry it off at 1246.

1203-6 As well as referring to Trojan misfortunes, these lines relate to the words of Cassandra at 447 where Agamemnon in common with other Greeks is said to be merely under the illusion that he is accomplishing great things. In reality, as Athena and Poseidon have prophesied, and Cassandra knows, the Greeks will be destroyed in their homecoming. Hence one can never rely on seeming good fortune to stay for long. A typical Euripidean sentiment, cf. *Hel.* 1140ff., *H.F.* 101ff., fr. 420.

"like a capricious man": for *emplēktos* "unstable", "capricious", cf. Soph. *Aj.* 1358. The addition of this image, *emplēktos ... anthrōpos* containing the notion of blind instability, to the already strong verb *pēdaō* "leap", transforms what might otherwise be a mere ruminative cliché into a strong protest. 'This is a whole world that is reeling, tottering, staggering in desperate vertigo' (Poole 226).

1209 "not for your victory ... with horses or bow": The wreath Hecuba is offering the boy is not for winning a chariot race or for archery but instead is to honour his death. The accusative participle *nikēsanta* is used as if Hecuba were going on to say *stephanō se* "I crown you" i.e. not having won a victory - but she then changes the construction to one requiring a dative - *soi*.

1210 *nomous* properly belongs outside the relative clause but has become incorporated within it.

1211 "practices respected, but not excessively, so": *ouk es plēsmonas therōmenoi* is literally "not pursuing these occupations to excess". In addition to metrical anomalies here, this phrase is extremely awkward since it is an irrelevant interruption of an important utterance by Hecuba. Such a generalisation at this point diverts attention from her strong note of regret.

1212 "precious things": *agalmata* is the word customarily used for decoration of the dead, cf. *Alc.* 613, *H.F.* 703, and I have translated thus to convey the sense of importance the Greeks attached to such practices.

223

b) 1216 to end   After Hecuba's speech over Astyanax' body there follows the decking of the corpse with robes and ornaments brought by Hecuba's handmaidens and a brief lament between Hecuba and the Chorus. This is followed by a short choral song preceding the entry of Talthybius with guards at 1260. Talthybius sets in motion the final portion of the play, giving his orders abruptly for Troy to be fired and for the women to depart. As Hecuba and the Chorus with bitter reluctance take their leave of Troy, they sing a last lyric lament in which they kneel down and beat the earth with bare hands crying out to raise the spirits of their dead husbands.

It is the rhythm of the lyrics in this closing section, together with the broken utterance of the women and their beating of the ground, which give the ending such impact. Their agitation several times breaks out from iambics (1216, 1226–1230, 1235–1238) into excited dochmiacs (1217–18, 1231, 1239), two of them with a row of resolved syllables within the line (1217 and 1239) indicating an urgency of communication which is enhanced at 1217 by the repeated *ethiges*.

The short choral intervention in anapaestic metre (1251–1259) divides the iambic sequences. The kommos (1287 to the end) returns to lyric iambics distinguished by a high number of resolutions, some lines consisting entirely of short syllables (e.g. 1288, 1300, 1313, 1328). Three of these dissolving lines are urgent apostrophes, to Zeus (1288), to Priam (1313) and the cry to Hecuba's own trembling limbs to lead her away (1328). These agitated appeals are also underlined by the string of vocatives (1288), the alliterative ring of the initial vowels in *olomenos gtaphos aphilos/atas emas aistos ei* (1313–1314), the repeated *iō* and *Priame* at 1312, and the double imperative at 1328 preceded by the repeated *iō*, and *tromera* at 1327.

Such metrical and stylistic devices combine with the powerful spectacle of these tired women on their knees striking the earth in a desperate appeal to make the dead hear. This collective act appropriately closes the play which is after all called by a collective title "The Trojan Women".

1216–17   "you who were once a great lord in my city": *ō megas emoi pot'ōn / anaktōr poleōs*. Does this refer to Astyanax or Hector? I think it must be to the former. Hecuba has been addressing Astyanax in the previous few lines and the Chorus continue her thought. A sudden apostrophe to Hector without preparation would be odd.

224

Though a child, Astyanax was still prince of the city, and his name carries the word *anaktor* within it, i.e. *astu - anaktōr*.

1221 The personalisation of Hector's shield, almost as if it were another body to be buried, and adorned, has a powerful effect here. Heracles' image of his bow talking to him as if it were another person at *H.F.* 1379ff. is a similarly moving instance of the attribution of personal qualities to an object. Euripides was a master at engendering pathos of this kind. I have already pointed out (see 173n.) the frequent addresses to Troy as if that city too were a well loved person. The shield of Hector is to be venerated; the arms of Odysseus hated.

1224-5 Odysseus is appropriately mentioned here as the chief architect of Astyanax' death.

1236 *pitulous* is a metaphor and refers to the quick motion of oar-strokes. See 1123n. and introduction to second stasimon, 799-859n.

1239-40 The text is daggered in two places here where the sense is incomplete as the lines stand.
Hekabē, sas enepe means "Hecuba, tell me of your ...": I have supplied "thought" to make up the gap.
ouk ēn ar' en theoisi is literally "there was not in the gods ... except my troubles". The general sense seems to be "the gods meant nothing but trouble for me and hatred for Troy".

1242 "my sacrifices were useless": the references to "sacrifices" is literal since the *"bou"* part of the word *ebouthutoumen* suggests victims of oxen.
Diggle is surely right to adopt Stephanus' *ei de mē* for the MSS *ei d'hēmas*. The point is that the gods *have* pretty well turned the world upside down; "had they not done that (*ei de mē*)" the Trojans would never have acquired fame. *ei d'hēmas* would mean "if the gods had overturned us we should have vanished from sight altogether", which is nonsense. Posthumous fame through songs and poetry is always some consolation to an ancient Greek. Cassandra in her speech at 394ff. stresses its importance for the Trojans even though disastrous circumstances were the cause.

1244-5 An allusion perhaps to the fame given the Trojan War in the Homeric poems and through the bards and rhapsodes. In the *Iliad*, Achilles consoles himself after

225

the insult to him by singing of "the fame of men", 9.
189, and in *Od*. 8. 72-92 Odysseus is greatly moved that
his own exploits are already in the bard Demodocus'
repertoire. To all the participants of the war against
Troy preservation of their deeds through song was the
only guarantee of their survival after death – cf. Helen's
words at *Il*. 6. 357-8 about her own and Paris' survival
as "things of song for the men of the future"; also *Od*.
8. 579-80.

1253 "torn apart": *kataknaptō* is a strong compound verb
meaning "to card wool" and then to "mangle" or "tear" –
literally "wretched mother, who mangled life's great
hopes".

1258 "waving": *dieressontas* is literally "rowing about". Might
the nautical metaphor here (untranslatable in English) not
indicate that the women still have ships on their minds or
at least that the poet wishes to keep the idea of them
constantly in play? I have commented elsewhere on the
recurring patterns of ship imagery (see also 1236 above)
throughout. That Euripides was capable of using metaphor
to indicate half-conscious attitudes is suggested at *Ba*.
1107-9 where Agave's confused state of mind is captured
in the image of a "climbing beast" who can talk. See
Dodds' note.

1264 "with gladness": strongly ironic in view of the prophesied
future for the Greeks.

1265 "so that my one order has double effect": *hin' hautos
logos echēi morphas duo* is literally "so that the same word
has two shapes". *Morphē* properly "shape" or "form"
seems to mean here something given tangible reality i.e.
put into concrete effect by the spoken word. The use of
this word here is both rare and striking. The double
implementation of the spoken order consists of the razing
of the city and the departure of the women.

1280 Hecuba's scepticism about the gods, shown elsewhere in
the play at 469 and 1240, is finally seen here to have
been all too justified. No help is at hand and at this
point the old Queen despairs and tries to commit suicide
by rushing into the flames. The moment is all the more
poignant as one remembers her courage and positive
advice to Andromache earlier, to live on at all costs.

1282-3 "Best for me to die with this country of mine as it
burns": the eight simple Greek words of this sentence,

not one wasted, are very eloquent.

1284 literally "you are in a possessed state", *enthousiais*.

1285 "no delaying": *pheidesth'* is literally "do not spare me".

1287 to the end is a *kommos* between Hecuba and Chorus, i.e.
a lyric dialogue, here in lyric iambic metre. In the course
of it the women kneel and beat the bare ground with
their hands (1305ff.). This was a customary way of
evoking the spirits of the dead.

1288 "son of Cronos" i.e. Zeus. The text is daggered here and
no sense can be made of the words as they stand,
"father, things unworthy of the (race) of Dardanian".
Dardaniou cannot agree with *tēs* ... *gonas* yet some
meaning like "things the race of Dardanus did not
deserve" or "things unworthy of the race of Dardanus to
suffer" is required.

1291 The Chorus' wry "he has seen" speaks volumes. Zeus is
omniscient, yet callous enough to let this happen.
"the great city": *megalopolis* is an epithet used by Pindar
at *Pyth.* 2.1., 7.1.

1295-7 Daggered by Diggle on metrical grounds and also
because he thinks it likely that the text has been
influenced by the scholion on these lines *to Ilion tōi puri
lelampen, homoiōs de kai ta Pergama kai ta teramna tōn
Pergamōn*, "Ilion is consumed with fire and so is
Pergamum and Pergamum's houses".

1298-9 The substance of Troy is being dissipated like smoke
on a wing of wind. It is also of course literally turning
into smoke as it burns.
"dissipates into nothingness": the verb *kataphthinei* here
gives an image both of disintegrating city and dissolving
smoke. Cf. 1320 where, as the city disintegrates into
dust, the dust is described as rising into the air like
smoke.

1300-1 Bracketed because Hermann thought they belonged
more appropriately after 1297 since they continue the
theme of burning buildings, a theme which is then
rounded off by a more general image of the whole land
disintegrating.

1307 The Chorus here refer to themselves in the singular
(*tithēmi*), yet speak of "husbands" in the plural. Such
confusion between their individual and collective identity
is common. See Kaimio (1970) 78.

1310 *algos*: "pain" is repeated.

1316 "unholy   butchery":   "unholy"   because   Priam   was
     slaughtered at the altar of Zeus. See 482, 3n.
1319,1322 "you will ... become nameless" and "the name of
     the land will be lost": cf. 1244-5.
1323 "vanished": on *phroudos* see 858n.
1325 Note how the words of the text do what in later drama
     stage directions would do. See Introduction p.17.
1326 "earthquake": *enosis* is repeated to emphasise the total
     upheaval and engulfment of the city.
1332 "to the ships of the Achaeans": the Greek ships have the
     last word after all. The play began with allusion to their
     sinister presence and ends with another. They have
     bounded the women's thoughts and feelings throughout,
     recurrent nautical imagery ensuring that they have never
     been far out of mind.

STYLISTIC INDEX

(This index refers to stylistic items discussed in the Introduction and Commentary.)

INDEX OF GENERAL SUBJECTS

References to names of scholars, authors and works, and major characters are not included on the grounds of their frequency throughout. NB. bibliographies on pp. 41-47.